A COMPREHENSIVE BIBLIOGRAPHY OF MODERN AFRICAN RELIGIOUS MOVEMENTS

Compiled by

Robert Cameron Mitchell

Harold W. Turner

with the assistance of

Hans-Jurgen Greschat

T O

MARJORIE AND MAUDE

42692

TABLE OF CONTENTS

INTRODUCTION

From the Ghost Dance of the Great Plains Indians in North America to the Melanesian Cargo Cults, the impact of Western culture and political domination has brought forth new forms of religious expression which possess, despite numerous diversities, a striking similarity of process and function. Nowhere have these movements been so widespread, assumed such a variety of forms and recruited so many adherents as in Africa south of the Sahara.

The earliest modern African religious movement in the sense in which the term is here used was probably the Antonin movement of prophetess Beatrice among the Bakongo /Congo (Leo.) and Angola/ at the end of the 17th century, consequent upon contact with the Portuguese. More recently, since late in the 19th century, new religious movements have sprung up in virtually every country south of the Sahara, but especially in South Africa, the Congo (Leo.), Nigeria and the Ivory Coast. Probably two million or more Africans are members of such movements today and, if Nigeria is at all typical, they are increasing more rapidly since independence than before.

The study of modern religious movements in Africa has gone through two stages and is approaching a third. At first they were described and evaluated principally by those directly affected, such as missionaries and colonial officials. Most of the literature from this period is to be found in periodicals, often rather obscure ones, or buried in books on a larger subject.

Scholarly studies of these movements were almost non-existent before the publication in 1948 of Sundkler's Bantu Prophets in South Africa (item 1262). This thorough and penetrating analysis of Zulu prophets in the context of both Christian and traditional culture inaugurated the second stage of study. Sundkler, although himself a Lutheran missionary, examined the Zulu independents as a religious phenomenon in their own right and asked questions regarding their causes, their social structure and their function. Since 1948 an ever increasing number of scholarly monographs and articles by theologians, historians and social scientists have been published, mostly on a specific movement or on a set of movements within a particular geographical area.

Currently an interest in placing the phenomenon in a larger theoretical framework through comparative studies is becoming evident. This is the third stage which we see approaching. As early as 1949, of course, Katesa Schlosser published an important comparative study of African prophets, Propheten in Afrika (item 184), but this was based on the relatively limited data available in the missionary and administrator sources of stage one. Now studies which utilize data from both stages as well as gathering further data of their own are beginning to appear such as David Barrett's study of independency across 200 African tribes (items 36, 37). One of our principal aims in compiling this bibliography is to contribute to this phase of the study of religious movements by making more accessible the existing rich and varied literature on the subject and, implicitly, by revealing the many gaps which necessitate further study.

Scope

This bibliography deals with the literature on non-Islamic modern African religious movements. Islamic movements are omitted not because of doubt as to their importance but because they belong to a separate geographical and cultural area which requires independent treatment.

The term modern is meant to limit the field to movements which have arisen in connection with the Western impact on African societies. The dividing line between what is peculiarly modern and what is merely a continuation of traditional religious innovationary movements is far from clear, and so-called "witchfinding" movements probably occurred among certain peoples long before the arrival of missionaries and traders. All doubtful examples have been included so that the final decision about their type may rest with the user of this bibliography.

The term religious limits us to movements which involve worship of the divine. This has, for example, led us to attempt to distinguish between literature which interprets Mau Mau as a political terrorist organization and that which recognizes a religious basis to Mau Mau; only the latter has been included here.

Movements is used as a general term both for the spontaneous popular manifestations of religion which rapidly sweep an area and then die away, and for the more stable phenomenon of syncretist cults or independent churches.

Comprehensiveness

As a comprehensive bibliography, an attempt has been made to include every available reference in any language to modern African religious movements that has been published and achieved more than local circulation. The inclusion of items of vastly uneven quality is therefore inevitable. Some are merely incidental references to religious movements in a book on a larger subject; others, though longer, may be superficial, derivative, narrowly polemical, or demonstrably false; and in this field, as in any other, writers have often been content to repeat the same tired references and cliches.

This wide and indiscriminate coverage has been determined by several considerations. First and most important is the fact that it is impossible to prejudge the value of seemingly minor references. An incidental reference to an otherwise unknown movement might provide the crucial clue to the prospective student who wishes to choose an area in which to do field research. Furthermore, references which might be both brief and derivative may nevertheless reveal the point of view of the author; it is important to understand the attitudes of such people as missionaries and administrators, for their response to these movements often affected the course of the movements themselves. Again, the changing attitudes of writers on the subject of African religious movements provides interesting material in itself for the sociology of knowledge. Finally, to provide some direction in separating the wheat from the chaff for any particular purpose we have annotated as many items as possible.

Works published locally by the African religious movements themselves form another category of items included because of their obvious importance as primary sources for the study of these movements. In the course of our own field work in Nigeria we have come across a considerable quantity of locally printed materials for the African and aladura independent churches including histories, biographies, constitutions, catechisms, theological works, polemics and hymn books. Only a selection of the more important of these Nigerian items is included in this bibliography, together with

every reference of this kind that could be collected for other
African countries. Although the non-Nigerian items we were able
to locate are few in comparison we strongly suspect that Nigeria
is not unique in the quantity and variety of its indigenous literature, and that further research will uncover more such material in
other countries. The difficulty with locally published material
is, of course, its relative unavailability to scholars. Many of
the Nigerian items listed have been deposited in the Department
of Religion at the University of Nigeria, Nsukka, or in the
Library of the University of Ibadan. Similar deposits have been
made, we understand, at Makerere University College, Kampala, Uganda.
It is to be hoped that such collections will increase in all areas
and that information about them will be made available to scholars.

It should be noted that our cutoff date for this bibliography
is December 1965: where possible, however, we include items
published after this date or items of special relevance which we
know are forthcoming.

Grouping

Material has been grouped in the following sections:
1. Theory: a small selection of important discussions concerning
    typology, causes and interpretations of these and similar
    movements in all parts of the world.
2. Africa: general material on the whole area, or items spanning
    more than one of our regional divisions.
3. Regions: West, Middle, East, Central, and Southern Africa,
    in this order.
4. Countries: based on current political units; in borderline
    cases a country has been allocated to the region with which
    its religious movements have more affinity. Within the
    regions, countries appear in alphabetical order.

Languages

English and French being the basic languages of African studies,
French items are not translated. An English translation of titles
in other languages is given in brackets, unless the original is
immediately obvious or throws no light on the section concerned.
Place names (unless included in titles), journal series, months,

etc., are given in English form throughout. The more sparing French use of capitals has been applied to all English titles, and usually only proper names are capitalized.

Periodicals and Dissertations

Except for the best-known journals, place of publication is shown in parentheses, together with the publisher or sponsor of journals that may be especially hard to trace. Serials references such as "3e annee" or "Jahrgang 3" are treated as if they were volumne numbers, in spite of a few resultant anomalies. In general, the style of the UNESCO bibliographies in the social sciences has been followed. Newspapers (i.e. journals appearing more often than weekly) are not covered here.

Abbreviations

Anon = anonymous or unknown author
bibl. = bibliography
edn. = edition
ed./eds. - editor/s
illus. = illustration
n.s. = news seriew / nouvelle series / neue Folge
vol. = volume
E.Tr. / F.Tr. / G.Tr. / I.Tr. / S.Tr. = English / French / German / Italian / Spanish translation.
IAI   = International African Institute
IFAN = Institut francais d'Afrique noire
U.P. = University Press
Where a digest or reprint etc., is available this is shown as follows and in parentheses:
A A   = African Abstracts (followed by volume and item number)
D A   = Dissertation Abstracts (U.S.)   "
F A   = Fiches Analytiques (Paris)   "
S A   = Sociological Abstracts   "
BMRS = Bobbs Merrill Reprint Series (with reference number)
MIC   = University Microfilms Inc., 313 North First Street, Ann Arbor, Mich., U.S.A. (with reference number)

Sources

In the original typescript of the bibliography we marked each item not personally inspected by us with an asterisk. Unfortunately this device was inadvertently dropped in the final stages of publication. Generally where material has been obtained from the bibliographies of others, and we have no further sources of information, the author is shown in parentheses at the end of the bibliographical details, under the following abbreviations:

B.Eth. = Bibliographie Ethnographique (Tervuren)

B.H. = Bohumil Holas	B.S. = B.G.M. Sundkler
B.W. = Bertin J. Webster	C.B. = C.G. Baeta
E.A. = Efraim Andersson	G.G. = Guglielmo Guariglia
G.S. = George Shepperson	I.S. = Ian Schapera
K.L. = Kenneth Little	K.S. = Katesa Schlosser
S.C. = Silva Cunha	Sectes = Devant les sectes non-chretiens
S. & P. = Shepperson & Price	V.L. = Vittorio Lanternari

Annotations

Items whose title is sufficiently explanatory, or about which little is known, have no annotation. Elsewhere the annotation indicates the main contents, special context, viewpoint or methodology, and the main ethnic reference. Every people or tribe mentioned is to be found in G.P. Murdock's Africa. Its people and their culture history. (New York: McGraw Hill, 1959, 456p. map). Murdock's spelling is also followed.

Where an item has more than one appearance or translation the references in the annotation are to the first appearance or to the English translation, unless otherwise stated. If further information is available in the standard abstracting services this is shown at the end of the annotation.

Cross references to other items in this bibliography are by means of author's name and item number.

Errors, Omissions and Acknowledgements

It is impossible to claim freedom from errors, especially when much of the preparation of this work was done in Africa without access to major libraries. The most that can be hoped for is the avoidance of serious mistakes, such as the non-existent items found in some of the bibliographies from which we have drawn.

We are aware that our coverage is incomplete in various ways, especially in the literature of languages other than English, French and German. Since our own work has lain principally in West Africa and especially in Nigeria, items from other areas may have been inadvertently omitted, particularly, we suspect, from South Africa. There is also a range of church and missionary society journals that remains unexplored.

Those who have so willingly answered enquiries are largely responsible for the degree of completeness and accurace achieved. Special mention must be made of assistance from Dr. Hans-Jurgen Greschat of the Seminar fur Religionsgeschichte at the Philipps-University of Marburg, who added to his own specialized labours in this field by undertaking many enquiries for us in Europe and beyond. We are very grateful also to the librarians of the following libraries: the Africana Library of Northwestern University, Columbia University Library, the Bodleian Library and the libraries of Rhodes House and the Institute of Social Anthropology in Oxford, the International African Institute library, London; University of Nigeria library, Nsukka, and the University of Ibadan library, Ibadan, in which we did the major part of our research.

We are especially grateful to Dr. Richard D. Schwartz, Chairman, Council for Intersocietal Studies; Dr. John Middleton, Professor of Anthropology and Dr. Gwendolen Carter, Directer, Program of African Studies; all of Northwestern University. Professor Schwartz made possible the duplication of a preliminary version of this bibliography. The original idea for this volume came out of a conference on the subject of modern African religious movements sponsored by the Program of African Studies which also assisted its publication. Professor Middleton, a co-chairman of the conference with Dr. Victor Turner, kindly undertook to arrange the preliminary details of the bibliography's publication in the absence of the authors in Africa.

Finally, we invite communications from readers regarding the inevitable corrections and additions to this bibliography.

June 1966   Robert Cameron Mitchell
                                   Harold W. Turner

                                   Department of Sociology
                                   Northwestern University
                                   Evanston, Illinois

                                   University of Leicester
                                   Leicester, England

A N N O T A T E D   B I B L I O G R A P H Y

THEORY

1. AMES, Michael M. "Reaction to stress: A comparative study of nativism," <u>Davidson</u> <u>Journal</u> <u>of</u> <u>Anthropology</u> (Seattle), 3 (1) Summer 1957, 17-29. (mimeo.)
   > A theoretical article which draws from non-African examples to illustrate a conceptual framework.

2. BASTIDE, Roger. "Messianisme et développement économique et social," <u>Cahiers</u> <u>internationaux</u> <u>de</u> <u>sociologie</u>, 8 (31) July-Dec. 1961, 3-14.
   > An important theoretical article on the role of messianic movements in modernization, with examples from the Congo.

3. CLEMHOUT, Simone. "Typology of nativistic movements," <u>Man</u>, 64 (art. 7) Jan.-Feb. 1964, 6-7.
   > Continues the anthropologists' discussions in Linton, item 10, Wallace, 15 & 16, Smith, 12 & 16, and Voget, 16, and incorporates categories from several of these earlier attempts.

4. DOUTRELOUX, M. A(lbert). "Prophetisme et culture," in M. Fortes & G. Dieterlin (eds.), item 87, 224-239.

5. ELIADE, Mircea. "Dimensions religieuses du renouvellement cosmique," in <u>Eranos</u> <u>Jahrbuch</u> (Zurich), 28, 1959, 241-275.
   > An evaluation of millenial movements in primitive societies; all have the general character of renewal, and should be classed with New Year festivals and initiations.

6. EMMET, Dorothy. "Prophets and their societies," <u>Journal</u> <u>of</u> <u>the</u> <u>Royal</u> <u>Anthropological</u> <u>Institute</u>, 86 (1) 1956, 13-23.
   > Examines Weber's charismatic theory of the prophet type; describes the social role of prophets, and offers a typology.

7. FERNANDEZ, James W. "African religious movements--types and dynamics," <u>Journal</u> <u>of</u> <u>Modern</u> <u>African</u> <u>Studies</u>, 2 (4) 1964, 531-549. Also summary in <u>African</u> <u>Studies</u> <u>Bulletin</u> (New York) 6 (4) Dec. 1963, 7. Also in J. Middleton and V. W. Turner (eds), item 156.
   > A single typology defined by the four quadrants of a bi-axial co-ordinate system (traditional-acculturative and instrumental-expressive), giving separatist, syncretist, nativist, and messianic types.
   > (FA 1, 1019) (AA 17, 8)

7A. KOPPERS, W. "Prophetism and messianic beliefs as a problem of ethnology and world history," <u>Proceedings</u> <u>of</u> <u>the</u> <u>IX</u> <u>International</u> <u>Congress</u> <u>of</u> <u>History</u> <u>of</u> <u>Religions</u> (Tokyo-Kyoto) <u>1958</u>. Tokyo: 1960, 39-50.

8. KOPYTOFF, Igor. "Classifications of religious movements: analytical and synthetic," in Melford E. Spiro (Chairman), Symposium on new approaches to the study of religion, Proceedings, American Ethnological Society, 1964, 77-90. Also in J. Middleton and V. W. Turner (eds), item 156.
    An analytical profile approach is advanced, based on a movement's internal social organization, larger setting, problem, ideology, goals, means, time-perspective and functions. Illustrated by the Suku Holy Water movement in the Congo (Leo.).

9. LANTERNARI, Vittorio. "Messianism: Its historical origin and morphology," History of Religions (Chicago), 2 (1) Summer 1962, 52-72.
    The "crisis theory."

10. LINTON, Ralph. "Nativistic movements," American Anthropologist, 45 (2) Apr.-June 1943, 230-240. (BMRS, A 146)
    An influential discussion of conservative religious reactions of tribal societies to Western impact, with an anthropological typology in terms of revivalist or perpetuative, and magical or rational features.

11. PEREIRA DE QUEIROZ, Maria Isaura. "Aspectos gerais do messianismo," (General aspects of messianism), Rivista de Antropologia (São Paulo), 8 (1) 1960, 63-76. (B. Eth.)
    A general account of messianism, prophets etc.

12. SMITH, Marian W. "Towards a classification of cult movements," Man, 59 (art. 2) Jan. 1959, 8-12.
    Surveys the anthropological contributions to this problem between 1943 (Linton, item 10) and 1958, and suggests three basic classifications, as nativistic, vitalistic, or synthetist.

13. TALMON, Yonina. "Pursuit of the millennium: the relation between religious and social change," Archives européennes de sociologie, 3 (1) 1962, 125-148.
    A comprehensive survey of millenial movements including discussion of Balandier, item 601.

14. THRUPP, Sylvia L. (ed.). Millennial dreams in action: essays in comparative study. The Hague: Mouton, 1962. 229p.
    Conference papers, Chicago 1960; case studies drawn from different societies and different historical periods. Several essays attempt to relate these to a more general perspective. The only essay specifically on Africa is Shepperson, item 987.

15. WALLACE, Anthony F. C. "Revitalization movements," American Anthropologist, 18 (2) Apr. 1956, 264-81.
    A theoretical framework for religious and other movements, viewing them as a response to strain and an attempt to remake culture to relieve the strain.

16. _____, VOGET, F. W., & SMITH, M. W. "Towards a classification of cult movements: some further contributions," Man, 59 (art. 25-27) Feb. 1959, 25-28.
    Continues the discussion from Smith, item 12. Voget distinguishes cultural, sociopsychological, and sociological "referents."

17. WILSON, Bryan R. "An analysis of sect development," American Sociological Review, 24 (1) 1959, 3-15. F.T.: "Typologie des sectes dans un perspective dynamique et comparative," Archives de sociologie des religions, 16, 1963, 49-63. (BMRS, S 316)
    Sects viewed as organizations which attempt to preserve their original value orientations; four types of sects are distinguished and the elements which promote or hinder the preservation of values are analyzed. No direct reference to Africa.

AFRICA GENERAL

18. ABEL, Armand, & DE HEUSCH, Luc (eds). Religions de Salut. Brussels: L'Institut de Sociologie Solvay, 1962, 228p. illus.
    See especially pp. 127-167, articles by De Heusch giving a phenomenology of ecstatic religions, possession cults, and initiation societies for Africa.

19. ADEJUNMOBI, T. A. "Polygamy," in V. E. W. Hayward (ed.), item 110, pp. 52-59.
    Reference to the attitude of independent churches towards polygamy.

20. AFRICAN STUDIES ASSOCIATION. "Report of the sixth annual meeting . . . San Francisco, 1963," African Studies Bulletin (New York), 4 (4) Dec. 1963.
    Pp. 7-8, summary of papers given in a session on the topic "African Religious Movements." Topics included typology, Holy Water movement among the Suku (Congo, Leo.) and the Aladura movement among the Yoruba (Nigeria).

21. _____. "Report of the seventh annual meeting . . . Chicago, 1964," African Studies Bulletin (New York), 7 (4) Dec. 1964.
    Pp. 27-29, references to Musama Disco Christo Church (Ghana), to Mau Mau, and to the "sects."

22. ALEXANDRE, P. "Marxisme et tradition culturelle africaine," Afrique et Asie (Paris), 67, Summer 1964, 8-25.
    Includes analysis of syncretistic cults in terms of their relation to the influence of Communism in Africa. (FA 1, 949)

23. ANON. "Resolutions of the All African People's Conference, Accra 1958," Current History (Philadelphia), 37 (215) July 1959, 41-46.
    P. 44, "Resolution on Tribalism and Religious Separatism"--brief statement, without further definition.

24. _____. News summaries and reports in Africa Research Bulletin (Political, Social and Cultural Series) (Exeter).
    Includes a regular section on religion, and covers a large range of African and other newspapers not included in the standard abstracting services. E.g.: 2 (1-6) Jan.-June 1965, p. 267A, Lenshina movement; p. 325B, Jehovah's Witnesses; 2 (9) Sept. 1965, pp. 372C-373A, Zimbabwe Church of the Orphans (founded 1962 but "steadily penetrated by elements of the banned People's Caretaker Council"), and Lenshina movement, in Zambia.

4

25. Archives de sociologie des religions, 3 (5) Jan.-June 1958.
     Special issue on messianism and millenialism; articles by various
     authors, see especially Balandier item 604; also articles in Nos.
     4 & 6, 1957, 1958.

26. BAËTA, C. G. "Conflict in mission: historical and separatist churches,"
     in G. H. Anderson (ed.), The theology of the Christian mission, New York:
     McGraw-Hill, 1961, 290-299.
     Theological analysis of the relationship between mission created and
     independent churches by a Ghanaian theologian.

27. _____ (ed.) (title unavailable) London: International African Institute.
     Forthcoming.
     Papers read at 7th International African Seminar on "The Impact of
     Christianity in tropical Africa," April 1965. See Barrett, item 37;
     Shepperson, 195; Webster, 574.

28. BALANDIER, Georges. "Les conditions sociologiques de l'art nègre,"
     Présence africaine, 10-11, 1951, 58-71.
     Reference to independent religious movements and their abstract
     symbolisms. (AA 3, 283)

29. _____. "Contribution à une sociologie de dépendance," Cahiers inter-
     nationaux de sociologie (Paris), n.s., 12, 1952, 47-69.
     Reactions to the colonial situation, including African religious
     movements.

30. _____. "Messianismes et nationalismes en Afrique noire," Cahiers inter-
     nationaux de sociologie (Paris), n.s. 14, 1953, 41-65. E. Tr.,
     "Messianism and nationalism in Black Africa," in P. L. van den Berghe
     (ed.) Africa: Social problems of change and conflict, San Francisco:
     Chandler, 1965, 443-460.
     Illustrated from the Congo area. (AA 5, 352)

31. _____. "Contribution a l'étude des nationalismes en Afrique noire,"
     Zaire, 8 (4) Apr. 1954, 379-389.
     Mau Mau, Kimbanguism and the role of messianic movements in
     nationalism. (AA 6, 471)

32. _____. "Les mythes politiques colonisation et de décolonisation en
     Afrique," Cahiers internationaux de sociologie (Paris) n.s., 33
     July - Dec. 1962, 85-96.
     Pp. 91-92, on new religious movements with revolutionary aims.

33. _____. "Réflexions sur le fait politique: le cas des sociétés
     africaines," Cahiers internationaux de sociologie (Paris), n.s. 37
     July - Dec. 1964, 23-50.
     P. 37, messianic leaders in modern political developments. (AA 16,
     364).

34. _____. "Mouvements messianiques et prophetiques en Afrique tropical,"
     Études sociologiques (Paris), 6 (1), p. 17.

35. BANTON, Michael. "African prophets," Race, 5 (2) Oct. 1963, 42-55.
     General article, suggests that the political functions of prophets
     are not so definite as some have suggested. (AA 15, 150)

36. BARRETT, David Brian. <u>Reaction to mission: an analysis of independent church movements across 200 African tribes</u>. Unpublished Ph.D. dissertation, Columbia University-Union Theological Seminary, 1965.
     A sociological analysis of the incidence of independency based on secondary sources and a mail questionnaire to missionaries in various tribal areas. Uses factor analysis techniques to isolate the variables associated with independency.

37. _____. "Reaction to Mission: An Analysis of Independent Church Movements across 200 African Tribes," in C. G. Baëta (ed.), item 27.
     A digest of the previous item. (FA 2 (1))

38. BASTIDE, Roger. "Les metamorphoses du sacré dans les sociétés en transition," (with English summary) <u>Civilisations</u> (Brussels), 9 (1) 1959, 432-443.
     Compares West African syncretist movements and Brazilian religion, Umbanda; the latter creates a balance between the masses and the Western oriented elites in power; Yoruba syncretist religions attempt to reconcile old and new values based on a demand for spiritual independence from the religious imperialism of Western ideas.

39. BAUMANN, Hermann, THURNWALD, Richard, & WESTERMANN, Diedrich. <u>Volkerkunde von Afrika</u> (Ethnology of Africa). Essen: Essener Verlag Anst, 1940, xv + 665. (K.S.)
     Pp. 141 f., la prophets; p. 230, Atta a Wal of the Dinka.

40. BEETHAM, T. A. "Christian discipline: law and gospel," in V. W. Hayward (ed.), item 110, 60-64.
     Reference to independent churches.

41. BENZ, Ernst (ed.). <u>Messianische Kirchen, Sekten und Bewegungen im Heutigen Afrika</u> (Messianic churches, sects, and movements in present-day Africa). Leiden: Brill, 1965, 128p. bibl.
     With an introduction by E. Dammann; and see items 66, 97, 175, 261, 1063.

42. BERNARDI, Bernardo. <u>Le religioni in Africa</u>. Rome: Institutio Italiano per L'Africa, 1961. 95p.
     Popular work: pp. 41-42 on "movimento profetico-salvifici" after Guariglia, items 99-101.

43. BEYERHAUS, Peter. "What is our answer to sects?" <u>Ministry</u> (Morija, Basutoland), 1 (4) July 1961, 4-13. Also G. Tr., "Was ist unsere Antwort auf die Sekten?" <u>Evangelische Missions-Zeitschrift</u> (Stuttgart), 18, 1961, 65-80.
     A missionary theologian evaluates independent movements.

44. BOHANNAN, Paul. <u>Africa and Africans</u>. New York: Natural History Press, 1964. 260p.
     Pp. 25-30, "separatist churches."

45. BOOTH, Joseph. <u>Africa for the African</u>. Baltimore, Md.: Published by Joseph Booth, Press of the Educator of Morgan College, 1897.
     By an important force towards Ethiopianism in Central and South Africa. See Shepperson & Price, item 986, for a summary of its contents.

46. BOUCHAUD, J. "Aspects modernes du paganisme africain," <u>Annales spiritaines</u> (Paris), 66 (7) 1956, 93-99. (B. Eth.)
   Includes discussion of messianism.

47. BRISBANE, Robert Hughes. "Some new light on the Garvey movement," <u>Journal of Negro History</u> (Washington, D.C.), 36 (1) Jan. 1951, 53-62.
   Pp. 56-57 claims Garvey had discussions with followers of Chilembwe and Kimbangu.

48. BROU, Alexandre. "Le prophetisme dans les églises protestantes indigenes d'Afrique," <u>Revue d'histoire des missions</u>, 8 (1) Mar. 1931, 71-84. Also in <u>Congo</u> (Brussels), 1 (5) July 1931, 708-720.
   Draws on Buell next item; includes Harris.

49. BUELL, Raymond Leslie. <u>The Native Problem in Africa</u>. New York: Macmillan, 1928; London: Cass, 1965; 2 vols.
   Vol. I: pp. 120-124, Ethiopianism; pp. 242-249, Watch Tower and Chilembwe; pp. 363, 368, 373-376, Thuku in Kenya; pp. 612 f., Malaki in Uganda; pp. 745-749, Nigerian movements in the 1920's. Vol. II: pp. 66-68, Harris; pp. 302-305, United Native Church, Nigeria; p. 563, Faith Tabernacle, Kinshasa, Belgian Congo; pp. 601-609, the "prophet movement" in Belgian Congo; pp. 730-733, the Garvey movement and Liberia. One of the earliest comprehensive treatments.

50. BUHLER, Alfred. "Die messianischen Bewegungen der Naturvölker und ihre Bedeutung für Probleme der Entwicklungständer" (Messianic movements among primitive peoples, and their meaning for the problem of developing countries), <u>Acta Tropica</u> (Basel), 21, 1964, 362-382.
   A general article including reference to Africa.

51. BUREAU, René. "Syncretismes et messianismes en Afrique noire," <u>Parole et Mission</u> (Paris), 24, 15 Jan. 1964, 132-135.
   Report on Bouaké conference, 1963.

52. CADEL, . "Les fétiches blancs remplacent-ils les fétiches noirs?" <u>Foyer chrétien</u> (Abidjan), July 1957. (B.Y.)

53. CARPENTER, George W. "The role of Christianity and Islam in contemporary Africa," in C. G. Haines, <u>Africa Today</u>, Baltimore: Johns Hopkins U.P., 1955, pp. 90-113.
   P. 110, brief reference to the role of "separatist sects."

54. CARTER, Gwendolen M. (ed.). <u>Five African states</u>. Ithaca: Cornell U.P., 1963.
   Pp. 83-85, messianic movements and Kitawala in Congo; p. 203, "messianic cults" in Dahomey; p. 402, Chilembwe.

55. CARY, Joyce. <u>The Case for African Freedom</u>. Austin: University of Texas Press, 1962.
   Pp. 61-62, brief generalization about African religious movements as anti-white and ephemeral.

56. CHESNEAUX, J. "Les hérésies coloniales. Leur rôle dans le développement des mouvements nationaux d'Asie et d'Afrique à l'époque contemporaine," <u>Recherches internationales à la lumière du Marxisme</u> (Paris), 6, Mar.-April 1958, 170-188.

57. CHODAK, Szymon. "Niektóre Socjologiczne aspekty funkcji religii w
     Czarnej Afryce" (Some sociological aspects of the functions of religion
     in Black Africa), Studia Socjologiczne (Warsaw), 2, 1961, 212-243.
          Includes new religious movements. (AA 16, 547.)

58. CHURCH CONFERENCE ON AFRICAN AFFAIRS, Christian action in Africa, New
     York: Africa Committee of the Foreign Missions Conference of North
     America, 1942.
          Pp. 62-64 on independent churches.

59. COLEMAN, James S. "Nationalism in tropical Africa," American Political
     Science Review, 48, (2) June 1954, 404-426. Also in: P.J.M. McEwan
     and R. B. Sutcliffe (eds.). The study of Africa, London: Methuen,
     1965,   156-183. W. J. Hanna (ed.) Independent black Africa, the
     politics of freedom, Chicago: Rand McNally, 1964, 208-234.
          Pp. 406-7 distinguishes traditionalist, syncretistic (including
          "religious separation"), and modernist movements. (AA 6, 330)

60. _____. "Current political movements in Africa," in W.O. Brown (ed.)
     The Annals of the American Academy of Political and Social Science
     (Philadelphia), 298, Mar. 1955, 95-108.
          Pp. 99-100, "messianic politico-religious movements," distinguished
          as "puritanical," "chiliastic," or "nativistic." (AA 7, 4).

61. COMHAIRE, Jean L. "Religious trends in African and Afro-American urban
     societies," Anthropological Quarterly (Washington, D.C.), n.s. 1 (4),
     Oct. 1953, 95-108.
          Pp. 95-99, Kimbanguism at Leopoldville; pp. 100-104, Lagos and
          "West African Nationalism." (AA 6, 6).

62. COOK, Lloyd Allen. "Revolt in Africa," Journal of Negro History
     (Washington, D.C.), 18 (4) Oct. 1933, 396-413.
          Pioneer comparative study of prophet risings.

63. CRONON, Edmund Davis. Black Moses. The story of Marcus Garvey and the
     Universal Negro Improvement Association. Madison (Wisconsin): University
     of Wisconsin Press, 1955.
          Pp. 177-183, Garvey's ideas on religion, and the African Orthodox
          Church.

64. CUNHA, Silva. Movimentos associativos na África Negra (Association
     movements in Black Africa), Lisbon: Junta de Investigacoes do Ultramar,
     Ministerio do Ultramar, 1956. 57p. illus., bibl.
          Sections 1-3, pp. 7-34, on classification, mystico-religious
          associations, and Watch Tower. English summary pp. 55-6.

65. _____. Aspectos dos movimentos associativos na África Negra. Vol. I,
     Lisbon: Junta de Investigacoes do Ultramar, 1958. 104p. illus. map.
     bibl.
          Pp. 17-76 discusses "movimentos mistico-religiosos nao africanos
          readaptados" including Mau-Mau, South African Ethiopian and Zionist
          churches (after Sundkler) Kibanguism, and a first hand account of
          "Lassyism." See also Cunha, item 620.

66. DAMMANN, Ernst. "Das Christusverständnis in nachchristlichen Kirchen und
     Sekten Afrikas" (The understanding of Christ in African post-Christian
     churches and sects), in Jesus Christus, Marburg: Marburger Theologische
     Studien I, 1963,   135-148. Also in E. Benz (ed.), item 41, 1-22.

67.   _____. Die Religionen Afrikas. Stuttgart: Kohlhammer, 1963. 302p.
      Also F. Tr. Les religions de l'Afrique. Paris: Payot, 1964. 272p.
            Pp. 276-280: post-Christian movements; & pp. 60, 80, 125, 149,
            265, 267 (Reformed Ogboni Fraternity, Nigeria). English
            translation expected.

68.   _____. "Bezeichnungen für die Führer nachchristlicher Kirchen und
      Sekten Afrikas" (Terms for the leaders of African post-Christian churches
      and sects), in Tagung für Allgemeine Religionsgeschichte 1963, Jena:
      Wissenschaftlichen Zeitschrift der Friedrich - Schiller Universitat,
      1964, pp. 113-117.

69.   _____. "Weihnachten in den nachchristlichen Sekten Afrikas" (Christmas
      in the post-Christian Sects in Africa), Afrika heute (Bonn), 24, 1964,
      340-342.
            On the comparative neglect of Christmas celebration.

70.   D'ANCY, M. "Itinéraire syncrétiste," Parole et Mission (Paris), 1 (2)
      July 1958, 219-251.
            The large number of "syncretist sects," and the possible causes -
            dissatisfaction with Christian forms, incomplete conversion, or
            residual paganism. These are not peculiar to Africa, but must be
            taken seriously. Pp. 239-246 on Congo movements; p. 240, Kitawala.

71.   DA SILVA, Rego A. Alguns problemas sociologico - missionários da África
      Negra. Lisbon: Junta de Investigacões de Ultramar, 1960. 137p.
            P. 68 brief mention of "movimentos antieuropeus" after Dufonteney,
            item 699, and Cunha, items 65 & 620.

72.   DAVIS, J(ohn) Merle (ed.). Modern industry and the African. London:
      Macmillan, 1933. xviii + 425p.
            Pp. 4-5, 371, brief reference to separatist churches and their
            causes; pp. 408-414, list of registered "separatist churches" in
            S. Africa.

73.   DEBRUNNER, H. W. "The influence of witchcraft," in Christianity and
      African culture, Accra: The Christian Council of the Gold Coast, 1955,
      pp. 46-50.
            Pp. 48-49 on "the sects" and witchcraft.

74.   DE OLIVEIRA, Herculano L. "Movimento messiânico-communista africano,"
      Portugal em África (Lisbon), 15 (1) 1958, 18-36.

75.   DE SAINT-CHAMANT, Jean. "Sectes et christianisme en Afrique Noire,"
      La Revue des deux mondes (Paris), 4, 1 Aug. 1962, 339-353. Also G. Tr.,
      "Sekten und Propheten im schwarzen Afrika," Schweizerische monatshefte
      für politik und kultur (Zurich), Jan. 1964, 1034-1046.
            The relations between religion, tribal tradition and politics.

76.   DE SARAM, B.J.H. African independent churches. London: Church Missionary
      Society, n.d. (1964), 3p. (mimeo.)
            A brief survey from secondary sources, together with recommended
            attitudes for the older churches, by the C.M.S. Africa Secretary.

77.   DESCHAMPS, Hubert. Les religions de l'Afrique noire. Paris: Presses
      Universitaires de France, 1954.
            Pp. 114-119, a brief survey of independent churches, prophetism and
            new cults.

78. DESROCHES, Henri. "Les messianismes et la catégorie de l'échec," _Cahiers internationaux de sociologie_, n.s. 35, July-Dec. 1963, 161-84.
   An historical and theoretical survey.

79. _____. (ed.). "Syncrétisme et messianisme en Afrique noire," _Archives de sociologie des religions_, 8 (16) July-Dec. 1963, 105-108.
   A report of the Seminar at Bouake, Ivory Coast, 1963.

80. DOUGALL, James W. C. "African separatist churches," _International Review of Missions_, 45 (179) July 1956, 257-266.
   General review of the origins and causes from a missionary point of view. (AA 8, 142)

81. _____. _Christians in the African revolution_. Edinburgh: Saint Andrew Press, 1963.
   Pp. 61-74, analysis of major literature from the point of view of mission policy.

82. DUFONTENY (Père)   . "Les sorciers comme chefs de rebellion," in Semaine de Missiologie, XIV, _La Sorcellerie dans les pays de Mission_, Brussels: L'Édition Universelle, 1937, 70-88.
   General article which views new religious movements as always "political-religious." P. 87 special discussion of Kimbangu.

83. DU PLESSIS, J(ohannes C.) _The evangelization of pagan Africa_. Cape Town & Johannesburg: Juta, 1929. xii + 408p.
   Pp. 121-122, Harris; pp. 349-351, Chilembwe; pp. 350-351, Ethiopianism and separatism; ch. 15, Malaki.

84. FABIAN, J. "Führer und Führung in den prophet-ischmessiani-schen Bewegungen der (ehemaligen) Kolonial-völker. Überlegungen zur Methode," (Leader and Leadership in messianic prophet movements of former colonial peoples), _Anthropos_ (Freiburg) 58 (5-6) 1963, 773-809. Bibl.
   On the role of charismatic leaders, with many African examples. (FA 1, 523)

85. FERNANDEZ, James W. "Politics and prophecy: African religious movements," _Practical Anthropology_ (Tarrytown, N. Y.) 12 (2) Mar.-Apr. 1965, 71-75.
   Functions and causation of African religious movements with fourfold typology: separatist, reformative, messianic and nativist. (FA 2 (1))

86. FISHER, Humphrey J. "Muslim and Christian separatism in Africa," in W. M. Watt (chairman), item 233, 9-23.
   Description of West African Muslim separatism, and comparison with some of the characteristics of Christian separatism.

87. FORTES, Meyer, & DIETERLIN, Germaine. _African systems of thought_. London: Oxford U.P. for I.A.I., 1965. viii + 392p.
   Pp. 224-290 include papers by Doutreloux, item 4; Pauw, 1219; Stenning, 934; and Sundlker 1266.

88. FRASER, Donald. _The new Africa_. London: Church Missionary Society, 1927. 202p. illus.
   Pp. 88-90, the undisciplined nature of separatist movements.

10

89. FROELICH, J. C. "Importancia del Islam, el Christianismo y las sectas en Africa negra" (The importance of Islam, Christianity, and the sects in black Africa), Europe-France Outremer (Paris), Jan. 1963. Similar title (probably the same article) in Actualidad Africana (Madrid), 143, Mar. 1964, 2 ff.

90. GARAUDY, R. "L'église, le colonialisme et les mouvements d'indépendence nationale," Cahiers du Communisme (Paris), 11, 1959.

91. GARVEY, Amy (ed.). Philosophy and opinions of Marcus Garvey or Africa for the Africans. New York: Universal Publishing House, 1926. Vol. II. Pp. 27-33, Garvey's view of Christ and true Christianity.

92. GEDAT, Gustav Adolf. Was wird aus diesem Afrika? (What will come out of this Africa?). Stuttgart: Steinkopf, 1938. 287p. (K.S.) P. 208, Ethiopianism.

93. GIORGETTI, F. "Brevi note sulla societa segreta africana Yanda o mani" (A brief note on the Handa or Mani secret society), Annali Lateranensi (Vatican City), 21, 1957, 9-29. (B. Eth.) On Mani sect, not of Zande origin but expanded among them.

94. GOLLOCK, Georgina A. Sons of Africa. London: Student Christian Movement, 1928. 247p. G. Tr., Sohne Afrikas. Berlin: Heimatdienst Verlag, 1930. 156p. F. Tr., Fils et filles d'Afrique. Paris: Société des missions évangéliques, 1946. Ch. 13, "Among the Prophets - a Study of African Heretics": includes Malaki of Uganda, Braide of Nigeria, Kimbangu of the Congo, and South African movements; pp. 198-202, on Harris.

95. GRANGETTE, G. "Syncrétismes et messianismes en Afrique noire," Parole et Mission (Paris), 4 (4) 15 July, 1961, 343-370. Sympathetic approach to causes of such movements, by a Dominican Father in Senegal. Pp. 346-349, specific references to "religion de san"; pp. 349-350, Harrisism; pp. 350-352, messianic sects.

96. GRESCHAT, Hans-Jürgen. "Die originalsprachliche Literatur des christlichen Syncretismus in Afrika" (The vernacular literature of Christian syncretist movements in Africa). Afrika und Übersee (Hamburg), 48 (4) 1964, 275-283. (actually published 1965.) A general survey of oral and printed religious literature in African languages.

97. _____. "Eine vorläufige Bibliographie zum Problem nachchristlicher Kirchen, Sekten und Bewegungen in Africa," (A provisional bibliography on post-Christian Churches, sects and movements in Africa), in E. Benz (ed.), item 41, 106-119; 158-165.

98. GROVES, C(harles) P(elham). The planting of Christianity in Africa. London: Lutterworth, vol. III, 1955, vol. IV, 1958; reissued 1964. Vol. III, p. 179, Ethiopianism in S. Africa; vol. IV, pp. 45-46, 123-124, Harris; pp. 62-63, Ethiopianism (Booth and Chilembwe); pp. 124-126, the Malakites of Uganda; pp. 126-127, Braide of Nigeria; pp. 127, 192, Kimbanguism in the Congo; pp. 128-130, 324, Ethiopianism in S. Africa; p. 188, African Universal Church, Ghana; p. 189, Babalola in Nigeria; pp. 236-237, separatism; pp. 352-354, separatism illustrated in the Apostolic Revelation Society of Ghana, and Cherubim and Seraphim of Nigeria.

99. GUARIGLIA, Guglielmo. "Prophetismus und Heilserwartungs-Bewegungen bei den Niedrigen Kulturen" (Prophetic and salvation movements in the lower cultures), Numen, 5 (3) 1958, 180-198.
   A classification of religious movements.

100. _____. Prophetismus und Heilserwartungs-Bewegungen als völkerkindliches und religionsgeschichtliches Problem. (Prophetic and salvation-movements as a problem in anthropology and history of religions). Vienna: F. Berger, 1959. xvi + 332p., maps, bibl.
   General world survey; especially pp. 197-239, African movements, in terms of syncretism, millennialism, vitalism, etc.; extensive bibliography.

101. _____. "I movimenti profetico-salvifici e le missioni" (Prophetic-salvation movements and missions), Le Missioni Cattoliche (Milan), 89 (8-9) Aug.-Sept. 1960, 258-269.

102. _____. "Movimenti profetico-salvifici in Africa e chiese separatiste nere" (Prophetic-salvation movements and black separatist churches in Africa), in La Chiesa e le trasformazioni sociali, politiche e culturali dell' Africa Nera, Milan: Vita e Pensiero, 1961, 133-152.

103. _____. "Les grandes characteristiques des sectes modernes (mouvements prophético-salvifiques) dans les terres de mission," in Museum Lessianum, item 161, pp. 13-27.

104. _____. "Gli aspetti etno-sociologici della fame nel mondo" (Ethno-sociological aspects of hunger in the world), in Il problema della fame nel mondo, Milan: Vita e Pensierio, 1964.
   Pp. 57-61 on prophetic-salvation movements, in Africa as elsewhere, as reactions to economic distress.

105. _____. "Pour une nouvelle typologie des 'mouvements prophétiques' au niveau ethnologique," in Actes du VIe Congres international des Sciences anthropologiques et ethnologiques . . . , Paris: Musée de l'homme, Tome II, 2nd. vol., 1964, pp. 393-398.

106. HAINES, Charles Grove (ed.). Africa today. Baltimore: Johns Hopkins U. P., (1955), 1959. xvi + 510p.
   The articles include several references to independency: pp. 161-162, Yoruba 'African' churches and Zionism by L. D. Turner; pp. 483-491, Mau Mau by Philip Mitchell; p. 110, independent churches by G. W. Carpenter.

107. HARR, Wilber C. The Negro as an American protestant missionary in Africa. Unpublished Ph.D. dissertation, University of Chicago, 1945. (S. & P.)

108. HARRIS, John H(obbis). Dawn in Darkest Africa. London: Smith Elder, 1912. xxxvi + 308p.
   Pp. 287-289, on African secession churches and their dangers.

109. HAYWARD, Victor E. W. (ed.). "African independent church movements," Ecumenical Review, 15 (2) Jan. 1963, 192-202. Also in International Review of Missions, 52 (206) Apr. 1963, 163-172. F. Tr. "Mouvements ecclésiastiques indépendentes en Afrique," Église vivante (Paris - Louvain), 15 (1) Jan.-Feb. 1963, 18-32.
   The Mindolo Consultation Statement of 1962; a sympathetic evaluation of these movements by the older churches.

110. _____. (ed.). <u>African independent church movements</u>. London: Edinburgh House Press, 1963. 94p. bibl.
    Some of the papers given at an Ecumenical consultation of African Independent Churches held at Kitwe, Zambia, in September 1962. Includes the consultation's statement, and a classification of modern African religious groups by H. W. Turner. See items: Adejunmoki, 19; Beetham, 40; Lehmann, 139; Mitchell, 157: Sundkler, 203; Welbourn, 939; Pauw, 1217.

111. HELANDER, Gunnar. <u>Must we Introduce Monogamy?</u> Pietermaritzburg (S. Africa): Shuter and Shooter, 1958. 69p.
    "A sympathetic study of polygamy as a mission problem in South Africa," but of general relevance to independent movements.

112. HERSKOVITS, Melville J(ean). <u>The Human Factor in Changing Africa</u>. New York: Knopf, 1962. 1v + 500p.
    Pp. 215-216, 417-429, separatist churches, messianic movements, etc., and their causes by an American anthropologist.

113. HODGKIN, Thomas. <u>Nationalism and colonial Africa</u>. London: Frederick Muller, 1956. 216p.
    Pp. 93-114, role of prophets and priests.

114. HOLAS, Bohumil Théophile. "Sur la position des religions traditionelles dans l'Ouest africain," <u>Monde non-chrétien</u> (Paris), n.s. 26 June-July 1953, 183-192.
    On the cartography and classification of religions in Africa; pp. 190-192, on "new cults." (AA 5, 570)

115. _____. <u>Le culte de Zié: Eléments de la religion Kono</u>. Paris: University of Paris, Faculté des Lettres, 1954. 275p., illus.
    Pp. 217-222, general discussion of neo-Harris churches.

116. _____. <u>Ouvrages et articles 1944-1962</u>. Paris: Paul Geuthner, 1962. 69p.
    A digest of the works of Holas, many of which are included in this bibliography.

116A. _____. <u>L'Afrique noire</u>. Paris: Bloud & Gay, 1964. 115p. illus.
    Includes separatist churches and prophet movements, concerned with a "black Christ" and escapist in tendency.

117. HUP, Walter. "Sekten und Splitterkirchen in Afrika" (Sects and splitter-churches in Africa), <u>Kirchenblatt fur die reformierte Schweiz</u> (Basel), 1964, 257-262.

118. INSTITUT DE SOCIOLOGIE SOLVAY. <u>Religions de salut</u>. Brussels: the Institute, 1962. 288 p.
    Especially pp. 127-167 by Luc de Heusch giving a phenomenology of ecstatic religions, possession cults, and initiation societies in Africa.

119. JOHNSON, William W. "The harvest work in Africa," <u>The Watchtower</u>, 32 (2) 1911. (G.S.)
    The Jehovah's Witness' history of their early work in Africa.

120. JUNG, H. "Die Entchristlichung unter den Neger-völkern" (The de-
Christianization of the Negro peoples), <u>Aussenpolitik</u> (Stuttgart), 11
(11) Nov. 1960, 750-757.
The transformation of Christianity among the Negro peoples of Africa,
Central and S. America, etc., into "sects, spiritism, and fetishism."

121. KARSTEDT, (Franz) Osker. <u>Probleme afrikanischer Eingeborenenpolitik</u>
(Problems of African native politics). Berlin: Mittler & Sohn, 1942.
vi+ 162p. (K.S.)
Pp. 95-104, Watch Tower, and Ngunzism in Angola; p. 112, Thuku, a
Kikuyu.

122. _____ and VON WERDER, Peter. <u>Die afrikanische Arbeiterfrage.</u> (The
African labour question). Berlin: de Gruyter, 1941. (K.S.)
Pp. 148-151, Watch Tower; p. 154, Chilembwe; p. 194f., Thuku in
Kenya; p. 234, Enoch Mgijima.

123. KAUFMANN, Robert. <u>Millénarisme et acculturation.</u> Brussels: Institut de
sociologie Solvay, 1964. 133p. bibl.
Primarily on the history, doctrine, and organization of the Watch
Tower, in Zambia and Congo (Leo); the "orthodox" and Africanized
sections. Extensive bibliography. (FA 1, 1227)

124. KIMBLE, George H. T. <u>Tropical Africa.</u> New York: Twentieth Century Fund,
1960. Vols. I and II.
Vol. I, p. 275, and II, pp. 205-6, on Aiyetoro; vol. II, pp. 90,
275-6, on syncretist and separatist movements; p. 279 on Watch
Tower, and p. 280 Garvey's African Orthodox Church as nationalist
influences.

125. KNOOB, Willi J. "Die Rolle des Propheten in den afrikanischchristlichen
Sekten." (The role of prophets in African Christian sects), <u>Ethnologica</u>
(Cologne), n.s., 2, 1960, 398-406.
Charismatic prophets correspond to traditional diviners, and fulfil
political and economic functions as well as religious. (AA 12, 286)

126. _____. <u>Die afrikanisch-christlichen Bewegungen unter den Bantu. Ein
Akkulturationsproblem.</u> (African-Christian movements among the Bantu. An
acculturation problem). Cologne: University of Cologne, 1961. 80p.
A doctoral dissertation on independent churches, based on secondary
sources.

127. KÖBBEN, A.J.F. "Prophetic movements as an expression of social protest,"
<u>International Archives of Ethnography</u> (Amsterdam), 49 (1) 1960, 117-64.
Bibl.
A valuable article discussing typology in terms of variations of
content and of form; criticism of Linton's and Wallace's classifications; extensive bibliography. (AA 11, 397)

128. KOPPERS, Wilhelm. "Prophetismus und Messianismus als völkerkundliches
und universalgeschlchtliches Problem" (The question of Prophetism and
Messianism in ethnology and universal history), <u>Saeculum</u> (Freiburg),
10 (1) 1959, 38-47.
P. 40, brief reference to Africa.

14

129. KUBAY, Laurel Betty. "Christian Women in Africa want their place in the Church," Ministry (Morija, Basutoland), 3 (4) July 1963, 180-184.
P. 182, brief reference to women as founders of "sects" in Africa.

130. KUPER, Leo. "Sociology--some aspects of urban plural societies," in R. A. Lystad (ed.), The African World, New York: Praeger, for African Studies Association (USA), 1965, 106-130.
Pp. 108-109, 123-124, mention the causes and influence of independent churches.

131. LANTERNARI, Vittorio. "Fermenti religiosi e profezie di libertà fra i populi coloniali" (Religious ferments and prophecies of freedom among colonial peoples), Nuovi Argomenti (Rome), 37 1959, 54-92.

132. _____. Movimenti religiosi di libertà e di salvezza dei populi oppressi. Milan: Feltrinelli, 1960. 366p., bibl. F. Tr. Les mouvements religieux de liberté et de salut des peuples opprimés. Paris: Maspero, 1962. 399p. E. Tr. The Religions of the Oppressed: a Study of Modern Messianic Cults. New York: Knopf, 1963, and Mentor Books, 1965. xvi + 286p.
(E. Tr.) Ch. 1: "Nativistic-Religious Movements in Africa: (Africa:) pp. 22-39, the Congo; pp. 39-49, S. Africa; pp. 49-50, Nyasaland; pp. 50-56, W. Africa; pp. 56-58, "other movements." Religious movements in colonial areas are reactions against oppression, anxiety and frustration, aggravated by alienation of lands, and race relations.
See also "A Book Review . . .," Current Anthropology, 6 (4) Oct. 1965, 447-465.
Fifteen reviews of Religions of the Oppressed, together with a precis of the book and reply to the reviewers by Lanternari. Note his complaints against the E. Tr.; and p. 454, Shepperson on the African material. (FA 2, 1878)

133. _____. "La chiesa e le religioni dissidenti d'Africa, d'Asia, Oceania e America," (The Church and the dissident religions of Africa . . .) Ulisse (Rome), 15 (7) 1962, 127-143.

134. _____. "Convegno Internazionale di Bouaké sui sincretismi e messianismi dell' Africa Nera" (The international colloquim at Bouaké on syncretism and messianism in Black Africa), Rivista di Antropologia (Rome), 50, 1963, 213-230. Bibl. (with English summary). (FA 2, 1877)

135. _____. "Profeti Negri e movimenti di liberazione in Africa" (Negro prophets and liberation movements in Africa), Sapere (Milan), Dec. 1964, 689-695.

136. _____. "Religione, società, politica nell' Africa Nera avanti e dopo la indipendenta" (Religion, society, and politics in Black Africa before and after independence), Nuovi Argomenti (Rome), 69-71 (in press, 1964).

136A. _____. "Syncrétismes, messianismes, néo-traditionalismes en Afrique noire," Archives de sociologie des religions (Paris), 19, Jan.-June 1965, 99-116. Bibl.

137. _____. "Developpements et tendances des mouvements religieux nouveaux de l'Afrique Noire: Comparison ethnique et historique," in Bouaké, item 206.
An intra-African comparison.

138. LATOURETTE, Kenneth Scott. The Christian world mission in our day. New
      York: Harper, 1954.
            Pp. 104-105, brief reference to African independents.

139. LEHMANN, Dorothea A. "Women in the independent African churches," in
      V.E.W. Hayward, item 110, pp. 65-69.
            The appeal to women, in South and Central Africa.

140. LESSING, Peter. Only hyenas laugh. London: Michael Joseph, 1964.
            Pp. 181-184, "new religions": separatist churches as "pseudo-
            Christianity" and playing an "increasingly important" part in African
            nationalism.

141. LEYS, Norman (Maclean). Kenya. London: Hogarth Press, (1924) 1926. 423p.
            Pp. 212 ff., Thuku in Kenya; pp. 341-350 on Chilembwe, an important
            early source and the basis for subsequent accounts.

142. LIENHARDT, R. G. "Some African 'Christians'," Blackfriars (Oxford), 33
      (382) Jan. 1952, 14-21.
            A positive approach to separatists, with a penetrating account of
            causes.

143. LINZ, M. "'Black Muslims' und Bantu-kirchen" ('Black Muslims' and Bantu-
      churches), Evangelische Missions-Zeitschrift (Stuttgart), 20 (1) 1963,
      21-26.

144. LOWIE, Robert H. "Primitive messianism and an ethnological problem,"
      Diogenes (Chicago), 19 Fall 1957, 62-72. (See also parallel edns. in
      French, German etc.)
            An interpretation of messianism and nativism; pp. 67-68, brief
            references to Africa. (AA 11, 12).

145. LUYKX, Boniface. "Christian worship and the African soul," A F E R
      (African Ecclesiastical Review) (Masaka, Uganda), 7 (2) Apr. 1965, 133-143.
            Pp. 136, 143, a Roman Catholic missionary on "the sects" in Africa,
            caused by demand for a congenial ritual; but are "deviations from
            normal worship and even from human culture."

146. MACONI, Vittorio. "Il profetismo in Africa" (Prophetism in Africa), La
      Missione (Milan), June 1956, 19-27.

147. MAIR, Lucy (P.). "Independent religious movements in three continents,"
      Comparative Studies in Society and History, 1 (2) Jan. 1959, 113-36.
            American Indian, Melanesian and African movements compared. See
            also Mead, item 152.

148. _____. New nations. London: Weidenfeld and Nicholson, 1963. 235p.
            Ch. 6, "New religions," including a summary of the course of Kimbanguism
            and a discussion of South African and other independent churches.

149. _____. "Witchcraft as a problem in the study of religion," Cahiers d'études
      africaines, 15 (4,3) 1964, 335-348.
            Pp. 347-348, the relation between anti-witchcraft and messianic
            movements. (AA 16, 193).

150. MAYCOCK, E.A. "The Church's duty to separatist religious sects," Daystar
      (London), 24 Apr. 1955, 6-7.
            An Anglican missionary on the need for a positive attitude, with recog-
            nition of some responsibility for causing these bodies.

16

151. MAZÉ, (Père). "Le prophetisme dans les Eglises protestantes d'Afrique,"
      Grands Lacs (Namur, Belgium), Apr. 1936. (B.H.)

152. MEAD, Margaret. "Independent religious movements," Comparative Studies in
      Society and History, 1 (4) June 1959, 324-329.
            Commentary on Mair, item 147.

153. MENDELSOHN, Jack. God, Allah and Juju: Religion in Africa today. New
      York: Nelson, 1962.
            Pp. 156-165 on "rebel churches in a restless land." Popular account.

154. MENDES-CORREA, A. A. "Sociedades secretas africanas e ciência social"
      (African secret societies and social science), Boletim da Sociedad
      Geografica (Lisbon), 72 (4-6) 1954, 219-34.

155. MIDDLETON, John & WINTER, E. H. (eds.). Witchcraft and sorcery in East
      Africa. London: Routledge & Kegan Paul, 1963. viii + 302p.
            Pp. 24-25 relates witchfinding movements to theory of witchcraft.
            See Douglas, item 694; and Middleton, 929.

156. _____ & TURNER, V. W. (eds.). Modern Religious Movements in Africa.
      Evanston, Ill.: Northwestern U. P., forthcoming.
            Essays resulting from a conference at Northwestern University, April
            1965; see items: Fernandez, 7; Kopytoff, 9; Turner, 222; Mitchell,
            515; Simpson, 551; Fernandez, 797; Hopkins, 925; Middleton, 931;
            Murphree, 998; Colson, 1018.

157. MITCHELL, Robert Cameron. "Christian healing," in V. Hayward (ed.), item
      110, pp. 47-51.
            Healing as a widespread characteristic of independent churches, with
            examples from the Aladura churches of Western Nigeria.

158. _____. "Africa's prophet movements," The Christian Century, 81 (47)
      18 Nov. 1964, 1427-1429.
            The Lumpa uprising in Zambia, 1964, in the general context of African
            prophet movements.

159. MUHLMANN, Wilhelm E. "Chiliasmus, Nativismus, Nationalismus" (Chiliasm,
      nativism, and nationalism), in A. Busch (ed.), Soziologie und Moderne
      Gesellschaft, Stuttgart: Enke, 1959, 228-242

160. _____ (ed.). Chiliasmus und Nativismus: Studien zur Psychologie,
      Sociologie und Historischen Kasuistik der Umsturzbewegungen. Berlin:
      D. Reimer (1961) 1964. 472p.
            Includes modern millenial phenomena in Africa, with roots both in
            frustrations consequent on culture contact, and in the "mutation" from
            mythical to historical thought resulting from the impact of the
            biblical viewpoint. See also essays by Sulzmann, item 613; Knoob,
            1051; and Mühlmann, 876.

161. MUSEUM LESSIANUM. Devant les sectes non-chrétiennes. Louvain: Desclée
      de Brouwer, n.d. (1962). 318p.
            Pp. 62-163 on African independent religious movements. Papers at the
            31st Semaine de Missiologie, by Roman Catholic scholars; see items:
            Van Bulck, 393; Anon, 618; Decapmaekers, 675; Doutreloux, 687; Masson,
            727; Pich, 887; Wagner, 1281.

162. NEILL, Stephen. _A history of Christian missions_. Harmondsworth, England: Penguin, 1964.
Pp. 497-502, challenge of independent churches to Christianity in Africa.

163. NIDA, Eugene A. _Message and mission_. New York: Harper and Bros., 1960.
Pp. 139-142, "nativistic movements" as including independent churches; by a Protestant missionary anthropologist.

164. OMONIYI, Prince Bandele. _A defence of the Ethiopian movement_. Edinburgh: 1908. xi + 124p. (S. & P.)
By a Yoruba.

165. OOSTHUIZEN, Gerhardus C. "The church among African forces," _Practical Anthropology_ (Tarrytown, N.Y.), 11 (4) July-Aug. 1964, 162, 164-165.
Contains generalizations about political, millenial and healing aspects of separatist movements, by a South African theologian.

166. _____. "Independent African churches: sects or spontaneous development?" _Ministry_ (Morija, Basutoland), 5 (3) Apr. 1965, 99-107.

167. _____. "The Misunderstanding of the Holy Spirit in the Independent Movements in Africa," in _Christusprediking in de Wereld_, Kampen (Holland): Kok, 1965, pp. 172-197.

168. PADMORE, George. _The life and struggles of Negro toilers_. London: Red International of Labour Unions, Magazine, . . . , 1931. 126p.
Pp. 84-87, Thuku and the Kikuyu Central Association--conflicts with Government; pp. 102-103, Kimbanguism.

169. _____. _How Britain rules Africa_. London: Wishart, 1936. 402p.
Pp. 365-367, on "tribal-'Religious' Organizations," especially Chilembwe, and Enoch Mgijima in South Africa.

170. _____. _Pan Africanism or Communism?_ London: Dobson, 1956, 463p. illus.
Pp. 87-104, Marcus Garvey's African Orthodox Church under Archbishop Alexander McGuire (West Indian), in U.S.A., with Black Christ and Black Madonna; influence alleged on dissident nationalist churches in Africa.

171. PARRINDER, (E.) G. "Worship in Protestant missions," _International Review of Missions_, 35 (138) Apr. 1946, 187-193.
The need for revision of Western forms of worship; the lead given by "African sects"--a brief reference.

172. PHILIPPS, J.E.T. "The tide of colour. I. Pan-Africa and anti-White," _Journal of the African Society_ (London), 21 (82) Jan. 1922, 129-135.
P. 130, brief reference to 1915 "Ethiopian rising" in Nyasa, and Nabingi society in Ruanda; pp. 133-134, American connections with Ethiopianism; p. 134, Congo secret sects.

173. POTEKHIN, I. I. "O nekotorykh zadachakh Afrikanistiki v svyazi s konferent-siey naradov Afriki" (Some problems of African studies arising from the Conference of the Peoples of Africa), _Sovetskaya Etnografia_ (Moscow), Mar.-Apr. 1959, 10-17.
The late head of the African Institute, Moscow, after the 1958 Accra Conference, urged Soviet Africanists to include the study of religious separatism, both mission and indigenous, as an obstacle to national unity. (AA 10, 459.)

174. RANGER, Terence O. "African attempts to control education in East and Central Africa, 1900 to 1939," Past and Present (Oxford), 32, Dec. 1965, 57-85.
        Independent schools and their connection with independent churches.

175. RAUM, O. F. "Von Stammespropheten zu Sektenführern?"(From tribal prophets to sect-leaders), in E. Benz (ed.), item 41, pp. 48-70.

176. REHWALDT, Hermann. Geheimbünde in Afrika (Secret Societies in Africa). Munich: Ludendorffs, 1941. 67p. (E.A. & K.S.)
        Pp. 15 ff., a national church for the Pedi; p. 17, Watch Tower; p. 21, Thuku in Kenya; pp. 53 ff., Kansapala in Angola, c. 1928.

177. RETIF, André. "Pullulement des 'églises' nègres," Études (Paris), 302 (7) Sept. 1959, 186-195.
        A Roman Catholic survey of various areas; interpretation as mixtures of paganism and Christianity, and as anti-white and political in nature.

178. RICHTER, Julius. Geschichte der evangelischen Mission in Afrika (History of the evangelical mission in Africa). Gutersloh: C. Bertelsmann, 1922. viii + 813p. (K.S.)
        P. 111, Harris; pp. 141 f., Braide; pp. 274 f., Ntsikana; pp. 364 ff., Ethiopianism; pp. 566-568, Booth; pp. 572-573, Chilembwe; et passim.

179. ROLAND, Marc. "L'Inde exporte en Afrique amulettes et philtres magique," Belgique d'Outremer (Brussels), 266, Apr. 1957, 307-309.
        Superstition remains strong among évolués who replace the traditional social and religious supports by magic and occult "medicines" bought from Indian catalogues at arbitrary prices. (AA 9, 542)

180. ROTBERG, Robert I. "The rise of African nationalism: the case of East and Central Africa," World Politics (Princeton, N.J.), 15 (1) Oct. 1962, 75-90. Also in P.J.M. McEwan and R.B. Sutcliffe (eds), The study of Africa, London: Methuen, 1965, 184-193.
        Pp. 84-87, the contribution of independent religious movements.

181. RUSSO, Antonio. "Profetismo e movimenti salvifico-messianici" (Prophetism and messianic-salvation movements), Rivista di Etnografia (Naples), 14, 1960, 78-85.
        Some reference to Africa, especially the Congo.

182. SANTOS, A Miranda. "Aculturação e saúde mental," (Acculturation and mental health), Portugal em África (Lisbon), Special issue, 17-18 (100-105) July 1960-1961.
        Pp. 369-370, 376, brief reference to messianic movements.

183. SASTRE, Robert. "Christianisme et cultures africaines," Tam-Tam (Paris), 6 (7) 1957, 12-23. Also E. Tr., "Theology and African Culture," Présence africaine (Paris), 24-25, Feb.-May 1959, 142-52.
        A Roman Catholic priest interprets messianism and independent churches as a response to Christianity in terms of spiritual emancipation.

184. SCHLOSSER, Katesa. Propheten in Afrika. Braunschweig: A. Limbach, 1949. 426p. bibl. map.
Important pioneer comparative survey of sixty-eight African prophets, divided into three types: traditional, Muslim and Christian. Extensive bibliography.

185. _____. "Der Prophetismus in niederen Kulturen" (Prophetism in primitive cultures), Zeitschrift für Ethnologie (Berlin), 75, 1950, 60-72.

186. SHAREVSKAYA, B. I. Religioznaya politika Angliyskogo imperializma v Angliyshikh koloniyakh Afriki. (The religious policy of British imperialism in British possessions in Africa). Moscow: GosPolitIzdat, 1950.
Includes African Christian sects interpreted as protest movements, by the chief Soviet writer on religion in Africa.

187. _____. Staryye i Novyye Religi Tropicheskoy i Yushnoy Afriki (Old and New Religions of Tropical and Southern Africa). Moscow: Izdatel'stvo Nauka, 1964. 387p. bibl.
Ch. 6, S. Africa; sect. 2, the "Ethiopian" movement. Ch. 7, Congo Basin: sect. 2, Kimbanguism and other movements, 1920-1950. Ch. 8, Tropical E. Africa, includes "anti-colonial religio-political movements." Ch. 9, Tropical W. Africa; sect. 2, The formation of independent churches and sects. A major Russian study with extensive bibliography including Russian works.

188. SHEPHERD, R.H.W. "The separatist churches of South Africa," International Review of Missions, 26 (104) Oct. 1937, 453-463.
A brief outline, with general comments on causes.

189. SHEPPERSON, George A. "Ethiopianism and African nationalism," Phylon (Atlanta), 14 (1) 1953, 9-18. Bibl.
Uses Ethiopian and Zionist categories in a general treatment of the political role of independent churches. (AA 5, 359.)

190. _____. "External factors in the development of African nationalism, with particular reference to British Central Africa," Phylon, 22 (3) 1961, 207-225.
Short discussion of prophets' role mentioning Chilembwe, Harris etc.

191. _____. "Pan-africanism and 'pan-africanism'," Phylon, 23 (4) Winter 1962, 351-2, 355, 357.
"Ethiopianism," the origins and applications of the term.

192. _____. "The comparative study of millenarian movements," in S. L. Thrupp (ed.), item 14, 44-52.
Various terms currently used of African movements are distinguished.

193. _____. "Church and sect in Central Africa," Rhodes-Livingstone Journal, 33, June 1963, 82-94.
A review article: Taylor and Lehmann, item 1045; Sundkler, 1262; Welbourn, 821; with further information.

194. _____. "Religion and the city in Africa: a historian's observations," in Urbanization . . . item 223, 141-150.
Pp. 147-149 on separatism.

195. _____. "Ethiopianism: past and present," in C. G. Baëta (ed.), item 27. (FA 2 (1))

197. SIERKSMA, F. Een nieuwe hemel en een nieuwe aarde (A new Heaven and a new
       Earth). The Hague: Mouton, 1961. 312p.
            Messianic ideas among primitive peoples; Africa mentioned, pp. 211-212.

198. SIK, Endre. Histoire de l'Afrique noire. Vol. II. Budapest: Akademia;
       Kiado, 1964. 346p. illus. bibl.
            African religious movements as having had an "important role in organi-
            zation of peasant movements" which were an early expression of class
            consciousness. P. 52 Chilembwe; p. 59 Malaki; p. 71 Braide; p. 78
            Harris; pp. 130-131, 292-293, Kimbangu, also pp. 130-131. French
            translation of Hungarian original.

199. SMYTH, H. H. & M. M. "An African balance sheet: 1960," Journal of Human
       Relations (Wilberforce, Ohio), 8 (3-4) Spring-Summer 1960, 831-843.
            Pp. 839-840, independent churches briefly treated under religious
            "liabilities."

200. SPECKER, J. "Heidnisch-christlicher Synkretismus in Afrika" (Pagan-
       Christian syncretism in Africa), in L'Afrique chrétienne II & III (Le
       Monde Religieux, n.s. 28). Lezay (Deux Sèvres): A. Chopin, 1960-1961.
            Ch. 5: "L'Émancipation africaine," 447-458.

201. SUNDKLER, B. (G.M.). "Propheten: Religionsgeschichtlich" (Prophets--as
       in history of religions), Die Religionen in Geschichte und Gegenwart,
       Tubingen: Mohr, 1961, Vol. V, cols. 611-613.
            African prophets, as phenomena in the history of religions.

202. _____. "Sektenwesen in den jungen Kirchen" (Sectarianism in the Younger
       Churches), in Die Religionen in Geschichte und Gegenwart, Tubingen: Mohr,
       1961, Vol. V, cols. 1664-1666.
            Independent churches in Africa.

203. _____. "What is at stake? (2)," in V. E. W. Hayward (ed.), item 110,
       30-32.
            A general statement on relationship of mission churches to independent
            churches; special reference to Nyanza independents in Kenya.

204. SURET-CANALE, Jean. L'Afrique noire occidentale et centrale: geographie,
       civilisations, histoire. Paris: Éditions sociales, 1958. (B.H.)
            Pp. 128-129 on religious movements as reaction to colonialism from a
            Marxist perspective.

205. _____. Afrique noire occidentale et centrale--l'ère colonial (1900-1945).
       Paris: Éditions sociales, 1964. 640p. (B.H.)
            Pp. 543ff. on religious movements.

206. Syncrétisme et messianisme en Afrique Noire. Paris: Ed. du Seuil.
            Papers presented to the Seminar on this theme at Bouaké, Ivory Coast,
            Oct. 1963. See following items: Lanternari, 137; Dieterlin, 245;
            Bureau, 272; Baëta, 291; Rouch, 388; Verger, 563; Raymaekers, 750;
            De Heusch, 803; Roumeguère, 1002; Schlosser, 1246; Sundkler, 1267.

207. TAMBARAM CONFERENCE SERIES. Vol. IV. The life of the Church. London:
       O.U.P., 1939.
            Pp. 404-407, on the importance of reckoning with independency.

208. TALMON, Yonina. "Pursuit of the millennium: the relation between religious and social change," <u>Archives européenes de sociologie</u>, 3 (1) 1962, 125-48.
A comparative study of some of the literature on millennial movements including Balandier, item 601.

209. TAYLOR, John V(ernon). "Saints or heretics?" in J. Hermelink <u>et al</u>. (eds.), <u>Basileia</u>. Stuttgart: Evangelische Missionsverlag, 1959, 305-312.
On the Cherubim and Seraphim, Lagos; the Lumpa church and Emilio's "Children of the Sacred Heart," Zambia.

210. TERRY-THOMPSON, Arthur Cornelius. <u>The history of the African Orthodox church</u>. New York: Beacon Press, 1956. 139p., illus.
On Garvey's church, which influenced African churches in South and East Africa.

211. THOMAS, L. V. "L'Église chrétienne d'Afrique noire," <u>Tam-Tam</u> (Paris), 7-8, Dec. 1963, 7-21.
Includes "deformations" of the Church found in syncretist movements and independent churches. (FA 1, 267.)

212. THWAITE, Daniel. <u>The seething African pot: A study of black nationalism, 1882-1935</u>. London: Constable, 1935. 248p.
Pp. 64ff. on African prophets, especially in Congo (Leo) and Angola; by an opponent of African nationalism.

213. TSHIMBAYEKE . "Mau-Mau au Kenya, Kibangisme et Kitawala au Congo belge," <u>Bulletin du Cercle Colonial Luxembourgeois</u>, 6, 1953, 3-6; 7, 1953, 5-8. (B.Eth.)

214. TURNER, Harold Walter. "African prophet movements," <u>Hibbert Journal</u> (London) 61 (242) Apr. 1963, 112-116.
A general survey of causes.

215. _____. "They hold a mirror to our weaknesses," <u>The Outlook</u> (Christchurch, New Zealand), 19 Sept. 1964, 5-7. Illus.
A popular survey of causes and features of independent churches.

216. _____. <u>Modern African religious movements: An introduction for the Christian Churches</u>. Nsukka: Department of Religion, University of Nigeria, revised edn. 1965. 10p. (mimeo.)

217. _____. "Methodology for modern African religious movements," <u>Comparative Studies in Society and History</u>, 8 (3) Apr. 1966, 12-25.
The location and identification of the phenomena, and the allocation to the most relevant disciplines.

218. _____. "Problems in the study of African independent churches," <u>Numen</u> (Leiden) 13 (1) Jan. 1966, 27-42.
The problems of evidence in religion, and of participation, commitment, objectivity, and detachment, in the African context.

219. _____. "Monogamy as a mark of the church?" <u>International Review of Missions</u> 55 (218) extracted July 1966.
A theological refutation of the view that polygamy disqualifies African groups from acceptance as Christian churches.

22

220. _____. "A typology for modern African religious movements," Journal of Religion in Africa (Leiden), 1, 1966. (forthcoming in 2 parts)
    A suggested terminology and classification, revising the outline given in Hayward, item 110, p. 13.

221. _____. "Prophets and politics; a Nigerian test-case," Bulletin, Society for African Church History (Aberdeen), 3, 1965 (expected 1966).
    The conflict between governments and prophets, with special reference to the prosecutions of Garrick Braide.

222. TURNER, Victor W. "The waters of life: some reflections on Zionist water symbolism," in J. Middleton and V. W. Turner (eds.), item 156.

223. Urbanization in African Social Change. Edinburgh: University Centre of African Studies, 1963. (mimeo.)
    See Hair, item 591; Shepperson, 194; Wallerstein, 229; and Mayer, 1194.

224. VAN DER POST, Laurens. Flamingo feather: a story of Africa. London: Hogarth, 1955. 341p. (G.S.)
    Fiction, after Prester John.

225. VAN LANGEN HOVE, Fernand. Consciences tribales et nationales en Afrique noire. Brussels: Institut royal des relations internationales, 1960. 468p.
    Pp. 195-222, general review of "reactions politico-religieuses"; pp. 368-374, Mau-Mau.

226. VAN WYCK, J. Alex. "Independent African churches: sects or spontaneous development?" Ministry (Morija, Basutoland), 4 (2) Jan. 1964, 59-63.
    A thorough general survey from a theological viewpoint. See the reply of Oosthuizen, item 1215.

227. VAZ, José Martins. "Problemas africanos," Portugal em África (Lisbon), n.s., 15 (90) Nov.-Dec. 1958, 322-333; 16 (91) Jan.-Feb. 1959, 38-52; (92) Mar.-Apr. 1959, 71-90.
    Includes reference to messianic movements.

228. VILAKAZI, Absalom. African religious concepts and the separatist movements. Paper read to the Second Annual Conference, American Society of African Culture, New York City, 1959. 10p. (mimeo.) (private circulation).
    Based on field work among his own people, the Zulu; sympathetic.

228A. VON SICARD, H. Ngoma Lungundu. Uppsala: Almquist & Wiksells, 1952.

229. WALLERSTEIN, Immanuel. "The political role of voluntary associations in middle Africa," in Urbanization . . ., item 223, 151-165.
    Pp. 159-161, "secessionist churches."

230. _____. "Voluntary associations" in J. S. Coleman and C. G. Rosberg Jr. (eds.), Political parties and national integration in tropical Africa, Berkeley, California: University of California, 1964, 308-339.
    Pp. 329-330 on new religious groups.

231. WARREN, Max A. C., in the C.M.S. News-Letter (London) 240, July 1961, 3-5, reflections on Field, item 308, and Welbourn, 821; 254, Nov. 1962, 3-4, on pentecostalism with reference to Mitchell, 514, and Turner, 262; 259, Apr. 1963, 3, on the Holy Chapel of Miracle in Nigeria.

232. ____. Christianity in the new Africa. London: Prism Pamphlets, 18, n.d. (1964).
Pp. 13-14 on 'African' churches, by the former General Secretary of the Church Missionary Society (Anglican).

233. WATT, W.M. (Chairman). Religion in Africa. Edinburgh: University Centre of African Studies, 1964. 130p. (mimeo.).
See H. J. Fisher, item 86; T. O. Ranger, 1000; G. Shepperson, 965.

234. WELBOURN, F(rederick) B. "The missionary culture," in D. M. Paton (ed.), Essays in Anglican self-criticism. London: S.C.M. Press, 1958. 238p.
Pp. 65-68, brief reference to independent churches, in connection with polygamy, nationalism and culture.

235. WERNER, Alice. Myths and legends of the Bantu. London: Harrap, 1933. 335p. illus.
Pp. 239-246 on traditional prophets and Chaminuka in Mashonaland, Mohlomi of the Basuto, and the religious origins of the Majimaji rebellion in Tanganyika.

236. WILLOUGHBY, W(illiam) C(harles). The Soul of the Bantu. New York: Doubleday Doran, 1928. 276p.
Pp. 104-112, Revelation by "possession"; 112-135, revelation by "prophets"--Chibisa, Makana, Mhlakaza, Marethe, Mgijima, Kimbangu, etc. et passim, see "prophets" in index.

237. WILSON, Bryan R. "Millennialism in comparative perspective," Comparative Studies in Society and History, 6 (1) Oct. 1963, 93-114.
A review article: Thrupp (ed.) item 14, Muhlmann (ed.) item 160, etc.

238. WORSLEY, Peter M. "Millenarian movements in Melanesia," Rhodes-Livingstone Journal, 21, 1957, 18-31. Also BMRS, A 248.
Includes comparative reference to millennial movements in Africa.

239. ZAJACZOKWSKI, Andrzej. "Magia i religia w czarnej Afryce" (Magic and religion in black Africa), Kultura i Spoleczenstwo (Warsaw), 4 (4) Oct.-Dec. 1960, 157-172.
Negro churches, and the integrative role of religious movements, chiefly in the Congo area.

240. ZEITZ, Leonard. Some African messianic movements and their political implications. Paper read to the second Annual Conference, American Society of African Culture. New York City, 1959, 42p (mimeo.) (private circulation).
A general account of South African movements; brief accounts of Harris, and the Watch Tower society; longer treatment of Kimbanguism.

WEST AFRICA

241. ANON. "The challenge of West Africa," The Foreign Field (London: Wesleyan Methodist), Sept. 1922, 221.
On the movements derived from Harris and Oppong.

242. BASTIDE, Roger. "Les metamorphoses du sacré dans les sociétés en transition," Civilisations, 9 (4), 1959, 432-443.
A comparison of West African religious movements and the Brazilian syncretist religion, Umbanda.

242A. BLYDEN, Edward Wilmot. The Return of the Exiles and the West African
       Church. London: 1891.

243.   CONSULTATION ON EVANGELIZATION OF WEST AFRICA TODAY. "The Evangelization
       of West Africa Today," International Review of Missions, 54 (216) Oct.
       1965, 484-494.
           P. 486, the "northward thrust" of independent churches; part of the
           Yaoundé statement, 1965.

244.   COOKSEY, Joseph James & MCLEISH, Alexander. Religion and civilization in
       West Africa: A missionary survey of French, British, Spanish and Portu-
       gese West Africa with Liberia. London: World Dominion Press, 1931.
       vi + 277p.
           Pp. 55-71, 135-141, 251, Harris; p. 67 Loxzema at Sassandra; p. 141
           Oppong.

245.   DIETERLIN, Germaine. "Le syncrétisme du mythe peul," in Bouaké, item 206.

246.   LE COEUR, Ch(arles). Le culte de la génération et l'évolution religieuse
       et sociale en Guinée. Paris: Leroux, 1932. 146p. (B.H.)
           Pp. 138ff., prophet Harris.

247.   LITTLE, Kenneth. "The urban role of tribal associations in West Africa,"
       African Studies (Johannesburg), 21 (1) 1962, 1-9.
           Pp. 2-3, 6, syncretistic adaptations of traditional cults. (AA 14,
           365.)

248.   _____. West African urbanization: A study of voluntary associations in
       social change. Cambridge: C.U.P., 1965. 179p.
           Pp. 35-46, "syncretist cults," a general description of their role in
           urban society, especially in Ghana; (after Fiawoo, item 304).

248A. LYNCH, Hollis R. "Edward W. Blyden: Pioneer West African nationalist,"
       Journal of African History, 6 (3) 1965, 373-388.
           Pp. 382-383, Blyden's influence on early Nigerian secessions. See
           fuller account in Lynch's Edward W. Blyden, Pan-Negro patriot, London,
           expected 1966.

249.   MUSSON, Margaret. Prophet Harris: The amazing story of old Pa Union Jack.
       Wallington (England): Religious Education Press, 1950. 111p. illus.
           Popular, imaginative, inaccurate reconstruction.

250.   PARRINDER, E. G. "The religious situation in West Africa," African Affairs
       (London), 59 (234) Jan. 1960, 38-42.
           Pp. 41-42, includes brief survey of independent movements, and their
           mixture of pagan and Old Testament elements. (AA 12, 177.)

251.   _____. "Africa's churches advance," West African Review (London), 33
       (409) Jan. 1962, 5-9.
           P. 9, on the "breakaway sects" and their inclusion in a united church.

252.   PILKINGTON, F. W. "'Old Man Union Jack': William Wade Harris, prophet of
       West Africa," West African Review (London), 23 (293) Feb. 1952, 122-125.
       Illus.

253. PLATT, W. J. _An African prophet, The Ivory Coast movement and what came of it._ London: S.C.M. Press, 1934. 157p.
    Prophet Harris of the Ivory Coast; pp. 81-83, some reference to Kimbangu; pp. 84-86, Sampson Oppong; by the Methodist missionary who "discovered" the Harris movement.

254. PRICE-MARS, Jean. _Silhouettes de nègres et de négrophiles._ Paris: Presence africaine, 1960. 213p.
    The second part based on F. D. Walker, item 396, includes a popular biography of prophet Harris.

255. RINGWALD, Walter. "Westafrikanische propheten" (West African prophets), _Evangelische Missionszeitschrift_ (Stuttgart), 1 (4) 1940, 118-122; (5) 1940, 145-155.
    In Nigeria and, particularly, in Ghana.

256. SAWYERR, Harry. "Christian evangelistic strategy in West Africa: Reflections on the centenary of the consecration of Bishop Samuel Adjayi Crowther on St. Peter's Day, 1864," _International Review of Missions,_ 54 (215) July 1965, 343-352.
    P. 347, "spiritual churches" cited as offering members spiritual healing through absolution.

257. SCHULTZ, L. "William Wade Harris und seine Massenbewegung" (W. W. Harris and his mass-movement), _Evangelisches Missions-magazin_ (Basel), n.s. 86 (5) May 1942, 83-92.

258. TAYLOR, John V. _C.M.S._ News-Letter (London), 287, Nov. 1965.
    Pp. 1, 3, brief references to the "separatist churches" and their evangelistic thrust northwards, and to their toleration of polygamy.

259. TURNER, Harold W. "The litany of an independent West African church," _Sierra Leone Bulletin of Religion,_ 1 (2) Dec. 1959, 48-55. Also in _Practical Anthropology_ (Tarrytown, N.Y.), 7 (6) Nov.-Dec. 1960, 256-262.
    An analysis of a Church of the Lord (Aladura) text; see Oshitelu, item 541. (AA 12, 64.)

260. ____. "Searching and syncretism: A West African documentation," _International Review of Missions,_ 49 (194) April 1960, 189-194. Also in _Practical Anthropology_ (Tarrytown, N.Y.), 8 (3) May-June 1961, 106-110.
    An analysis of the religious literature possessed by a member of an Aladura church. (AA 12, 65.)

261. ____. "The catechism of an independent West African church," _Sierra Leone Bulletin of Religion,_ 2 (2) Dec. 1960, 45-57; Also in _Occasional Papers_ (International Missionary Council, London), 9 April 1961, 10p. (mimeo.) G. Tr., "Katechismen unabhängiger westafrikanischer Kirchen," in E. Benz (ed.), item 41, 72-88.
    An analysis of a text from the Church of the Lord (Aladura); comparison with two Ghanaian and two Kimbanguist catechisms. See Oshitelu, item 541. (AA 12, 336.)

262. ____. "The Church of the Lord: the expansion of a Nigerian independent church in Sierra Leone and Ghana," _Journal of African History,_ 3 (1) 1962, 91-110. (AA 14, 523.)

263. _____. "Pagan features in West African independent churches," <u>Practical Anthropology</u> (Tarrytown, N.Y.), 12 (4) July-Aug. 1965, 145-151.
    Pagan features are not confined to the independent churches, nor derived entirely from indigenous religions; some are regular features in Christian history, or derive from imported occultism and magic.

264. _____. <u>Profile through preaching</u>. <u>A study of the sermon texts used in a West African independent church</u>. London: Edinburgh House Press, 1965. 88p.
    The Church of the Lord (Aladura): visual profiles derived from an analysis of 8,000 texts, showing its Biblical emphases; with an Anglican comparison.

265. _____. <u>African independent church</u>. vol. I, <u>History of an African independent church, the Church of the Lord (Aladura)</u>. vol. II, <u>African independent church: The life and faith of the Church of the Lord (Aladura)</u>. Oxford: Clarendon Press, 1966.
    A comprehensive study, including phenomenological description and theological analysis.

266. WALKER, F(rank) Deaville. <u>The day of harvest in the white fields of West Africa</u>. London: Cargate Press, n.d. (1925). 80p. illus.
    Ch. 1, prophet Harris in Apolonia, with photo; pp. 16-18, Sampson Oppong, with photo; pp. 71-79 on Platt and the Harris movement.

267. _____. <u>Harris le prophète noir</u>. Privas (Ardèche), Pasteur Delattre, 1931. 191p. illus. map.

268. WILSON, H. S. "E. W. Blyden on religion in Africa," <u>Sierra Leone Bulletin of Religion</u>, 2 (2) Dec. 1960, 58-66.
    Especially pp. 64-65 on Africanizing Christianity, his role in the foundation of the United Native African Church in Lagos, and the references to Blyden's works given there.

<u>CAMEROUN</u>

269. BRITISH GOVERNMENT. <u>Report by His Britannic Majesty's Government to the council of the League of Nations on the administration of the British Cameroons for the year 1925</u>. London: HMSO, 1926. Colonial No. 22.
    P. 21, brief report of a witchfinding movement in the Fontem area.

270. _____. <u>Report on Cameroons under British mandate for the year 1930</u>. London: HMSO, 1931. Colonial No. 65.
    Pp. 9, 12, a brief account of prophetess Makaïya in Bamenda and Mamfe Divisions in 1930.

271. BRUTSCH, L. R. "Origine et développement d'une église indépendante africaine. L'Eglise baptiste camerounaise," <u>Monde non-chrétien</u> (Paris), n.s. 12, Oct.-Dec. 1949, pp. 408-424.
    The Cameroun Baptist Church. Includes documentary appendices on dismissal of a Baptist pastor, and extract from <u>Journal officiel du Cameroun français</u>, 5 July 1949, containing constitution of the Church.

272. BUREAU, R. "L'absence de syncrétisme et de messianisme au Cameroun méridionale: causes et significations," in Bouaké, item 206.

273. COLIGNON, A. <u>La véritable histoire de Marie aux léopards</u>. Paris: 1933. (E.A.)
      Prophetess Sombe or Maria among the Kundu, 1915.

274. HODGKIN, Thomas. "The French Cameroons," <u>West Africa</u> (London), 27, 27 Nov. 1954, 1109; and 4 Dec. 1954, 1133.
      Lotin Same's Native Baptist Church in Douala, including reference to the role of the Garvey movement's ideas. (AA 6, 561)

274A. HORNER, Norman A. <u>Cross and crucifix in mission</u>. New York: Abingdon, 1965. 223p.
      Pp. 51-52, the "Ngoumba Independent Church" (correct name: Église protestante africaine) among the Ngoumba; a secession from the Presbyterian Church of Cameroun on the issue of their tribal language.

275. HUGHES, W. <u>Dark Africa and the way out</u>. London: Sampson, Low, 1892. 155p.
      Pp. 31, 71, 72, on the Native Baptist Church.

276. JABOT, J. M. <u>Sous les manguiers en fleurs</u>. <u>Histoires de Bantous</u>. Paris: Éd. de Belles-Lettres, 1922. 225p.
      Includes reference to prophetess Sombe or Maria, among the Kundu, 1915.

277. MALLO, Eugène. "Rapports entre jeunes églises," <u>Flambeau</u> (Yaoundé), 5, Feb. 1965, 37-39.
      Brief definitions of two kinds of independent churches--by secession, or by new formation; brief evaluation of independents in the Cameroun context.

278. MVENG, Engelbert. <u>Histoire du Cameroun</u>. Paris: Présence africaine, 1963. 533p.
      Pp. 457-458, the Native Baptist Church and other independents.

279. RUDIN, Harry Rudolph. <u>Germans in the Cameroons 1884-1914</u>: <u>A case study in modern imperialism</u>. London: Cape, 1938. vii + 456p.
      Pp. 361-3, on Native Baptist Church.

<u>DAHOMEY</u>

280. LOMBARD, J. "Cotonou, ville africaine," <u>Études dahoméennes</u> (Porto Novo, Dahomey, I.F.A.N.), 10, 1953, 179-187.
      Pp. 186-8 on new religions imported from Nigeria including the Cherubim and Seraphim Society and the United Native African Church. (AA 7, 35)

281. PARRINDER, E. G. "Les Sociétés-religieuses en Afrique occidentale," <u>Présence africaine</u>, n.s. 17-18, Feb.-May 1958, 17-22. (Series no. 18-19 on spine).
      A brief account of several independent churches in Porto Novo. (AA 10, 334.)

GHANA

282. ACQUAH, Ioné. Accra survey. London: University of London Press, 1958.
      Pp. 148-150, a brief survey with statistics of churches founded by
      Africans in Accra.

283. ANON. In The Methodist Recorder (London), 6 May 1915, 4 May 1916,
      3 May 1917.
      Missionary reports on the Harris mass movement in W. Ghana.

284. _____. "M.P.'s talk about the sects," Christian Messenger (Accra,
      Presbyterian), 6 (3), Mar. 1965, pp. 1, 6. Continued as "Should sects
      be controlled," in 6 (5), May 1965, 2.
      A report of a debate in the Ghana National Assembly on the alleged
      abuses connected with indigenous prophets and their "sects."

285. APPIAH, J. Jehu. Christ mpiadua hu dom asornhu abakonsem. Koforidua:
      1943. (C.B.)
      In Fanti, by the founder of the Musama Disco Christo Church.

286. _____. Musama Disco Christo Church History. Koforidua, Ghana: Fanzaar
      Press, n.d. (C.B.)
      Originally written in Fanti.

287. APTER, David E. The Gold Coast in transition. Princeton, New Jersey:
      Princeton U.P., 1955. xvii + 355p.
      P. 152, members of "nativistic or messianic cults" tend to avoid
      Western culture, seeking solace in religious beliefs but not in a
      particular form of social life.

288. ARMSTRONG, Charles W. "The appeal of Apolonia," The Foreign Field
      (London: Wesleyan Methodist), April 1915, 209-11.
      The area where Harris had recently initiated a mass movement.

289. _____. The winning of West Africa. London: Wesleyan Methodist Mission-
      ary Society, 1920. 64p.
      Ch. iv, "The Apolonian movement"; a summary of the work of Harris
      in West Ghana.

290. BAËTA, C. G. Prophetism in Ghana: A study of some 'spiritual' churches.
      London: S.C.M. Press, 1962. 169p.
      A study by a Ghanian theologian of nine independent churches in
      Ghana including the Church of The Twelve Apostles, Musama Disco
      Christo Church, The Saviour Church, The Apostolic Revelation Society
      and The Prayer and Healing Group of the Evangelical Presbyterian
      Church at Etodome. Three of the other four groups are outgrowths
      of Nigerian Aladura churches. Appendix C gives the text of the
      Apostolic Revelation Society's catechism.

291. _____. "Cultes syncrétiques au Ghana," in Bouaké, item 206.

292. BARTELS, F. L. The roots of Ghana Methodism. Cambridge: Cambridge
      U.P. 1965.
      Pp. 161-163, Majola Agbebi in 1902, early Ethiopianism and the
      Basel Mission in 1905, the African Methodist Zion Church under
      Pinanko; pp. 174-178, prophet Harris; p. 188, African Methodist
      Episcopal Zion Church. By a Ghanaian historian.

293. BRUCE, Ernest. "I grew up with history," African Challenge (Lagos),
     Apr. 1957, 6-10.
          Personal reminiscences of prophet Harris by a Ghanaian Methodist
          minister.

294. BUSIA, K. A. Report on a social survey of Sekondi-Takoradi. London:
     Crown Agents for the Colonies, 1950. 164p.
          P. 78, the Hope and Honesty inter denominational societies; pp. 79-80,
          Tigare.

295. CARSTAIRS, G. M. "A view from the shrine," The Listener (London), 65
     (1666) 2 Mar. 1961, 387-389. Illus.
          Comparison of modern W. African and Indian shrines and their priests
          --using Field, item 308.

296. CERULLI, Ernesta. "La setta dei Water Carriers" (The Water Carriers
     Sect), Studi e materiali per la storia delle religioni (Rome), 34 (1),
     1963, 27-29.
          A syncretist Harris derivative in the Nzemba tribe with healing
          emphasis.

297. CHING, D(onald) S. Ivory Tales. London: Epworth, 1950. 126p.
          Pp. 95-124, a summary account of Harris, by a Methodist missionary.

298. CHRISTENSEN, James Boyd. "The Tigare Cult of West Africa," Papers of the
     Michigan Academy of Science, Arts and Letters, 39, 1954, 389-398.
          A neo-pagan cult. (AA 6, 528.)

299. _____. "The adaptive functions of Fanti priesthood," in W. Bascom &
     M. J. Herskovits (eds.), Continuity and change in african cultures.
     Chicago: University of Chicago Press, 1959, 257-278.
          A concise analysis of the impact of Christianity upon traditional
          Fanti religion, with a concluding section on "new cults" which
          discusses Tigare.

300. DEBRUNNER, Hans W. Witchcraft in Ghana. London: Brown, Knight and
     Truscott (1959) 1961. Illus.
          Chps. 20 and 21 on "African healing churches and witchcraft" and a
          "witchhunting prophet."

301. _____. A church between colonial powers. London: Lutterworth, 1965.
     368p.
          Pp. 269-281, Prophet Do's prayer movement, and Prophet Wovenu's
          Apostolic Revelation Society; p. 283, Apostolic Faith Mission;
          pp. 284, 287, Sect of the Second Adam; and ch. 22, passim.

302. DE WILSON, George. The biography of Prophet John Mensah. Cape Coast
     (Ghana): the author, n.d. (c. 1960). 42p.
          On the founder of the independent Church of Christ, 1959, at Cape
          Coast.

303. DICKSON, Kwesi A. "The 'Methodist Society': A sect," Ghana Bulletin of
     Theology, (Legon), 2 (6) June 1962, 1-7.
          A secession in Ghana in the 1860's.

304. FIAWOO, D. K. The influence of contemporary social changes on the magico-religious concepts and organization of Southern Ewe-speaking people of Ghana. Unpublished Ph.D. dissertation, Edinburgh University, 1959. (K.L.)
        Reference to various neo-pagan movements: Atike, Blekete and their role in social change. See Little, item 248.

305. _____. "Urbanization and religion in Eastern Ghana," Sociological Review (Keele), n.s. 7 (1) July 1959, 83-97.
        Pp. 93-94, the communal life of the Apostolic Revelation Society at Tadzewu and general remarks. (AA 13, 513.)

306. FIELD, M. J. "Some new shrines of the Gold Coast and their significance," Africa (London), 13 (2) April 1940, 138-149.
        Revival of traditional methods to deal with new problems.

307. _____. Akim-Kotoku, an 'oman' of the Gold Coast. London: Crown Agents for the Colonies, 1948. viii & 211p.
        Pp. 171-197, on new cults relating traditional practices to modern life.

308. _____. Search for security: an ethno-psychiatric survey of rural Ghana. London: Faber and Faber, 1960. 478p.
        Pp. 87-104, Ashanti healing shrines from a psychological perspective.

309. GIBSON, Stephen J. "How the gates are lifted on the Gold Coast," The Foreign Field (London: Wesleyan Methodist) Jan. 1920, 59.
        Brief reference to Harris.

310. GOODY, Jack. "Anomie in Ashanti?" Africa (London), 27 (4) 1957, 356-62.
        A criticism of Ward, item 332, asserting that increased malaise due to European contacts is not proven.

311. GOUDIE, William, in The Methodist Recorder (London), 56 (2998) 6 May 1915, 5.
        An early first hand report by a missionary on the effect of Harris' work in Apolonia, Ghana.

312. GROTTANELLI, Vinigi L. "Asongu worship among the Nzema: A study in Akan art and religion," Africa (London), 31 (1) Jan. 1961, 46-60.
        P. 49, brief account of Deazate, an iconoclast in S. W. Ghana in 1954. (AA 12, 314.)

313. _____. "Pre-existence and survival in Nzemba beliefs," Man, 61 (art. 1) Jan. 1961, 1-5.
        P. 1, brief reference to a prophet in 1954.

314. HALIBURTON, G(ordon) M. The Prophet Harris and the Methodist Church. London: Paper for African History Seminar, School of Oriental and African Studies, Feb. 1963. 8p. (mimeo.)
        An account of the Methodist reaction to the influence of Harris in Apolonia, from 1914 to 1926.

315. _____. "The Anglican Church of Ghana and the Harris movement of 1914," Bulletin, Society for African Church History (Nsukka, E. Nigeria), 1 (3-4) Dec. 1964, 101-6.
        On John Swatson, mulatto evangelist in West Ghana, who was influenced by Harris.

316. ____. "Sampson Oppong, the calling of a prophet," Bulletin, Society for African Church History (Aberdeen), 2, Dec. 1964. (expected 1966).

317. ____. "The late Sampson Oppong, Ashanti Prophet," West African Religion (Nsukka, E. Nigeria), 5, Feb. 1966, 1-3.
     An obituary notice.

318. HARTENSTEIN, Karl. Anibue: die 'Neue Zeit' auf der Goldkuste und unsere missionsausgabe (The 'New Era' in the Gold Coast, and our missionary task). Stuttgart: Evangelische Missionsverlag, 1932.
     D.T., Anibue: de 'Niewe Tijd' op de Goudkust en onze zendingstaak. Culumborg: 1933. 175p.
     Pp. 83-86 on Prophet Chei among the Ewe in Ghana.

319. HAYFORD, Joseph E. Casely. William Waddy Harris: the West African reformer: the man and his message. London: C.M. Phillips, 1915.
     Hayford's impression of Harris through personal contact with his preaching at Axim, Gold Coast; by a Gold Coast lawyer and nationalist.

320. HAYFORD, Mark Casely (ed.). The year-book and report, The Baptist Church and Mission and the Christian Army of the Gold Coast. London: the Church, n.d. (1913). 127p.
     The independent church founded by the author, who was ordained in 1898 by Majola Agbebi of Nigeria for the Gold Coast work.

321. HORLER, Edmund C. "Stretching out her hands to God," The Foreign Field (London: Wesleyan Methodist), July 1917, 153.
     A missionary on the opportunity provided in Apolonia (W. Ghana) by the Harris converts.

322. JAHODA, Gustav. "Traditional healers and other institutions concerned with mental illness in Ghana," International Journal of Social Psychiatry (London), 7 (4), 1961, 245-268.
     Includes examination of a prayer healing church as a new institution to deal with new problems. (AA 14, 282)

323. KIMBLE, David. A political history of Ghana: The rise of Gold Coast nationalism 1850-1928. Oxford: Clarendon, 1963. xviii + 587p.
     Pp. 163-166, A.M.E. Zion, Church of Gold Coast, Church of God, Nigritian Church, Musama Disco Cristo, Harris and Oppong.

324. RINGWALD, W. "Experiment Goldküste" (Gold Coast Experiment), Evangelische Missions-zeitschrift (Stuttgart), 12, 1955, 1-18, 40-48, 72-83.
     Especially p. 81 for Musama Disco Christo church, and p. 41 for translation of "An Abuakwa Son's Prayer," taken from the Ashanti Pioneer n.d., -- a nationalized version of the Lord's Prayer.

325. SACKEY, Isaac. "A brief history of the A.M.E. Zion church, West Gold Coast District," Ghana Bulletin of Theology (Legon), 1 (3) 1957, 16-20.
     An "ethiopian" type of independent church founded under American auspices in the Gold Coast, 1903. By a Ghanian clergyman of this church.

326. SMITH, J. Noel. The Presbyterian Church of Ghana, 1835-1960: a younger church in a changing society. Unpublished Ph.D. dissertation, Edinburgh University, 1963. (K.L.)
     Reference to Ghanian separatist churches.

327. SOUTHON, A. E. <u>Gold Coast Methodism</u>: <u>the first hundred years</u>, <u>1835-1935</u>.
London: Cargate Press, 1934. 158p. illus.
Pp. 141f., on Sampson Oppong.

328. 'SPECTATOR.' "Why so many sects?" <u>Christian Messenger</u> (Accra: Presbyterian),
6 (8) Aug. 1965, 2.
A "healing revival crusade" in Accra, 1965, led by Osei-Bonsu; see
latter's reply in 6 (9) Sept. 1965, 8.

329. STOEVESANDT, G. "The sect of the Second Adam," <u>Africa</u> (London), 7 (4)
Oct. 1934, 479-482.
A defunct community in Ghana which sought a return to primitive
paradise, c. 1911.

330. THOMPSON, E. W. "The village pastor and his training," <u>The Foreign Field</u>
(London: Wesleyan Methodist), Sept. 1922, 232-233.
P. 232, the author's meeting with Sampson Oppong.

331. VAN TRIGT, F. "De Profeet Harris" (The Prophet Harris), <u>Afrika Ontwaakt</u>
(Oosterbeek, Tafelberg, Holland), 19 (4) Apr. 1948, 59-61.
An account of Harris derived from the journal of Fr. Stauffer, the
Roman Catholic priest at Axim, when Harris visited there.

332. WARD, Barbara E. "Some observations on religious cults in Ashanti,"
<u>Africa</u> (London), 26 (1) Jan. 1956, 47-61.
Reasons for dissatisfaction with the Church in Ashanti, and
development of new witchfinding cults in the 1940's. (AA 8, 44.)

333. WEINBERG, S. Kirson. "'Mental healing' and social change in West Africa,"
<u>Social Problems</u> (Spencer, Indiana), 11 (3) Winter 1964, 257-299.
Pp. 264-268, role of Christian "faith healers" in supplanting the
native doctors' position in traditional society.

334. WESLEYAN METHODIST MISSIONARY SOCIETY. London: <u>Reports</u>: No. 107
(for 1920) 1921, 79-80; No. 108 (for 1921) 1922, 79; No. 112 (for 1925)
1926, 86-87.
On Sampson Oppong.

335. WIEGRABE, P. "Un nouveau culte indigène à la Côte d'Or," <u>Journal des
Missions évangéliques</u> (Paris), 5 (21) Oct. 1950, 378-380.
The Tigare cult in Ghana.

336. WILLIAMSON, Sidney George (Kwesi A. Dickson, ed.). <u>Akan religion and the
Christian faith</u>: <u>A comparative study of the impact of two religions</u>.
Accra: Ghana U.P., 1965.
Pp. 28-30, 162-165, assessment of role of independent churches in
Akan, as "marginally Christian" and not as important as in Ibadan
and South Africa.

337. WITTER, T. "On the fringe of the Ashanti mass movement," <u>The Foreign
Field</u> (London: Wesleyan Methodist), Sept. 1922, 223-225.
Description of the Sampson Oppong movement. See also editorial,
p. 221.

GUINEA

338. PAULME, Denise. "Un mouvement féminin en pays kissi (Sept. 1948),"
      Notes africaines (Dakar), 46, Apr. 1950, 43-44.

IVORY COAST

339. AMON D'ABY, F. J. La Côte d'Ivoire dans la cité africaine. Paris:
      Larose, 1951. 208p. illus. map.
          Pp. 151ff., Prophet Harris, by an Ivory Coast scholar.

340. ANON. "The like that was never told," The Methodist Recorder (London),
      65 (3491) 9 Oct. 1924, 11.
          An appeal by the Wesleyan Methodist Missionary Society for workers
          among the Harris Christians, with information on the movement.

341. _____. "Thirty thousand African Christians without a pastor," The Foreign
      Field (London: Wesleyan Methodist), Dec. 1924, 59-62. Illus.
          Platt's "discovery" of the Harris churches.

342. _____. "West African prophet found," South African Outlook (Lovedale),
      57 (672) 2 May 1927, 97-98.
          The French Protestant missionary Benoit's discovery of Harris in
          Liberia.

343. _____. "Rapport d'un meurtre dû au tékékpan," Élite éburnéenne: science
      et culture (Abidjan), 9, Nov.-Dec. 1955. (B.H.)
          The divinity in a new cult in Ivory Coast.

344. _____. "Comptes rendus de la réunion sur le thème: tradition et
      modernisme en Afrique noire, Bouaké, Côte d'Ivoire, Janvier 1962,"
      Images de Toumliline (Azrou: Morocco), May-July-Sept. 1962. (B.H.)
          Pp. 87ff., "syncretism" and the Harris movement.

345. BERNUS, Edmund. "Ahouati, notes sur un village Dida," Études éburnéenes
      (Abidjan), 6, 1957, 213-230.
          Pp. 217-219, on a Harris church, Chratchoche.

346. BIANQUIS, Jean. Le prophète Harris ou dix ans d'histoire religieuse à la
      Côte d'Ivoire (1914-1924). Paris: Société des missions évangéliques de
      Paris, 1924. 40p. (B.H.) Also in Foi et Vie (Paris), 16 Nov. & 1 Dec.
      1924.
          A Protestant missionary compares several contemporary views of the
          Harris movement.

347. BOULNOIS, Jean. Gnon-Sua, dieu des Guérés. Paris: Fournier, 1933,
      132p. (B.H.)
          Pp. 108ff., prophet Harris in the Ivory Coast.

348. CHING, D(onald) S. "La vie du prophète Harris," Envol (Abidjan), May
      1955. (B.H.)

349. DE BILLY, Eduard. En Côte d'Ivoire, mission protestante d'AOF. Paris:
      Société des missions évangéliques, 1931. 182p. illus.
          Pp. 13-19, 27, 36-43 on Harris, by a Protestant missionary.

350. _____. "Le prophète Harris en Côte d'Ivoire," Envol (Abidjan), March 1955. (B.H.)

351. DESANTI, Dominique. "Attio le guérisseur," Constellation (Paris), 166, Feb. 1962. (B.H.)
    A young healer at Bregbo, Ivory Coast, in the Harris tradition.

352. _____. Côte d'Ivoire. L'Atlas des voyages rencontre. Lausanne: 1962. Illus.
    Impressionist; includes a chapter on Harris churches, and an interview with Jonas Ahui (or Awi), the older Ebrié leader among the Harris churches.

353. DIETERLIN, Germaine (ed.). Textes sacrés de l'Afrique noire. Paris: Gallimard, 1965. 287p.
    Pp. 98-106: "Cantiques harristes," with introduction by, and reprinted from, J. Rouch, item 389.

354. DJORO, A. Les mouvements marginaux du protestantisme africain: les Harristes en Côte d'Ivoire. Paris: École pratique des hautes études, section des sciences religieuses, 1956. 315p. (mimeo.)

355. FENTON, Thomas. Black harvest. London: Cargate Press, 1956. 160p.
    Pp. 39-76, imaginative but informative reconstruction of the development of a Protestant church subsequent to Harris, by the former superintendent of the Methodist Mission.

356. GORJU, Joseph. "Un prophète de la Côte d'Ivoire," Les missions catholiques, 2400, 4 June 1915, 267-268.
    A sympathetic account of prophet Harris by a Roman Catholic missionary.

357. GRIVOT, R. "Le cercle de grand Lahou," Bulletin de l'Institut français d'Afrique noire (Dakar), 4 (1-4) Jan.-Oct. 1942, 7-154.
    Pp. 82-89, Harris, Botto Adaï, Nianga and other "cults" in Ivory Coast.

358. HARRINGTON, Peter. "An interview with the 'Black Prophet'," The African Missionary (Cork, Ireland) vol. 1914-1918 (18) Mar.-Apr. 1917, 13-16. F. Tr., "Une interview avec le Prophète noir," Écho des Missions africaines de Lyon (Lyon), 16 (5) Sept.-Oct. 1917, 155-161; (6) Nov.-Dec.
    A Roman Catholic describes a meeting with Harris in 1915.

359. HARTZ, Joseph. "Ein sonderbarer schwarzer Prophet" (A strange black prophet), Afrikanisches Missionsglocklein (St. Pierre, Bas-Rhin, France), 3 (3) Mar. 1925, 56-60.
    By the Superior of the Missions africaines de Lyon, who knew Harris.

360. HIMMELHEBER, H(ans). "Massa-Fetisch der Rechtschaffenheit," (A Massa-fetish of uprightness) Tribus (Stuttgart), n.s., 4-5, 1954-1955. (Pub. 1956), 56-62.
    The massa cult among the Senoufo. (AA 10, 37.)

361. HOLAS, Bohumil. "En marge de l'étude d'un culte ouest-africain," Monde non-chrétien, n.s. (27) 1953, 267-280; (28) 1953, 399-429.

362. _____. "Bref aperçu sur les principaux cultes syncrétiques de la basse Côte d'Ivoire," Africa, 24 (1) Jan. 1954, 55-60.
    Harris and subsequent prophet cults, especially Deima.

363.   _____.   "Note sur l'apparition du 'vide spirituel' en Côte d'Ivoire et
        sur ces conséquences," Revue de psychologie des peuples (le Havre)
        9 (4) 1954, 398-404. (B.H.)
            Includes cults "de Massa," or "de la Corne"; emphasizes the impossi-
            bility of a spiritual vacuum in African society, as the background to
            new religious movements. (AA 7, 31)

364.   _____.   "Changements modernes de la pensée religieuse baoulé (Côte
        d'Ivoire)," Monde non-chrétien, (Paris), n.s. 31, July-Sep. 1954, 265-275.
            A new cult, L'Ayéré kpli or tétékpan, hostile to ancestral beliefs,
            and of universal outlook. (AA 7, 30.)

365.   _____.   "Le prosélytisme en Côte d'Ivoire," La Vie intellectuelle (Paris),
        28 (87) Dec. 1956, 31-41. (B.H.) Also in Recontres (Paris), 48, 1957,
        155-167.
            The Harris movement on the coast; the Ayéré kpli cult among the
            Baoulé of the centre; the massa cult of the Senoufo in the north;
            first given as a paper, "Mouvements prosélytiques en Côte d'Ivoire,"
            at W. African Institute of Social and Economic Research, Ibadan,
            1955, and included in the mimeo report, pp. 151-159.

366.   _____.   "Fondements spirituels de la vie sociale sénoufo. (Region de
        Korhogo, Côte d'Ivoire)," Journal de la Société des africanistes (Paris),
        26 (1-2) 1956, 9-32.
            Pp. 28-32, new cults--"de la Corne" (or massa), and Nya. (AA 9, 21.)

367.   _____.   Les Sénoufo (y compris les Minianka). Paris: Presses Universi-
        taires de France, 1957. 183p. bibl. maps.
            Pp. 155-158, "Le culte de la Corne" (Ram's Horn Cult), a modern
            adaptation of the traditional Poro cult.

368.   _____.   Changements sociaux en Côte d'Ivoire. Paris: Presses Universitaires
        de France, 1961. 119p. illus.
            Pp. 59-64, new "cults" in traditional societies, especially the Oubi
            of the southwest.

369.   _____.   La Côte d'Ivoire: Passé-present-perspectives. Abidjan: Centre
        des sciences humaines, n.d. (c. 1962). 99p.
            Pp. 73-74, brief summary of Harris and Harris movements.

370.   _____.   Le séparatisme religieux en Afrique noire (L'exemple de la Côte
        d'Ivoire). Paris: Presses universitaires de France, 1965. 410p.
        bibl. illus.
            A major study of the cult of the prophet Boto Adaï with texts; the
            Harris movement and its successors; new cults, especially Ayéré kpli,
            and massa. Indices of vernacular terms, and of "Prophets and cults"
            in Africa; extensive bibliography. The index of cults and the
            bibliography need correction.

371.   JOSEPH, Gaston. "Une atteinte à l'animisme chez les populations de la
        Côte d'Ivoire," Bulletin du Comité d'études historiques et scientifiques
        de l'A.O.F., 1916, 344f; 1917, 497f.
            Same material as in item 372.

372.   _____.   La Côte d'Ivoire. Paris: Fayard, (1917) 1944. xii + 234p.
        maps.
            Pp. 97-104, Harris and his followers.

36

373. KING, Louis L. "Indigenous hymnody of the Ivory Coast," Practical Anthropology (Tarrytown, N. Y.), 9 (6) Nov.-Dec. 1962, 268-270.
    Includes brief reference to the practice and influence of prophet Harris.

374. LAUBIER, R. "Le Harrisme se répand en Côte d'Ivoire," Tribune des nations (Paris), 17 June 1956.

375. LEJEUNE, Ad. "Religions nouvelles," Echo des Missions africaines de Lyon (Lyon), 46 (5) 1947, 11-13.
    The Adaï and Déima cults of the Ivory Coast.

376. LOBSIGER, G. "Une religion nouvelle en Côte d'Ivoire (Résumé de la conference de D. Paulme-Schaeffner)," Bulletin annuel du Musée et de l'Institut d'Ethnologie de la ville de Genève, 5, 1962. (B.H.)

377. MARTY, Paul. Études sur l'Islam en Côte d'Ivoire. Paris: E. Leroux, 1923. 496p. maps.
    Pp. 13ff. on the Harris movement.

378. MATTHIESEN, H. Harris. Et nutidseventyr fra Elfenbenskysten (Harris: a modern story from the Ivory Coast). Copenhagen: 1928. (EA)

379. MORGANTHAU, Ruth Schachter. Political parties in French-speaking West Africa. Oxford: Clarendon Press, 1964.
    Pp. 8, 182, 344, the slight political role of Harris churches in the Ivory Coast.

380. NEVEUX, Maurice. Religion des noirs. Fétiches de la Côte d'Ivoire. Alençon: Laverdure, 1923. 33 p.
    Pp. 15ff. on Prophet Harris.

381. OETTLI, Walter. Drei berühmte Afrikaner (Three famous Africans). Stuttgart: Evangelische Missionsverlag, 1931. 45p.
    Includes prophet Harris, following Walker, item 396.

382. PAULME, Denise. "Une religion syncrétique en Côte d'Ivoire: le culte déïma," Cahiers d'études africains, 3 (1) 1962, 5-90. Bibl. illus.
    Déïma, founded by Marie Lalou who was inspired by the doctrine of prophet Harris. Translation and commentary of 12 texts of the cult; prayers, catechism, testaments and doctrine. (AA 15, 33)

383. _____. Une société de Côte d'Ivoire hier et aujourd'hui: Les Bété. The Hague: Mouton, 1962. 200p. illus.
    Pp. 180-194 on "cultures nouveaux," Asye and Tetegba.

384. _____. "Sur un mythe africain récent d'origine de la mort," in Actes du VIe Congrès international des sciences anthropologiques et ethnologiques. Paris: Musée de l'Homme, Tome II, 2e. vol., 1964, 449-452.
    A myth in the Marie Lalou cult, Ivory Coast, with biblical and islamic features. (FA 1, 665.)

385. PLATT, W. J. (ed.). News notes from West Africa (England), 1, Jan. 1926, 1-5; 2, Apr. 1926, 2-3; 3, July 1926, 3. Also F.Tr., Courrier de l'A.O.F.
    The continuing Harris movement as taken up by the Methodists, and reported in a circular letter to missionary supporters.

386. _____. An African prophet: The Ivory Coast movement and what came of it.
London: SCM Press, 1934. 157p.
Prophet Harris; pp. 81-83 Kimbangu; 84-86 Sampson Oppong in Ghana.
By a Methodist missionary who worked with the Harrist movement.

387. _____. From fetish to faith. London: Edinburgh House Press, 1935. 160p.
Ch. 5, "The Prophet Movement," a first hand account of the Harris
movement as it existed in the 1920's.

388. RAYNAUD-MATHEIS, Franziska. Elfenbeinküste. Bonn: 1962.
Pp. 132f., on Harris.

389. ROUCH, Jean. "Introduction à l'étude de la communauté de Bregbo," Journal
de la société des africanistes (Paris) 33 (1) 1963, 129-202. Illus. bibl.
On Ebrié lagoon, east of Abidjan; a description of the community of
Albert Atcho, a young healer in the Harris tradition, by a French
anthropologist. (AA 16, 216)

390. _____. "Aspects du Harrisisme en Côte d'Ivoire," in Bouaké, item 206.
Rouch has also made a film entitled "M. Albert Atcho, prophète," on
a healer at Bregbo in the Harris tradition.

391. ROUX, A. "Un prophète: Harris," Présence africaine (special number,
Le monde noire), 8-9, 1950, 133-40.
An anecdotal account of Harris and his role in bolstering Protestant
strength in the Ivory Coast.

392. TAUXIER, L(udovic-Marie-Julien). (also as Louis). Religion, moeurs, et
coutumes des Agni de la Côte d'Ivoire. Paris: Geunther, 1932. 257p.
illus.
P. 190, the effect of Harris on the resistance of the Agni to the
administration.

393. THOMPSON, E. W. "The Ivory Coast adventure," The Methodist Recorder
(London), 65 (3491) 9 Oct. 1924, 10. Illus.
The Methodist "discovery" of the Harris converts in the Ivory Coast,
with photos of Harris.

394. _____. "The Ivory Coast: A study in modern missionary methods," International Review of Missions,17 (68) Oct. 1928, 630-644.
An account of the Methodist takeover of the Harris churches.

395. VAN BULCK, G. "Le prophète Harris vu par lui-même. (Côte d'Ivoire, 1914),"
in Museum Lessianum, item 161, 120-124.
Important extracts from the journal of a Roman Catholic missionary
who interviewed Harris.

396. WALKER, F. Deaville. The story of the Ivory Coast. London: Cargate
Press, 1926. 82p. illus.
Chs. 2 & 3 and Addendum: a popular account of the Harris movement
and the later takeover by the British Methodists. By a Methodist
missionary historian. (A third, revised edition, 1930, not seen.)

397. _____ (as F.D.W.) "The prophet Harris found at last," The Foreign Field
(London: Wesleyan Methodist), Feb. 1927, 107-112. Illus.
Pastor Benoit's visit to Harris in 1926.

398. _____ (as F.D.W.). "More about the Prophet Harris," The Foreign Field
      (London: Wesleyan Methodist), Mar. 1927, 136-141. Illus.
            Harris' own account of his life as told to Benoit; good illustrations.

399. WESLEYAN METHODIST MISSIONARY SOCIETY. London: Reports: No. 101 (for
      1914) 1915, 163-166; No. 102 (for 1915) 1916, 149-150; No. 106 (for
      1919) 1920, 73-74; No. 107 (for 1920) 1921, 80-81; No. 112 (for 1925)
      1926, 81-85; and others from 1923-1928.
            The Harris movement, at first in Apolonia, Gold Coast, then in
            Ivory Coast.

400. ZOLBERG, Aristide R. One party government in the Ivory Coast. Princeton:
      Princeton U.P., 1964. xiv + 374p.
            Pp. 37-38, "no evidence" of Harrisism having any contemporary
            political significance.

LIBERIA

401. BROWN, Kenneth I. "Aladura baptism," Hibbert Journal (London), 62 (245)
      Jan. 1964, 64-67.
            Account of a Church of the Lord (Aladura) baptism in Monrovia.

402. _____. "Services, rites, and ceremonies of the Church of the Lord
      (Aladura)," Practical Anthropology (Tarrytown, N. Y.), forthcoming 1966.
            The author participated in river baptism, holy communion, churching
            of twins, circumcision, etc., in the Monrovia headquarters branch
            of this Nigerian church.

403. CASON, John Walter. The growth of Christianity in the Liberian environ-
      ment. Unpublished Ph.D. dissertation, Columbia University, New York,
      1962, 484p. maps, bibl.
            Pp. 296-297, Harris; pp. 450-453, the Church of the Lord (Aladura).
            (MIC. 62-2858) (DA 23 (2) pp. 728-729)

404. FRAENKEL, Merran. Tribe and class in Monrovia. London: O.U.P. for
      I.A.I., 1964. xii + 244p.
            Pp. 151-195 on churches and societies discusses the increasing number
            of "independent local churches" founded in Monrovia since World War II.

405. WILLIAMS, Walter B. God's avenging sword. n. place: n. pub., 1928. 8p.
            An American Methodist missionary who met Prophet Harris, and
            interpreted a physical disability suffered by Harris at the time as
            a judgment on his criticism of the mission.

406. WILLIAMS, Walter B. & Maude W. Adventures with the Krus in West Africa.
      New York: Vantage Press, 1955. 147p.
            Pp. 141-142, "the Real Story of the 'Prophet Movement'"--i.e., Harris.

MALI

407. CARDAIRE, Marcel. L'Islam et le terroir africain. Bamako - Koulouba:
      IFAN, 1954.
            Especially pp. 37-38, the origin of the "religion de l'homme de
            Wolo," San district, Mali.

408. HOLAS, B. "Le Nya: changements spirituels modernes d'une société ouest-
      africaine," Acta tropica (Basel), 12 (2) 1955, 97-122. Illus. (B.H.)
         The Minianka, a Senoufo group; the cults of Nya and of massa.
         (AA 8, 34).

NIGERIA

409. ABA COMMISSION OF ENQUIRY. Notes of evidence. Lagos: Government Printer,
      1930. 990p.
         Pp. 964-971, evidence by missionaries on the Aba women's riots of
         1929, and their limited religious reference.

410. ABRAHAM, R. C. Dictionary of modern Yoruba. London: University of
      London Press, 1958. 776p.
         Pp. 623-624, under "sosi" (church) a discussion of Yoruba independent
         churches after Parrinder, item 543.

411. ADAMS, R. F. G. "Oberi Okaime: A new African language and script,"
      Africa (London) 17 (1) Jan. 1947.
         A "revealed" language in a section of the Spirit movement, E. Nigeria,
         from 1927; now the Oberi Okaime Church.

412. ADEDIPE, R. A. Igbeyawo mimo (Holy Marriage). Ado Ekiti, W. Nigeria:
      Ilori Press, 1949. 48p.
         One of several books in Yoruba by a leader of the Christ Apostolic
         Church.

413. ADEJOBI, Emmanuel Owoade Ade. The observances and practices of the Church
      of the Lord (Aladura) in the light of Old and New Testament. Lagos:
      the author, 1965. 14p.
         Biblical warrants for the Church practices, with a general apologetic,
         by the leading minister of the Church.

414. ADEMAKINWA, J. A. Iwe itan ijo wa lati egbe Okuta-iyebiye Ijo Faith
      Tabernacle Apostolic Church de Christ Apostolic Church (History of our
      Church from Diamond Society, Apostolic Church to Christ Apostolic Church).
      Lagos: Pacific Printing works, 1945. 180p.
         By a member of this church, in Yoruba.

415. AFRICAN CHURCH ORGANISATION. Report of proceedings of the African Church
      Organisation for Lagos and Yorubaland, 1901-1908. Liverpool: African
      Church Organisation, 1910. 104p.
         Origin, history and statistics.

416. AINA, J. A. Present day prophets and the principles upon which they work.
      Ibadan: the author, n.d. (c. 1932). 16p.
         Reissued, Nsukka, E. Nigeria: Department of Religion, University of
         Nigeria, 1964. 10p. (mimeo.) with introduction by H. W. Turner.
         A defence of the Aladura movement by an early leader, with an attempt
         at a theology of the place of holy water in the movement.

417. AINA, J. Ade. Odun medogbon Ijo Aladura ni ilu Ibadan (Silver Jubilee of
      the Establishment of the Aladura Church in Ibadan). Ibadan: the author,
      n. d. (1949). 27p.
         Includes a general history of the early Aladura movement, by one of
         its leaders, who founded several Aladura churches before his death
         in 1965, in Yoruba.

418. AJAYI, J. F. Ade. "Nineteenth century origins of Nigerian nationalism,"
      Journal of the Historical Society of Nigeria (Ibadan) 2 (2) Dec. 1961,
      196-210.
            P. 205, E. W. Blyden's advocacy of an "Independent West African
            Church"; pp. 207, 209, secessions in Calabar and Lagos.

419. _____. Christians missions in Nigeria, 1841-1891. The making of a new
      elite. London: Longmans, 1965. 317p.
            Pp. 266-273, E. W. Blyden's advocacy of an independent African Church.
            By a Nigerian historian.

420. AKINYELE, Isaac Babalola. Akanse awon eko ati alaye kikun lori awon . . .
      (Special lessons and elucidations on the 10 commandments). Ibadan:
      Iranlowo Press, 1953. 108p.
            One of the earliest of a series of more than twelve pamphlets in
            Yoruba on religious subjects written by one of the founders of the
            large Christ Apostolic Church in Nigeria.

421. _____. The place of divine healing in the church. Ibadan: Government
      Printer, 1962. 7p.
            A lecture delivered to the students of Immanuel College, Ibadan,
            giving an apologia for the Christ Apostolic Church's practice of dis-
            allowing the use of medicine.

422. ALUTU, John O. A groundwork of Nnewi history. Nnewi, E. Nigeria:
      Homeland Information Service, 1963.
            Pp. 298-303, on the National Church of Nigeria by a Nigerian author.

423. ANON. Reports on the Braide movement in Western Equatorial Africa Diocesan
      Magazine (Newcastle-on-Tyne, England).
            22 (152) Aug. 1917, 212; 23 (164) Aug. 1918, 194-196, summary of
            report of commission of enquiry into the movement; 24 (175) July
            1919, 171-173, the "new prophet movement."

424. _____. "Aiyetoro," Nigeria Magazine (Lagos), 55, 1957, 356-386. Illus.
            A pictorial account of a visit to the Holy Apostle's Community; a
            sequel to Duckworth, item 469.

425. _____. The Times British Colonies Review (London), Third Quarter 1957,
      p. 19.
            On the Holy Apostles community at Aiyetoro.

426. _____. "Cherubim and Seraphim," Nigeria Magazine (Lagos), 53, 1957,
      119-34. Illus.
            A popular account of the history and main features of an Aladura
            church. (AA 9, 298).

427. _____. "'Communism' in Aiyetoro," West African Review (London), 30
      (381) June 1959, pp. 469-471.
            A Nigerian religious community.

428. _____. Good health! The church's ministry of healing (West African Study
      Project No. 6). World Student Christian Federation, 1961. 16 p. (mimeo.)
            Pp. 8-9, superficial reference to Aladura and pentecostal healers
            in Nigeria.

429. ____. "Is spiritual healing a way of making money?" Africa (Surulere,
     Lagos), 12, Feb. 1962, 19-22.
          Journalistic article on the Cherubim and Seraphim churches in Nigeria.

430. ____. "Obituary notice," Journal of the Royal African Society (London),
     11 (43) Apr. 1912, 363-364.
          P. 362, brief reference to influence of Blyden on the Lagos secessions.

431. ____. in Qua Iboe Mission Quarterly (Belfast), 145, May 1930, 160.
          The aftermath of the 1927 "spirit movement" in E. Nigeria.

432. ____. "A survey of the year 1938," International Review of Missions, 28
     (109) Jan. 1939.
          P. 57, brief reference to "the Church" gathering converts from
          Babalola's work, and to the African Apostolic Church.

433. ANYIAM, Frederick Uzoma. Among Nigerian celebrities. Yaba (Nigeria):
     the author, 1960. 71p.
          Pp. 15-17, "Garrick Sokari Braide, Nigeria's Greatest Prophet."
          A reasonably accurate hagiography.

434. AUTHORITY, S.O.A. The happy city "Aiyetoro." Okitipupa (W. Nigeria):
     The Holy Apostles Community, 2nd. edn., 1960. 77p. map.
          Official history of the community, by one of their leaders.

435. AYANDELE, E. A. "An assessment of James Johnson and his place in
     Nigerian history," Journal of the Historical Society of Nigeria (Ibadan),
     2 (4) 1963, 486-516; 3 (1) 1964, 73-101.
          Discusses his role in the formation of the "African" churches in
          Lagos. (FA 1, 854)

436. AYORINDE, J. A. "Oba Sir Isaac Babalola Akinyele, Kt., Olubadan -
     Ibadan," Odu: Journal of African Studies (Ibadan), 1 (2) 1965, 78-82.
          Obituary on an early leader and later President of the Christ
          Apostolic Church; in Yoruba.

437. BABALOLA, Joseph Ayo. Iwe imototo ati iwa mimo (The book of hygiene and
     holy living). Ilesha, W. Nigeria: Ola-Iya Printing Works, 1959. 50p.
          By the Prophet leader of the 1930 Aladura revival; edited by D. O.
          Babajide; in Yoruba.

438. BANFIELD, A. W. "Report," The Church Missionary Review (London), 67
     (808), Aug.-Sep. 1916.
          P. 477, on the Braide movement from the Bible Society's agent in
          W. Africa.

439. BATUBO, A. B. The dawn of Baptist work in Eastern Nigeria. Port Harcourt:
     the author, 1964. 52p.
          Especially on Majola Agbebi's work, and Baptist secessions, by a
          Nigerian Baptist layman.

440. BENIN, Oba of. Addresses. . . in connexion with Aruosa (Edo National
     Church of God . . .) Benin City (Nigeria): the Church, 1946. 17p.
          A neo-pagan church.

441. BEYIOKU, Akin Fagbenro (Horatio Antus Williams). The origin of Ijo Orunmila organization. Lagos: Alafia Press, 1944. c.10p.
A Nigerian nativist church based on traditional Yoruba religion's Ifa cult. Traces the various offshoots of this group. By its founder.

442. BILL, S. A. (Mrs.) "The revival," Qua Iboe Mission Quarterly (Belfast), 136, Feb. 1928, 4-5.
On the "spirit movement" in Ibibio land, 1927; by the wife of the founder of this mission.

443. BOHANNAN, Paul. "Extra-processual events in Tiv political institutions," American Anthropologist, 60 (1) 1958, 1-12. Also in S. & P. Ottenberg (eds.) Cultures and societies of tropical Africa. New York: Random House, 1960, 328-344. (BMRS, A 17)
Five anti-witchcraft movements are described and related to the Tiv political system which requires periodic movements to restore its elasticity. The movements disappeared after their purpose was accomplished.

444. BRADBURY, R. E. The Benin kingdom and the Edo-speaking peoples of South-Western Nigeria. London: I.A.I., 1957. 212p.
Pp. 163-164, new semi-Christian cults, from 1929.

445. BRYANT, G. McLeod. Whither Africa. Richmond, Va.: John Knox Press, 1961.
Pp. 67-68, the Aiyetoro community in Nigeria.

446. BURNS, Alan Cuthbert. History of Nigeria. London: Allen and Unwin (1929) 1963.
P. 229, a summary account of the Braide movement.

447. _____. Colour prejudice. London: Allen & Unwin, 1948. 164p.
F. Tr., Le préjugé de race et de couleur. Paris: 1949.
P. 34, the race factor as a cause of independent movements.

448. CALABAR & OWERRI PROVINCES, Commission of Enquiry. Report of the Commission of Enquiry appointed to inquire into the disturbances in the Calabar and Owerri Provinces, December 1929. Lagos: Government Printer, 1930. 159p. + Appendices.
Pp. 19-20, 106, religious aspects of the "Aba riots"; the Spirit movement of 1926, see Appendix III (i), pp. 10-11; the "dancing women" of 1925, idem, pp. 11-12.

449. CARY, Joyce. The African witch. London: M. Joseph (1936) 1951. 309p.
Fiction. Preface p. 9, cites accounts of Watchtower and "other primitive sects" as one source of his material; one character is Coker, a "local revivalist agitator"; set in Northern Nigeria.

450. CHAMBERS, Michael. "Jesus of Oyingbo," New Society (London), 3 (80) 9 April 1964, 13-15. Illus.
Emmanuel Odumosu and the Universal College of Regeneration in Lagos; development from "simple messianism" to complex economic organization.

451. CHERUBIM AND SERAPHIM, ETERNAL SACRED ORDER OF. Holy hymn book. Lagos: the Order, n.d. (after 1957). 197p.
201 hymns and 9 canticles selected from a larger Yoruba hymnbook of this Aladura church, one of a number of Cherubim and Seraphim groups.

452.   ____. The "order": rules and regulations, duties of workers, & forty
        days lenten programme. Lagos: the Order, n.d. (c. 1959). 76p.
            Rules, officers, teaching, orders of service for various occasions,
            lectionaries, and Bible study helps.

453.   CHERUBIM AND SERAPHIM, SACRED ORDER OF. Daily Bible reading pamphlet 1965.
        Lagos: the Order, 1965. 52p.
            The 14th edn. of a yearbook of this church, containing lectionary,
            directory of officers and centres, and a history.

454.   CHRIST APOSTOLIC CHURCH. Orin ihinrere: gospel songs. Ibadan: the
        Church, 3rd. ed., 1961. 687p.
            803 hymns, mostly chosen from a wide range of English hymnbooks,
            together with some original compositions; all in Yoruba, for the
            largest Nigerian Aladura church.

455.   CHURCH MISSIONARY SOCIETY (Anglican). Proceedings. London: the Society,
        annually.
            E.g.: 1916-1917, pp. 3-4, 26 and 1918-1919, p. 32 on the Braide
            movement in the Niger Delta.

456.   CHURCH OF THE LORD (ALADURA). Hymn book. Ogere (W. Nigeria): the Church,
        n.d. (1958). 344p.
            300 hymns, some original, for an Aladura church; in English and
            Yoruba editions. At least three smaller churches derivative from
            this Church have their own hymnbooks.

457.   COKER, E. O. The order: constitution and bylaws of the Eternal Sacred
        Order of the Cherubim and Seraphim. Enugu: Dek's Press, n.d. 37p.
            One of a number of Aladura constitutions, orders of worship etc.,
            which have been published in Nigeria, in this case for the E.
            Nigeria wing of the Cherubim and Seraphim.

458.   COKER, Jacob Kayinde. Polygamy defended. Lagos: Karaole Press, 1915.
        22p.
            A defence of polygamy against the Minute of the Church Missionary
            Society which condemned it. By an "African" churchman.

459.   COKER, S. A. Three sermons on the Christian ministry. London: Unwin,
        1904. 32p.
            A theological statement by the Superintendent, African Church, Lagos,
            in support of episcopacy.

460.   ____. The rights of Africans to organise and establish indigenous
        churches unattached to and uncontrolled by foreign church organisations.
        Lagos: Tikatore Press, 1917. 48p.
            A lecture delivered by Coker, an "African" churchman, occasioned by
            his defense of the Christ Army Church.

461.   COLEMAN, James S. Nigeria, background to nationalism. Berkeley: Uni-
        versity of California Press, 1958.
            Pp. 174-178, 302-303: "Nativistic" and secession movements as aspect
            of nationalism; concentrates on those connected with white domination,
            and on National Church of Nigeria and the Cameroons.

462. COMHAIRE, J. L. "La vie religieuse à Lagos," Zaïre (Brussels), 3 (5) May 1949, 549-56.
    Pp. 553-554, mention of African Church and "prophetic sects."

463. DAFIDI, (A.A. Abiola-Jacobs). Itan, igbe aiye alagba Wm. Folarin Sosan (Life history of the Rev. Wm. Folarin Sosan). Ibadan: Lisabi Press, 1957. 17p.
    A biography of a leader of the Cherubim and Seraphim in W. Nigeria; in Yoruba.

464. DALLIMORE, H. "The Aladura movement in Ekiti," Western Equatorial Africa Church Magazine (Newcastle-on-Tyne, England) 36 (443) May 1931, 93-97. Illus.
    A first-hand contemporary account of the Babalola prophet movement by a C.M.S. missionary who initially attempted to work with it.

465. DARAMOLA, Dapo. "The free love isle gives up its secrets," Drum (Lagos), 165, Jan. 1965. Illus.
    Journalistic account of the Aiyetoro Community.

466. DAVIDSON, Basil & ADEMOLA, Adenekan (eds.). The new West Africa: Problems of independence. London: Allen & Unwin, 1953.
    P. 68, "dissident churches"--the "Nigerian National church."

467. DELANO, Isaac O. Notes and comments from Nigeria. London: United Society for Christian Literature, 1944. 64p.
    Pp. 31-34, the "African" Church; pp. 34-36, the original Faith Tabernacle Church; ch. 9, The Order of Seraphim and Cherubim - a Nigerian's descriptive account, with questions as to the adequacy of such forms of Christianity for the future.

468. _____. One church for Nigeria. London: Lutterworth, 1945. 48p.
    Pp. 29-45, brief accounts of "African Churches," Cherubim and Seraphim, Faith Tabernacle, "Praying Christians" and a plea for union of all Christian bodies.

469. DUCKWORTH, E. H. "A visit to the apostles and the town of Aiyetoro," Nigeria Magazine (Lagos), 36, 1951, 386-440. Illus., map.
    Based on a five-day visit by the editor of Nigeria; little on the religious features. (AA 3, 202.)

470. DUVAL, L. M. Baptist missions in Nigeria. Richmond, Va.: Foreign Mission Board, Southern Baptist Convention, 1928. 213p.
    Pp. 118-119, on the Lagos Native Baptist Church, by a Southern Baptist historian.

471. EDO NATIONAL CHURCH OF GOD. The book of the Holy Aruosa, according to the ancient Binis. Benin City (Nigeria): Edo National Church of God, 1946, Vol. I, 19p; 1948, Vol. II, 6p.
    The mythology and legends of the Aruosa or Edo National Church, "re-established" in 1945 by the Oba (King) of Benin.

472. EKIT, Richmael (ed.). Do you know the Spirit movement of 1927 in Ibibio Land? Edem Urua Ibiono (Itu, E. Nigeria): the author, n.d. (1964). 54p.
    Biographical accounts of Ekit and other leaders in the Spirit Movement, published for the Oberi Okaime Church.

473. EMANUEL, C. A. (Abiodum Akinsowon). Iwe itan tabi isipaya orun ti Olorun
     fi han (Book of vision or revelations of heaven shown by God). Lagos:
     Bethel Press, 1940. 9p.
        A pamphlet in Yoruba giving an account of the visions received in
        1925 by Mrs. Emanuel, one of the founders, with Moses Orimolade
        Tunolashe, of the Cherubim and Seraphim.

474. EPELLE, E(mmanuel) M. T(obiah). The Church in the Niger Delta. Aba
     (E. Nigeria): Niger Delta Diocese, 1955. 128p.
        Pp. 51-54 on the Braide Movement, by a Nigerian Anglican historian.

475. _____. The Church in Opobo. Opobo (E. Nigeria): St. Paul's Church
     Parochial Committee, n.d. (1958). 69p.
        Especially chs. 4 and 5 on Braide and other secessions.

476. _____. Bishops in the Niger Delta. Aba (E. Nigeria): Niger Delta
     Diocese, 1964. 196p.
        Pp. 136-139, Bishop James Johnson and the Braide movement.

477. FERGUSON, John. "Western Nigeria," Hibbert Journal (London), 61 (240)
     Oct. 1962, 10-12.
        Brief comment on "the sects," especially Aiyetoro community and
        Orunmilaism.

478. GOD'S KINGDOM SOCIETY. Theocratic songs of praise. Warri (Mid-West
     Nigeria): the Society, n.d. (1954). 184p.
        193 hymns, etc., mostly original, together with psalms and other
        biblical material adapted for an African "Judaistic" Society derived
        from Jehovah's Witnesses; in English.

479. GRIMLEY, John B. & ROBINSON, Gordon E. Church growth in Central and
     Southern Nigeria. Grand Rapids, Mich.: Eerdmans, forthcoming.
        Chapter 4 in the Southern Nigeria section describes Nigerian
        independent churches and analyzes the factors behind their growth.

480. GROVES, W. T. "A Nigerian prophet," The Herald (London: Primitive
     Methodist Missionary Society), 9 (6) June 1916, 84-87. Illus.
        An illiterate prophet of the Braide movement at Azumini, E. Nigeria,
        1916; the decrease in gin sales, burning of ju-ju houses, and "the
        blacks to be rules through a black church." By a Methodist mis-
        sionary.

481. HANNEY, G. H. "A term at Oron," The Herald (London: Primitive Methodist
     Missionary Society), 9 (3) Mar. 1916, p. 40.
        A "new sect, the African church."

482. HAU, K. "Oberi Okaime, script, texts and counting system," Bulletin
     IFAN (Dakar), Series B, 23 (1-2), Jan.-April 1961, 291-308.
        The revealed script and language of a section of the Spirit Movement
        in E. Nigeria from 1927. (AA 13, 216).

483. H.D. "Repentence at Bakana," Western Equatorial Africa Church Magazine
     (Newcastle-on-Tyne, England), (n.s. 504) Mar.-Apr. 1936, 23-24.
        Presumably about the Braide movement. Exact reference is uncertain.

484. IDOWU, E. Bolaji. Olodumare: God in Yoruba belief. London: Longmans,
     1962. 222p.
         Pp. 211-215, "syncretistic sects," especially Orunmilaism and Reformed
         Ogboni Fraternity.

485. _____. God in Nigerian belief. Lagos: Federal Ministry of Information,
     1963. 40p.
         Nigerian Broadcasting Corporation "October Lectures," pp. 37-38,
         new religious movements.

486. _____. Towards an indigenous church. London: O.U.P., 1965. viii + 60p.
         A Nigerian Methodist theologian gives a positive evaluation of the
         role of Nigerian independent churches in making Christianity
         indigeneous. P. 9, the National Church of Nigeria and the Aruosa
         Church in Benin City; pp. 41-47, the appeal of the Aladura churches
         of Yorubaland.

487. IGE, Oye. "Joseph Babalola--A twentieth century prophet," The African
     Historian (Ibadan, University of Ife), 1 (3) March 1965, 38-42.
         An account of the Aladura prophet, Babalola, based on Mediayese,
         item 507. (A student journal.) (FA 1, 1385)

488. IJOMAH, B. I. C. & UMEH, Nat. "This woman saw Jesus? Veronica - fake or
     stigmatist?" Eagle (Onitsha, Nigeria), May 1964, 16-17.
         A Roman Catholic prophetess at Nsukka, E. Nigeria.

489. IKECHIUKU, Joseph. The immutable rules and conducts of St. Joseph's
     Chosen Church of God selected through the revelation of God. Sapele
     (Mid-West Nigeria): the author, n.d., 55p. illus.
         Contains a creed; rules for worship, baptism, various festivals,
         marriage, burial, and the organization of the Church, which was
         founded by the author in 1945.

490. ILOGU, Edmund. "The problem of indigenization in Nigeria," International
     Review of Missions, 49 (194) April 1960, 167-82.
         Pp. 169-170, 178, 182, the importance of the older churches not
         leaving indigenization to the "semi-Christian sects," which are
         wrong forms of indigenization. (AA 12, 55)

491. IYALIA, N. B. The most Rev. James George Campbell, D.B.P., Senior
     Patriarch of the West African Episcopal church and the Presiding Patriarch
     of the Christ Army Church G.B.C. Nigeria; a brief account of his mis-
     sionary labours. Lagos: Oluwole Press, 1945. 16p.

492. JEFFREYS, M. D. W. "African tarantula or dancing mania," The Eastern
     Anthropologist (Lahore, India), 6 (2) Dec. 1952-Feb. 1953, 98-105.
         Pp. 101-102, the Spirit movement of 1927, E. Nigeria, and its
         similarity to Myalism and other movements.

493. JOHNSTON, Geoffrey. "A project in local church histories," West African
     Religion (Nsukka, E. Nigeria), 4, July 1965, 8-13.
         Report on results of a church history project for Nigerian theological
         students; includes reference to Garrick Braide movement and United
         African Church in Eastern Nigeria.

494. JOHNSON, James. "Elijah II," Church Missionary Review (London), 67, Aug. 1916, 459.
   On Garrick Braide, E. Nigeria, 1915-16, by the Nigerian Anglican Assistant Bishop concerned.

495. JUWE, Sylve Mubundu. Why (sic) is the National Church of Nigeria and the Cameroons and the God of Africa. Asaba (Mid-West Nigeria): the author, n.d., 41p.
   An apologia for this "church."

496. KALE, S. I. & HOGAN, H. Christian responsibility in an independent Nigeria. Lagos: Christian Council of Nigeria, 1961.
   Pp. 86, 101-3, 114 mentions independent churches; a report by a Nigerian-American team.

497. KAUFMANN, Herbert. Nigeria. Bonn: Schroeder, 1962.
   P. 264, brief mention of "syncretistic sects" after Parrinder, item 543.

498. KOPYTOFF, Jean Herskovits. Liberated Africans and the history of Lagos colony. Unpublished D.Phil. thesis, University of Oxford, 1960.
   P. 489, United Native African Church. (Recently published.)

499. LAGOS, (ANGLICAN) DIOCESE OF. Reports and minutes of proceedings . . . of the Synod . . . Lagos: the Diocese.
   E.g.: 1920, p. 11, itinerant prophets; 1922, pp. 11-14, the clash with the first Aladura society; 1924, p. 78; 1928, p. 23, the "Seraphim" movement; 1931, pp. 8-10, "fancy sects," 1933, pp. 10-11, non-fraternization with the "so-called African Churches"; 1935, p. 16, prophet movement in Bassa country; 1936, pp. 25-26, questions the "African" claims of independents, and maintains a stand against polygamy; 1948, p. 81, reports return of earlier seceders; 1958, p. 48, a new attitude of co-operation with the African Church Bethel.

500. LEITH-ROSS, Sylvia. African women. London: Faber, 1939; Routledge & Kegan Paul, 1965. 367p.
   Eastern Nigeria: pp. 299-301 on "sects" as spiritually dangerous and anti-government; pp. 250-253, denominations in Port Harcourt.

501. LUCAS, J. Olumide. Lecture on the history of St. Paul's Church, Bread-fruit, Lagos (1852-1945). Lagos: St. Paul's Church, n.d. (1946?). 72p. illus.
   Pp. 26-29, background to the secession of 1891 and the United Native African Church; pp. 35-38, the 1901 secession of the African Church; by the minister of the Anglican parish most involved.

502. MACAULAY, Herbert. The history of the development of missionary work with special reference to the United African Church. Lagos: Adedimeta Printing Works, 1942. 37p.
   By a leading Nigerian nationalist who was not a member of the church. In English and Yoruba.

503. MARIOGHAE, Michael & FERGUSON, John. Nigeria under the cross. London: Highway Press, 1965. 126p.
   Pp. 51-60, discussion of causes and character of Nigerian "sects," and description of the Aiyetoro Community.

504. MARTIN, Samuel W. *Where Jesus found me*. (U.S.A.): the author, n.d. (1921). 32p.
    The life history and apologia for missions in Africa, of the African founder of the Pilgrim Baptist Mission of Nigeria (Inc.), ca. 1938, at Issele-Uku. An appendix contains testimonials from prominent U. S. citizens.

505. MAXWELL, J(ohn) Lowry. *Nigeria, the land, the people, and Christian progress*. London: World Dominion Press, n.d. (c. 1927). 164p.
    Pp. 83-84, survey of the earlier secession churches, and the Braide movement; pp. 112-113, statistical survey of "independent churches," based on 1921 census.

506. McCLELLAND, Elizabeth. "The Experiment in Communal Living," *Comparative Studies in Society and History*, 9 (1) Oct. 1966.
    On the Aiyetoro Holy Apostles' Community.

507. MEDAIYESE, J. A. *Itan igbedide woli J. A. Babalola fun ise ihinrere*. (The rise of prophet Babalola for the work of the Gospel). Ibadan, Nigeria: Christ Apostolic Church, n.d. (c. 1960). 104p. Illus.
    A biography of Babalola by the General Superintendent of his church, and his contemporary; in Yoruba.

508. MEEK, C. K. *Law and authority in a Nigerian tribe*. London: O.U.P., 1937.
    The Ibo: p. 86, the 1927 "spirit-movement"; pp. 201-202, the 1925 women's movement at Atta, Owerri Province.

509. MESSENGER, John C., Jr. *Anang acculturation: A study of shifting cultural focus*. Unpublished Ph.D. dissertation (Anthropology), Northwestern University (U.S.A.), 1957. (Mic. 57-4414).
    Pp. 275-281 on religion as cultural focus, with reference to Christ Army Churches.

510. _____. "The Christian concept of forgiveness and Anang morality," *Practical Anthropology* (Tarrytown, N.Y.), 6 (3) May-June 1959, 97-103.
    The acceptance of the Christian doctrine of a forgiving deity, found in prayer churches, as a factor behind Anang immorality. (AA 14, 65)

511. _____. "Religious acculturation among the Ibibio," in W. R. Bascom and M. J. Herskovits (eds.), *Continuity and Change in African Cultures*, Chicago: University of Chicago Press, 1959, 279-299.
    Pp. 286-299, the Spirit movement of 1930-1938 and its effects as seen in 1951; nativist reactions and ensuing syncretism in all churches.

512. _____. "Reinterpretations of Christian and indigenous belief in a Nigerian nativist church," *American Anthropologist*, 62 (2), Apr. 1960, 268-278.
    The Christ Army Church among the Anang Ibibio of S. E. Nigeria, 1950, its organization and beliefs. (AA 12, 217.)

513. _____. "Anang art, drama and social control," *African Studies Bulletin* (New York), 5 (2) May 1962, 29-35.
    Pp. 34-35, a drama association presents a skit ridiculing the Christ Army Church, especially its possession and healing aspects. (AA 15, 220.)

514. MITCHELL, Robert Cameron. The Aladura churches in Ibadan. Paper read to
      the sociology research seminar, University of Ibadan, 1962. 11p. (mimeo.)
      Analysis of a 1961-1962 survey of independent churches in Ibadan
      which shows their rapid rate of expansion since 1950; typology.

515. _____. "The Babalola revival: a non-arrested prophet movement," in
      J. Middleton and V. W. Turner (eds.), item 156.

516. MORRILL, W. T. "The Ibo in twentieth century Calabar," Comparative
      Studies in Society and History, 5 (4) July 1963, 424-448.
          P. 443, "prayer-houses," syncretist and semi-commercialized, drawing
      upon members of the older churches.

517. MORTON-WILLIAMS, P. "A discussion of the theory of elites in a West
      African (Yoruba) context," in Conference of the West African Institute of
      Social and Economic Research, March 1955, Ibadan: the Institute, 1955,
      25-32. (mimeo.)
          P. 28 places witchfinding movements in the context of the theory of
      charismatic movements.

518. _____. "The Atinga cult among the South-western Yoruba: A sociological
      analysis of a witchfinding movement," Bulletin IFAN (Dakar), Series B,
      18 (3-4) July-Oct. 1956, 315-334.
          Analysis of the impact a witchfinding movement had among the Western
      Yoruba in the early 1950's.

519. NATIONAL CHURCH OF NIGERIA AND THE CAMEROONS. Hymns and prayers for use
      in the . . . Church . . . Aba (E. Nigeria): the Church, n.d. (1948). 54p.
          57 hymns, some original, some with varying degrees of adaptation from
      Christian hymns or Western poetry, together with prayers and a creed,
      expressing the beliefs of a neo-pagan and nationalistic associate of
      the early Zik political movement; in English.

520. _____. Catechism of the National Church professing the natural religion
      of Africa. Aba (E. Nigeria): Research Institute of African Religion,
      n.d. 20p.
          Catechism, creed and a few hymns of the National Church of Nigeria.

521. NIGER DELTA CHURCH BOARD (Anglican). Reports or minutes of proceedings
      of the . . . Church Board . . . Lagos: C.M.S. for the Board.
          E.g.: 1916, pp. 60-85, the three day discussion of the Braide
      movement; 1917, pp. 53-63; 1918, pp. 8-9, 17; 1919, pp. 35, 39, 50,
      all on the same topic; 1921, printed in Diocesan Magazine (see item
      577A), and 1921-1931 (again published separately) passim, on the
      later effects of the movement, especially 1929, p. vi.

522. NIGER, (Anglican) DIOCESE ON THE. Reports of proceedings . . . of the
      Synod . . . Onitsha: the Diocese.
          E.g.: 1931, p. 55; 1940, pp. 4, 9, 18, 19 on various secession groups.

523. NIGERIA, CHRISTIAN COUNCIL OF. Annual reports. Lagos, etc.: the Council.
          E.g.: 1934, p. 17, on faith healing; 1947, p. 23, invitations from
      two "secessionist groups" in E. Nigeria to the American Church of
      the Nazarene; 1964, pp. 34-35, relations with three independent
      churches; pp. 50-54, see Turner, item 557.

50

524. NWANGORO, Bob. "The City of Salem," Drum (Lagos), Oct. 1956, 7-9. . Illus.
     A journalistic account of Gideon Urhobo and his God's Kingdom
     Society, with headquarters at Warri, Mid-West Region; this is an
     African version of Jehovah's Witnesses.

525. NWANGWU, Jonathan. "I am Jesus Christ," Eagle (Onitsha, E. Nigeria),
     Sept. 1964, 7-10, 12-13. Illus.
     Odili Nwanjuani, an Ibo messianic founder of the "Uwaoma Church"
     near Onitsha; full verbatim report of his beliefs.

526. NZEKWU, Onuora. Wand of noble wood. London: Hutchinson, 1961.
     Novel by Nigerian author. Pp. 74-6 presents Cherubim and Seraphim
     society as popular because it recognizes the good in traditional
     religion.

527. OBATERO, O(luremilekun) I(gbekele), & FLOYD, B(arry) N. "The 'Holy City'
     of Aiyetoro: A geographic appraisal," Nigerian Geographical Journal
     (Ibadan), expected 1966.

528. O'CONNELL, James. "Government and politics in the Yoruba African
     Churches: the claims of tradition and modernity," Odu. University of
     Ife Journal of African Studies, 2 (1) July 1965, 92-108.
     A review article on Webster, item 572.

529. OJI, B. A. Originality of religion revealed. Aba (E. Nigeria): Re-
     search Institute of African Mission Press, 1960. 58p.
     A personal apology for the "National Church of Nigeria," especially
     in relation to Christianity and Islam; prefaced by report of a
     lecture by Azikiwe in 1951 on "Philosophy of African Religion, with
     special reference to the God of Africa."

530. OKARA, Gabriel. "One night at Victoria Beach," in G. Moore & V. Beier,
     Modern Poetry from Africa, pp. 98-99. Harmondsworth, England: Penguin,
     1963.
     Poem, Aladura prophets at prayer.

531. OKE, G. A. A short history of the United Native African Church 1891-
     1903. Lagos: Shalom Press, 1918.
     History of one of Nigeria's "African" churches by an "African"
     churchman.

532. _____. A short history of the U.N.A. 1904-1924. Lagos: Shalom Press,
     1936.
     An extension of the previous reference.

533. OKPALAOKA, C. I. (ed.). A report on the Holy City of Aiyetoro. Nsukka
     (E. Nigeria): Sociological Association, University of Nigeria, 1962.
     23p. (mimeo.)
     A descriptive report by Nigerian undergraduate sociology students,
     after a three day visit to the community in 1962.

534. OLAGUNJU, Bili. "The prophets of Nigeria," Flamingo (London), 5 (3)
     Dec. 1965, 32-35.
     Journalistic account of four Lagos prophets and their predictions
     of doom.

535. OLAYEMI, Sam. "I am Jesus," Drum (Lagos), July 1957, 22-23. Illus.
A journalistic account of the "Spiritual Kingdom" of Ededem Bassey, Ikot Ekpene, E. Nigeria.

536. OLUSHOLA, J. A. "The Church's loss of power," African Challenge (Lagos), 10 (4) April 1960, 5.
The weak spiritual state of the older churches in Nigeria as reason for popularity of the Aladura churches.

537. OMOYAJOWO, J. A. Witches? A study of the belief in witchcraft and of its future in modern African society. Ibadan: Daystar Press, 1965. 44p.
Pp. 23-24, witch finders--Bamucapi in Central Africa and first hand report on Atinga movement in Nigeria. P. 40, brief discussion of "local prophets" and witchcraft.

538. _____. Your dreams. Ibadan: Daystar Press, 1965. 57p.
Pp. 24-29, account of how Aladura prophets interpet dreams; by a Methodist clergyman.

539. ONYIOHA, K.O.K. Christianity, Islam and Godianism in Nigeria. Enugu: the author, 1964. 15p. Illus.
A lecture at the University of Nigeria, by the leading figure in Godianism, successor to the National Church of Nigeria.

540. OSHITELU, Josiah Olunowo. Awon asotele ohun ti yio bere si sele tabi inu odun 1931 (Prophecies that will happen in 1931). Ibadan: Lisabi Press, n.d., (c. 1930). 16p.
The first of a series of printed prophecies by the founder of the Church of the Lord (Aladura). He has also published a Handbook of Worship and Constitution, and other works for the Church.

541. _____. Catechism of the Church of the Lord . . . and the holy litany . . . with the church prayer drill. Ogere (W. Nigeria): the author, 1948. 22p.
By the founder of the 'Church of the Lord (Aladura)'. See Turner, items 259 & 261 for analysis of these texts.

542. PARNIS, R. O. "A visit to Aiyetoro," Nigerian Field (London), 30 (1) Jan. 1965, 37-40. Illus.
Impressionistic account of a brief visit to Aiyetoro.

543. PARRINDER, E. G. Religion in an African city. London: Oxford U.P., 1953.
Pp. 107-132, general description of independent churches in Ibadan with list of the churches found in an appendix.

544. _____. Witchcraft: European and African. London: Faber and Faber, (1958) 1963.
Pp. 170-180, Bamucapi in Central Africa, and a first hand account of Atinga movement in Dahomey and Nigeria, c. 1950.

545. _____. "Indigenous churches in Nigeria," West African Review, 31 (394) Sept. 1960, 87-93. Illus.
A sympathetic general survey. (AA 14, 223.)

52

546. PEEL, John D. Y. <u>The Aladura churches of Yorubaland</u>. Paper read to the
research seminar, Department of Sociology, University of Ibadan, 1965.
9p. (mimeo.)
    The Christ Apostolic Church and the Cherubim and Seraphim.

547. PILTER, M. T. "More about Elijah II," <u>Church Missionary Review</u> (London),
68 (815) Mar. 1917, 142-145.
    A missionary on the Braide movement in E. Nigeria, 1915-1916.

548. SADLER, G. W. <u>A century in Nigeria</u>. Nashville: Foreign Mission Board,
Southern Baptist Convention, 1950. 151p.
    Pp. 90-91, on the Lagos Native Baptist Church, by a Southern
    Baptist historian.

549. SAHLMANN, Herbert. "Der Stadtstaat Aiyetoro - eine Siedlung der Holy
Apostles Community in Nigeria" (The city-state of Aiyetoro - a settlement
of the Holy Apostles' Community . . .), <u>Geographische Rundschau</u>
(Braunschweig, W. Germany), 16 (10) 1964, 399-404. Illus.
    An "un-African" development, based on old tribal traditions and
    ancient Christian customs, and led by a young élite. By an early
    European visitor to the community.

550. SIMPSON, C.E.E.B. "An African village undertakes community development
on its own," <u>Mass Education Bulletin</u> (London), 2 (1) Dec. 1950, 7-9.
    Earliest published account of Aiyetoro by the local administrative
    officer. (AA 3, 70.)

551. SIMPSON, George E. "Religious changes in southwestern Nigeria," in
J. Middleton and V. W. Turner (eds.), item 156.

552. SKLAR, Richard L. <u>Nigerian political parties</u>. Princeton, N. J.:
Princeton U.P., 1963. 578p.
    Pp. 253-255, 466, 494, the Reformed Ogboni Fraternity in Benin
    politics.

553. SOYINKA, Wole. "The trials of brother Jero," in W. Soyinka, <u>Five plays</u>,
London: O.U.P., 1964, pp. 199-234.
    A humorous one act satire on an Aladura prophet in Lagos by a leading
    Nigerian playwright.

554. _____. <u>The interpreters</u>. London: Deutsch, 1965.
    Pp. 37, 160 ff., Aladura prophets; a novel set in Lagos and Ibadan.

555. TALBOT, P. A. <u>The peoples of Southern Nigeria</u>. London: O.U.P., 4 vols.,
1926.
    Vol. II, p. 275; vol. IV, containing the official 1921 census
    returns, pp. 118-123, reference to the Braide and other independent
    movements.

556. TURNBULL, Thomas N. <u>What God hath wrought: a short history of the
Apostolic Church</u>. Bradford: Puritan Press, 1959. 186p.
    An official history: pp. 71-87, how the Apostolic Church in Nigeria
    developed in connection with the Aladura movement.

557. TURNER, H. W. "The relationship of churches in the renewed church in Nigeria," in A Renewed Church in Nigeria, 14th Report, Christian Council of Nigeria, Lagos: the Council, 1964, 50-54.
Includes discussion of relations between older and independent churches.

558. _____. "The late Sir Isaac Akinyele, Olubadan of Ibadan," West African Religion (Nsukka, E. Nigeria), 4, July 1965, 1-4.
An obituary of an outstanding leader in the Aladura movement from 1925-1964.

559. _____. "Independent religious groups in Eastern Nigeria," West African Religion (Nsukka, E. Nigeria), 5, Feb. 1966, 7-18; 6, expected 1966.
A provisional check-list of material on independent churches, prophets, etc., in the National Archives, Enugu.

560. UBA, Sam. "I was raised from the grave to banish sickness," Drum (Lagos), 175, Nov. 1965 (7p.).
A reporter's interview with Ezenwayi (Mrs. Samuel Nwahune), an Anglican religious healer at Mbieri, near Owerri, E. Nigeria.

561. UCHENDU, Victor C. "Missionary problems in Nigerian society," Practical Anthropology (Tarrytown, N.Y.), 2 (3) May-June 1964, 105-117.
Pp. 106, 110, references to National Church of Nigeria, "Jesuses," and "African Churches"; by a Nigerian anthropologist.

562. _____. The Igbo of Southwest Nigeria. New York: Holt, Rinehart and Winston, 1965. xiii + 112p.
P. 104, mention of short lived "nativistic religious movement," Ekumeku, which sparked messianic excitement.

563. VERGER, Pierre. "Les formes syncrétiques du cult d'Ifa au Nigeria," in Bouaké, item 206.

564. WARD-PRICE, H(enry) L(ewis). Dark subjects. London: Jarrolds, 1939. 287p.
Pp. 241-243, sympathetic account of the Babalola movement by a British colonial officer who was concerned with it.

565. WEAVER, Edwin I. "A leadership training programme (For independent churches in Eastern Nigeria)," Messages and Reports, Africa Mennonite Fellowship, Bulawayo . . . , 1965, 33-37.
By a missionary co-operating with independent churches.

566. _____. "Nigeria Mennonite Church," Messages and Reports, Africa Mennonite Fellowship, Bulawayo, 1965, 60-63.
An indigenous church developed from independent groups since 1959, and its continuing co-operation with other independent churches in E. Nigeria.

567. WEBSTER, Douglas. "A 'spiritual church'," Frontier, 6 (2) Summer 1963, 116-120. Illus. Also in Practical Anthropology, 11 (5) Sept.-Oct. 1964, 229-232, 240.
The Holy Chapel of Miracle; a description of a service and its atmosphere, by an Anglican theologian.

54

568. WEBSTER, James Bertin. "Agege plantation and the African church, 1901-
      1920," Nigerian Institute of Social and Economic Research Conference
      Proceedings, March 1962, 124-130. (mimeo.)

569. ____. "The African Churches," Nigeria Magazine, 79, Dec. 1963, 254-266.
      Illus.
          The earlier independent churches in Lagos and Yorubaland; many good
          illustrations.

570. ____. "The Bible and the Plough," Journal of the Historical Society of
      Nigeria (Ibadan), 2 (4) Dec. 1963, 413-434.
          The development of commerce advocated by T. F. Buxton and Henry Venn,
          as attempted by mission societies in W. Africa, and by independent
          churches at Ifako, Agbowa and Agege in Nigeria. (FA 1, 849.)
          (AA 16, 582).

571. ____. "Source material for the study of the African Churches," Bulletin,
      Society for African Church History (Nsukka, E. Nigeria), 1 (2) Dec. 1963,
      41-49.

572. ____. The African Churches among the Yoruba: 1888-1922. Oxford:
      Clarendon Press, 1964. xvii + 217p., illus. bibl.
          A historical study of a series of secessions from mission churches
          in Nigeria, creating parallel African-led denominations of consider-
          able strength. The "African" churches resemble the African Ethiopian
          churches in their nationalistic feelings and lack of such practices
          as faith healing. Pp. 92, 94-96, the Braide movement in the Niger
          Delta. Extensive bibliography of the writings of African churchmen
          themselves.

573. ____. "Christianity in Nigeria," Historia (Ibadan), 2 (1) Apr. 1965,
      48-55.
          Pp. 51-52, the "African Churches"; p. 53, the Aladura movement;
          pp. 53-55, revivals of traditional religion - Orunmila, and M.
          Ojike's attempt at a "national church." In a student journal.

574. ____. "The attitudes and policies of the Yoruba African Churches towards
      polygamy" in C. G. Baeta (ed.), item 27.

575. WESLEYAN METHODIST MISSIONARY SOCIETY. London: Reports No. 117 (for
      1930) 1931, 79-80.
          "Strange prophets" in Ilesha and Ifaki areas, W. Nigeria.

576. ____. Annual Reports, Nigeria District (West Africa).
          E.g., 1931, pp. 18-19, 22, 26, 34; 1934, p. 20, on the Aladura
          movement.

577. WESTERN EQUATORIAL AFRICA, (ANGLICAN) DIOCESE OF. Reports and minutes of
      proceedings . . . of the Synod. Lagos: the Diocese.
              E.g., 1916, pp. 25-26, 43-46, Appendix I, 61-7, on the Braide prophet
          movement in the Delta area; 1917, pp. 23-24, 45, Appendix I, idem;
          1918, pp. 53, 57, App. II, 61-62, idem. Anglican reactions to the
          Braide movement.

577A.   WESTERN EQUATORIAL AFRICA (ANGLICAN) DIOCESAN MAGAZINE (London):   22
        (n.s. 152) Aug. 1917, p. 212, Braide movement; 23 (164) Aug. 1918,
        pp. 194-196, summary of report of Commission of enquiry into the prophet
        movement; 24 (175) July 1919, pp. 171-173, the "New Prophet Movement";
        26 (197-198) May-June 1921, contains report of Niger Delta Church Board
        of 1921, with references to the same movement; also p. 164, prophets;
        36, May 1931, pp. 89-91, comments on the Aladura movement.

578.   WESTGARTH, J. W.   "The movement at Uyo," Qua Iboe Mission Quarterly
        (Belfast), 135, Nov. 1927, 260-264.
            On the Spirit movement of 1927 in Ibibioland; a first-hand account
            by a missionary involved.

579.   _____.   "The old medicine man," Qua Iboe Mission Quarterly (Belfast),
        138, Aug. 1928, 47.
            The "spirit movement."

580.   _____.   "The power of God," Qua Iboe Mission Quarterly (Belfast), 139,
        Nov. 1928, 57.
            Further on the Spirit movement.

581.   _____.   The Holy Spirit and the primitive mind.   London: Victory Press
        (36 Clapham Crescent), 1946.   64p.
            A sympathetic account of the spirit movement.

582.   WILES, M.   "Letter from Nigeria," Theology (London), 60 (449) Nov. 1957,
        457-8.
            Lists a few independent churches and discusses causes.

583.   WOBO, M. Sam.   A brief resume of the life course of Dr. J. O. Ositelu
        (Part 1).   Ode Remo, W. Nigeria: Degosen Printing Works, 1955.   15p.
            Biography of the founder of the Church of the Lord (Aladura) by a
            former disciple.

SIERRA LEONE

584.   BANTON, Michael.   "An independent African church in Sierra Leone,"
        Hibbert Journal (London), 55 (1) Oct. 1956, 57-63.
            A service at the Church of the Lord (Aladura).   (AA 8, 211).

585.   _____.   West African city.   London: O.U.P. for I.A.I., 1957.
            Pp. 140-141 brief description of the Church of the Lord, and the
            reasons why Sierra Leone has relatively few independents.

586.   FYFE, Christopher.   "Four Sierra Leone recaptives," Journal of African
        History, 2 (2) 1961, 77-85.
            Pp. 83-84 on W. Jenkins, an Ibo recaptive who led the African
            Baptist Church, Freetown, in the 1840's.

587.   _____.   "The West African Methodists in the Nineteenth Century," Sierra
        Leone Bulletin of Religion, 3 (1) June 1961, 22-28.
            Secessions from mission-connected Methodism: by Rawdon St. (1822),
            by O'Connor and the recaptives as the W. African Methodist Church
            (1844); their renewal of mission connections in 1861 and 1859.

588. _____. "The Countess of Huntingdon's Connexion in nineteenth century Sierra Leone," Sierra Leone Bulletin of Religion, 4 (2) Dec. 1962, 53-61.
Especially pp. 57, 60, the secession of two congregations of re-captives from the African settler-dominated Connexion in 1847; their joining the Wesleyan Mission in 1886.

589. _____. A history of Sierra Leone. London: Oxford U.P., 1962. 773p.
Pp. 232-233, 290, West African Methodist Church; p. 233, African Baptist Church; pp. 233, 469, secession from Countess of Huntingdon Connexion; pp. 286, 329, 418, T. G. Lawson and the (Baptist) Church of God; all were nineteenth century independent developments.

590. _____. "The Baptist Churches in Sierra Leone," Sierra Leone Bulletin of Religion, 5 (2) Dec. 1963, 55-60.
Pp. 58-60; W. Jenkins and the African or Ibo Baptist Church, from 1838; T. G. Lawson and the (Baptist) Church of God.

591. HAIR, P. E. H. "Christianity at Freetown from 1792 as a Field for Research," in Urbanization . . ., item 223, pp. 127-140.
Pp. 136-138 on new church groups.

592. LYNCH, Hollis R. "The Native Pastorate controversy and cultural ethno-centrism in Sierra Leone, 1871-1874," Journal of African History, 5 (3) 1964, 395-413.
The failure of an attempt to found an independent church in the 1870's. (AA 17, 70.)

593. NDANEMA, I. M. "The Martha Davies Confidential Benevolent Association," Sierra Leone Bulletin of Religion, 3 (2) 1961, 64-67.
One of the semi-independent women's movements in Freetown, founded 1910; by a Sierra Leone minister.

594. PORTER, Arthur Thomas. "Religious affiliation in Freetown, Sierra Leone," Africa (London), 23 (1) Jan. 1953, 3-14.
Mostly on the older churches and their secessions; p. 10, brief reference to Martha Davies Confidential Band.

595. PORTER, Arthur T(homas). Creoledom. London: O.U.P., 1963.
P. 79, late 18th. c. separations among the original settlers; pp. 80, 83, mid-19th. c. fissions; p. 86, later "separatist churches"; ch. 8, passim, the effects of desire for social prestige on affiliation to the "sects" or the "organized churches."

596. TUBOKU-METZGER, C. E. "Sectarianism and divided Christendom: The African situation," in Report of Proceedings, Anglican Congress 1963. London: S.P.C.K.: 1963, pp. 38-40.
Sympathetic reference to independent groups in Freetown--Rev. Decker's Church, Mother Jane Bloomer, and the Church of the Lord-- by a Sierra Leone minister.

597. WALLS, Andrew Finlay. "The Nova Scotian settlers and their religion," Sierra Leone Bulletin of Religion, 1 (1) June 1959, 19-31.
Pp. 28-31, on the independent chapels in Freetown, first half of the 19th. c.; see further references given there.

MIDDLE AFRICA

598. ANDERSSON, Efraim. Messianic popular movements in the Lower Congo.
London: Kegan Paul, 1958. xiii + 287p. Illus. Bibl.
A major study. Discusses the term "prophet," and the movements
related to Kimbanguism in French and Belgian Congo from 1921 to the
1950's: Ngunzism or the Kimbangu movement, Matswanism, the Ngunzist
Salvation Army, Mpadi's Khaki Church, and the Munkukusu movement.
Also examines outside influences, including Jehovah's Witnesses, the
Salvation Army, and Marcus Garvey.

598A. ANON. "Nel Nome del Padre, di André Matsua e di Simon Kimbangu" (In the
Name of the Father, of André Matsua and of Simon Kimbangu), Nigrizia
(Verona), 2, 1958, 2-4.

599. BALANDIER, Georges. "Évolution, évolués," France Outre-Mer (Paris),
243. Dec. 1949, 322-3.
Includes politico-religious movements as aspects of the social
evolution in Gabon and the "Middle Congo." (AA 1, 536)

600. _____. "Messianisme des Ba-Kongo," Encyclopedie Coloniale et Maritime
Mensuelle (Paris), 1 (12) Aug. 1951, 216-220.
Kimbanguism, Matswanism, Amicalism, and Kakism. (AA 4, 43)

601. _____. Sociologie actuelle de l'Afrique noire. Dynamique des changements
sociaux en Afrique centrale. Paris: Presses Universitaires de France,
(1955) 1963. xii + 532p.
Revised and enlarged edition: pp. 65-67, Ngol and Mulifa cults;
pp. 219-232, 270-276 etc., Bwiti; pp. 396-416 Amicalisme; pp. 417-
504, Congo Kimbanguism and messianism. Comparison between Fang and
Bakongo messianism.

602. _____. "Afrique ambigue," Les Temps modernes (Paris), 12 (126) July 1956,
42-83.
Contains material on Matswanism, Kimbanguism, and the Bwiti of
Gabon, later published in the book of same title.

603. _____. Afrique Ambigue. Paris: Plon, 1957. 211p. illus. Also G.Tr.
Zwielichtiges Africa.. Stuttgart: Schwab, 1959. Also E.Tr. Ambiguous
Africa. Forthcoming, 1966.
Ch. vii, "Mouvements contraires."

604. _____. "Brèves remarques sur les messianismes de l'Afrique congolaise,"
Archives de sociologie des religions (Paris), 3 (5) Jan.-June 1958, 91-95.
(AA 10, 370)

605. BOUCHARD, J. "Messianisme des Ba-Kongo," Encyclopédie coloniale et maritime mensuelle (Paris), 1 (12) Aug. 1951. (B.H.)

606. CHALIAND, Gerard. "Problèmes du nationalisme angolais," Les Temps
modernes (Paris), 21 (231) Aug. 1965.
P. 277, brief reference to the "messianic movement" of Simao Toco
among Angolese emigrants to Congo.

607. DE POSTIOMA, A. "A heresia do Antonianismo," Portugal em África, 14
(114) 1962, 378-381. (B.Eth.)
An expression of independency in the old Portugese period of the Congo.

608. DE VECIANA VILALDACH, Antonio. La Secta del Bwiti en la Guinea Española
      (The Bwiti sect in Spanish Guinea). Madrid: Instituto de Estudios
      Africanos, 1958. 63p. bibl.
          Digest of information on a syncretistic movement active also in Gabon.

609. MARGULL, Hans-Jürgen. Aufbruch zur Zukunft (Breaking out into the future).
      Gutersloh: Gerd Mohn, 1962. 128p.
          A theological study of chiliastic and messianic movements in Africa
          and S. E. Asia as post-Christian; section 3, Kimbangu and Matswa.

610. NIPPGEN, J. "Une société secrète chez les Ba-Congo de l'Afrique tropical,
      la société de la 'mort' et de la 'resurrection'," Revue anthropologique
      (Paris), 32 (3-4) 1922, 119-121.

611. P. E. B. "Nel Nome del Padre, di André Matswa e di Simon Kibangu"
      (In the name of the Father, of André Matswa, and of Simon Kimbangu),
      Nigrizia (Verona), 2, Feb. 1958, 2-4. Illus.

612. PINTASSILGO, Antonio Rodriques. "Seitas secretas no Congo" (Secret
      societies in Congo), Portugal em África (Lisbon), 10)60) Nov.-Dec.
      1953, 361-371.
          Kimbanguism in Congo influenced three prophetic-political movements
          in Cabinda - Ngwima (1916), Ngunza prophets, and Mayangi. (AA 6, 224.)

613. SULZMANN, Erika. "Die Bewegung der Antonier im alten Reiche Kongo"
      (The St. Anthony movement in the ancient Congo Kingdom), in W. E. MÜHLMANN
      (ed.) item 160, 81-85.
          The cult of St. Anthony as the basis for a national church independent
          of Rome, early in the 18th. century.

614. TASTEVIN, C. "Nouvelles manifestations du prophétisme en Afrique equator-
      iale et en Angola," Comptes Rendus de l'Academie des sciences coloniales
      (Paris), 16 (3) Feb. 1956, 149-153.
          Includes Kimbanguism, the "Religion du Salut," Toko's "Étoile rouge,"
          and a "prophète du Christ" from the then French Congo. (AA 9, 181)

615. THIEL, V. "Le Kakinisme (mouvement politico-religieuse en pays Balari),"
      Annales spiritaines (Paris), 59 (6) July 1949, 91-92.

616. THOMPSON, Virginia & ADLOFF, Richard. The emerging states of French
      Equatorial Africa. Stanford, Calif.: Stanford University Press, 1960.
      xii + 595p. bibl.
          Pp. 304-314, helpful summary of role of "messianic cults."

617. ZIEGLE, H. "Notes sur la psychologie des Bantous de l'Afrique Centrale,"
      Cahiers d'Outre-Mer (Bordeaux), 4 (13) Jan.-Mar. 1951, 23-38.
          Includes the effects of Christianity on traditional religion, seen
          in the 'heresy' of Kimbanguism, and in the continuation of ancestral
          rites in the Salvation Army of the Middle Congo. (AA 4, 342.)

ANGOLA

618. ANON. "Sectes nouvelles en Angola," in Museum Lessianum, item 161,
pp. 140-143.
    Prophets Simon Toco, Zacharias Bonzo, Mayange (of Cabinda) and,
    particularly, Lassy.

619. BENTLEY, W. Holman. Pioneering on the Kongo. London: Religious Tract
Society, 1900. 2 vols., 478p,448p. illus.
    Vol. I, pp. 290-292, Kiyoka anti-fetish movement from 1872 in
    N. Angola. Vol. II, p. 151, Kimbanguism.

620. CUNHA, Silva. Movimentos associativos na África Negra (Associative movements in black Africa), vol. II (Angola). Lisbon: Junta de Investigacões
do Ultramar, 1959. 90p. illus. map. bibl.
    Volume II discusses movements in Angola of two types: "de forma
    primitiva e conteudo novo" and "mistico-religiosas de forma econtudo
    novos." The former include Os Santos e Santas and Grupo do Espirito
    Santo. The latter are Tocoism, Lassyism, Dieudonné, and Watch
    Tower. See also Cunha, item 65.

621. _____. "Tocoismo," Ultramar (Lisbon), 5, 1961, 141-175. (B.Eth.)
    An extract from Cunha, previous item.

622. CUVELIER, J. Relations sur le Congo du Père Laurent de Lucques (1700-
1717). Brussels: Institut royal colonial belge, 1953.
    Prophetess Béatrice, reincarnation of St. Anthony, early 18th. c.

623. DE ANDRADE, Mario. "Angolese nationalism," Présence africaine (English
edn.), 14-15 (42-43), 1962, 7-23.
    Brief references to Simão Toco's messianic movement, pp. 12, 22, by
    the president of a liberation movement.

624. DE OLIVEIRA, Herculano L. "Movimento messiânico-comunista africano"
(African messianic-communist movements), Portugal em África (Lisbon),
2nd. ser. 15 (1) 1958, 18-36.

625. DOS SANTOS, Eduardo. "Do sincretismo mágico e religioso nos fundamentos
ideológicos do terrorismo no noroeste de Angola" (On magical and religious
syncretism in the ideological bases of terrorism in N. E. Angola),
Garcia de Orta (Lisbon), 10 (1) 1962, 77-91. Bibl. (B.H.)

626. _____. "O Noroeste angolano e os movimentos profético-salvíficos" (The
natives of N. W. Angola and prophetic-salvation movements), Ultramar
(Lisbon), 17, 1964, 32-73.

627. EDWARDS, Adrian C. The Ovimbundu under two sovereignties: A study of
social control and social change among a people of Angola. London:
O.U.P. for IAI, 1962. xvii + 169p.
    Pp. 160-161. An account of a "contra-acculturative" movement which
    arose in 1955 combining features of cargo-cults and anti-witchcraft
    campaigns.

628. FRAZÃO, Serra. Associacões secretas entre os Indígenas de Angola (Secret
societies among the natives of Angola). Lisbon: Editora Maritimo-
Colonial, 1946. 325p. (S.C.)

60

629. GRAHAM, Robert H. Carson. Under seven Congo kings. London: The Carey Press, 1931. 293p. illus.
    By a Baptist missionary in Angola. Pp. 186, 188, Kimbanguist movement in the Portugese Congo; cites an American revivalist mission as a precursor to the movement.

630. MERCIER, Emanuel. "La nuova ondata, Ha nome cipambule" (The new outbreak is called Cipambule), Nigrizia (Verona), 17 (11) Nov. 1959, 13-15. Illus. (B.Eth.)
    "Some notes on a new spirit and the sect of its believers: Cipambule, with the Tshokwe of Angola."

CONGO (BRAZZA.)

631. ANON. "Matswa," Monde non-chrétien, n.s. 26, June 1953, 202-210. An extract from "Le probleme le plus délicat du XXe siècle en A.E.F.," La Lettre écarlate (Brazzaville), 3rd. ed., 1 April 1953.
    A summary of the career of André Matswa, with good documentation.

632. _____. "Rise and fall," West Africa (London), 2412, 24 Aug. 1963, 941. Illus.
    A biographical account of Abbé Fulbert Youlou and his inheritance of the support given Matswa.

633. BALANDIER, Georges. "Naissance d'un mouvement politico-religieux chez les 'Ba-Kongo' du Moyen'Congo," in Proceedings of the III International West Africa Conference held at Ibadan, Nigeria, December, 1949. Lagos: Nigerian Museum, 1956, 334-336.
    Kimbanguism, Amicalism and Kakisme.

634. _____. Sociologie des Brazzaville noires. Paris: Armand Colin, 1955, 274p.
    Pp. 224-226: a Matswanist follower.

635. DURIEZ, M. J. Etude de Balalisme. Paris: Centre des hautes études d'administration musulmane, Section Islam - Afrique noire, 1950. (mimeo.)
    Amicalism or Matswanism, by a French administrator.

636. RENAULT, L. "Abbe Fulbert Youlou et Matsoua," Bulletin d'Information de la France d'Outre-Mer (Paris), 324, Nov. 1956.

637. YOULOU, Fulbert. Le Matsouanisme. Brazzaville: Imprimerie centrale, 1955.
    By a national, the Abbé Youlou, a former Roman Catholic priest who became prime minister.

CONGO (LEO.)

638. ABBELOOS, R. V. "De sekte 'Lilwa' bij de volkstam der Bambole" (The 'Lilwa' sect among the Bambole tribes), Band. Leopoldstad, 8 (8) Aug. 1949, 311-313.

639. ALDÉN, Karl. Kingoyifolket (The Kingoyi people). Stockholm: 1936. 91p. (E.A.)
    Includes Ngunzism (Kimbanguism) in the Congo in the 1930's.

640. ____. "The prophet movement in Congo," International Review of Missions, 25 (99) July 1936, 347-353.
A vivid account of a night meeting in the bush, with ecstatic practices; by a Swedish missionary in the Kimbanguist area.

641. ____. "Forsamlingsvard in Ngunzatider" (Assemblies at the time of Ngunzism), in G. Palmoer (ed.), Masteren pa Kongos Stigar. Stockholm: 1941. (E.A.)
Pp. 310-319, Ngunzism.

642. ALEXANDRE, J. K. "Kibangisme, het nationalisme in Kongo" (Kimbanguism, the Congo nationalism), Ontwakend Afrika (Brussels: Assumptionist Fathers), 25 (88), 1960.

643. ANDERSSON, Efraim. "Profetrörelsen i Kongo, dess ursprung och innebörd" (Prophet movements in the Congo, their origin and nature), Svensk Missionstidskrift (Uppsala), 27 (1) 1939, 29-45.

644. ____. Afrikanen väljer Kristus. Omvändelsen hos naturfolken i Kongo. (The African chooses Christ. The conversion of primitive people in the Congo). Stockholm: Svenska Missionsförbundets forlag, 1943. 176p.
Pp. 72-73, 108, 116-117, 120-121, on Kimbangu; pp. 70-73, prophet Harris of Ivory Coast.

645. ____. "Nkita-en extatisk sekt hos Teke i Kongo" (Nkita: an ecstatic sect at Teke in Congo), Svensk Missionstidskrift (Uppsala), 43, 1955, 15-25.

646. ANET, Henri. "À propos du Kibangisme," Congo (Brussels), 5 (2) 1924, 771-773.
A refutation of charges that Protestant missionaries had promoted Kimbanguism.

647. ANON. "Fétiche indigène de guerre Tonga-Tonga," Congo (Brussels), 2, 1921, 423-438.
The Epikilipikili movement of 1904 in the Bena Dibele region of the Belgian Congo.

648. ____. "Le garvéyisme en action dans notre Colonie," Congo (Brussels), 2 (4) 1921, 575-576.
Kimbanguism regarded as Garveyism.

649. ____. "L'affaire Kibango," Congo (Brussels), 3 (1), 1922, 63-64.

650. ____. "À propos du Kimbangisme," Congo (Brussels), 5 (2) 1924, 380-388. From an article by P. Dufonteny in Bulletin, La Ligue pour la Protection et l'Evangélisation des noires. (Liege) No. 4 (1924).
Blames Kimbanguism on Protestantism and the activities of Protestant missionaries.

651. ____. "Un prédecesseur de Mwana Lesa," Revue de droit et de jurisprudence du Katanga (Elizabethville), 2 (4) 1926, 97. See also following issues for Mwana Lesa: 2 (8), 201-204; 2 (9), 225-230; 2 (10), 242-247; 2 (11), 274-276; 3 (1), 328-332.

62

652. _____. "Quelques notes sur le Kibangisme," La Revue de l'Aucam (Louvain), 6, March 1931, 66-74. (K.S.)

653. _____. "Kitawala," Bulletin de juridictions indigènes et du droit coutumier congolais (Elizabethville), 12 (10) July-August 1944, 231-236. (B.Eth.)
    Watchtower in Congo.

654. _____. "Autour de Kitawala," Essor du Congo (Elizabethville), 29 Sept., 6 Oct., 10 Nov., 1945.

655. _____. "Le 'Munkukusa'," Missions de Scheut (Brussels), 7, 1952, 132. (B.Eth.)
    A "superstitious movement" in Lower Congo provoked by the "difficulties of life."

656. _____. "Émeutes à Léopoldville," Présence africaine, 23, Dec. 1958 - Jan. 1959, 113-122.
    Pp. 119-121, relation between the Abako political movement and Kimbanguism in the 1959 riots.

657. _____. "Kibanguisme," Afrique Ardente (Brussels), 31 (110) 1959, 1-7. (B.Eth.)
    Its role in the events of Leopoldville, 1959.

658. _____. "Een Politiek-godsdienstige sekte," (A political-religious sect), Ontwakend Afrika (Brussels: Assumptionist Fathers), 24 (84) 1959, 16-19. (B.Eth.)
    Kimbangu and Kimbanguism.

659. _____. "Influence politico-religieuse au Congo belge - expansion du Kibanguisme," Notes et Documents (Rome: White Fathers), 1, Jan. 1960, 39-40. (Reprinted from Fides, 5 Dec. 1959.)

660. _____. "Le Kitawala au Congo," Notes et Documents (Rome: White Fathers), 15, April 1961, 196.

661. _____. "Articles of association," Moniteur congolais (Secretariat-Général, Leopoldville-Kalina), 2nd part, 19, 23 Aug. 1961, 80-81.
    Contains the articles of association of the "Church of Jesus Christ . . . through prophet Simon Kimbangu."

662. _____. in Archives de sociologie des religions (Paris), 7 (13) Jan.-June 1962, 191-192.
    A résumé of M. Sinda's dissertation, see item 759; notes an emphasis on political rather than religious sociology; reports (Pt. I) Kimbanguism as religion becoming political, and (Pt. II) Matswanism as a political movement becoming religious.

663. _____. "Sectes dans l'Est du Congo ex-belge," in Museum Lessianum, item 161, 91-101.
    Pp. 96-100, Kitawala.

664. BAPTIST MISSIONARY SOCIETY (Gt. Britain). London: Annual reports. 130th. year, 1922, pp. 45-49; 131st. year, 1923, pp. 47-49; 132nd. year, 1924, pp. 72-73.
    Local reports on the "prophet movement" of Simon Kimbangu.

665. BAZOLA, E. La conversion au Kimbanguisme et ses motifs. Leopoldville: Université Lovanium (Memoire de Licence en Science pédagogiques). 199p.

666. BELVAIN, A. "Matsoua et Kimbangu, sont-ils les sauveurs de l'Afrique noire?" Liaison (Brazzaville), 61, 1958, 11-13.

667. BERNARD, G. "The nature of a sociological research: religious sects in the west of the Congo," Cahiers économiques et sociaux (Leopoldville), 2 (3) Nov. 1964, 261-269.
    A suggested typology; Kimbanguism in relation to Congolese social developments, both colonial and post-colonial.

668. _____ & CAPRASSE, P. "Religious movements in the Congo: a research hypothesis," Cahiers économiques et sociaux (Leopoldville), 3 (1) Mar. 1965, 49-60.
    Comparative accounts of Jehovah's Witnesses, the Mpadist church (Mission des Noirs) and the Kimbanguist Church of Jesus Christ. (FA 1, 1727) (Digest also in Geneva-Africa, 4 (2) 1962, 323.)

669. BERTSCHE, James. Kimbanguism: a separatist movement. Unpublished M.A. (Anthropology) thesis, Northwestern University, Evanston, Ill., 1963.
    A review of the literature and some new material, by a Mennonite missionary in the Congo (Leo).

670. _____. "The Kwilu rebellion," Messages and Reports. African Mennonite Fellowship, Bulawayo, 1965, 74-76.
    The 1964 revolt and its "overlay of supernatural claims and beliefs," by a missionary captured by the rebels.

671. _____. "What are independent churches saying to traditional Christianity?" in Messages and Reports. Africa Mennonite Fellowship, Bulawayo, 1965, 26-30.
    A sympathetic discussion with reference to Kimbanguism, after a historical survey.

672. BIEBUYCK, M. O. "La société kumu face au Kitawala," Zaïre (Brussels), 11 (1) Jan. 1957, 7-40.
    Shows the relationship between the Kitawala movement (Jehovah's Witnesses) and the political, social and religious aspects of Kumu society. (AA 9, 196)

673. BITTREMIEUX, Léo. La société secrète des Bakhimba au Mayombe. Brussels: Institut royal colonial belge, 1936. 327p.
    A Roman Catholic missionary on traditional cults. Pp. 237-239, new religions and a brief description of Kimbanguism.

674. BORRISON, C. N. Katalog och beskrivning över S.M.F.S. vandringsmuseum. (Catalogue and description of the Swedish Mission Covenant Society travelling museum). Malmo: 1925. (E.A.)
    Pp. 23ff., Nkimba cult or secret society in the Congo.

675. BOSSCHE, Jean Vanden. Sectes et associations secrètes au Congo belge. Leopoldville: Ed. du Bulletin Militaire, 1954. 101p. (B.Eth.)

64

676. BRAECKMAN (Père). "Le Kibangisme. Aspirations indigènes," in Report, III Semaine de Missiologie. Louvain: Édit. du Museum Lessianum, 1925, 159-163.
A Roman Catholic account.

677. BROUSSARI, N. "Watch Tower oder Kitawala im Kongo" (Watch Tower or Kitawala in the Congo), Hémecht a Missio'n, 1, 1947, 19-20; 2, 1947, 50-51; 3, 1947, 85-87.

678. CHOMÉ, Jules. La passion de Simon Kimbangu. Brussels: Présence afri- caine, 1959. 134p. bibl.
A Belgian lawyer using local sources examines the trial of Kimbangu, criticizes the colonial government, and rehabilitates Kimbangu.

679. CHURCH OF JESUS CHRIST (Kimbanguist Church). Office du Prophète Simon Kimbangu (Nkanda Bisambu bis tata Simon Kimbangu). (Leopoldville), La Reunion des pasteurs kimbanguistes, n.d. (1960-1962?). 115p. illus.
Contains a life of Kimbangu (French); the liturgy of the "Church of Jesus Christ . . ." (French and Kikongo); ten hymns in Kikongo.

680. COMHAIRE, Jean L. "Sociétés secrètes et mouvements prophétiques au Congo belge," Africa (London), 25 (1) Jan. 1955, 54-59. Also in Revue coloniale belge (Brussels), 10 (230) May 1955, 292-294.
Reviews De Jonghe, item 688; surveys later developments; traces messianism to syncretists cults of the 18th. c. (AA 7, 218.)

681. COUSSEMENT, D. Grégoire. "La secte de Punga et du Mama Okanga," Bulletin des juridictions indigènes et du droit coutoumier congolais (Elizabeth- ville), 3, May 1935, 64-67.
A secret mutual-protection society in Katanga in the 1930's.

682. CRABBÉ, R. "La situation religieuse au Congo," Congo An V. Eurafrica et Tribune du Tiers-Monde (Brussels), 8 (7-8) July-Aug. 1964, 48-50.
A brief repetition of the common Belgian attitude of the last forty years, in a special issue in the fifth year of the Congo Republic (Leo).

682A. D'ANNA, Andrea. Da Cristo a Kimbangu (From Christ to Kimbangu). Bologna: Ed. Nigrizia, 1964. 158p.

683. DAUBECHIES (Mgr.). "Le Kitawala," Tendances du temps (Elizabethville), 19 (58) 1961, 5-18.
Translation of a publication in Kibemba. (AA 14, 161).

684. DEBERTRY, Léon. Kitawala. Elisabethville: Éditions Essor du Congo, 1953. 274p. map.
Fiction, in French; a chapter at the end, pp. 259-274, summarizes the history of Kitawala in S. E. Congo.

685. DECAPMAEKER (Père). "Le Kimbanguisme," in Museum Lessianum, item 161, pp. 52-66.
By a Roman Catholic missionary in the Congo; describes contemporary Kimbanguism and quotes Kimbanguist documents.

686. DE COCKER, M. "Essai de parallélisme biblico-congolais," Zaïre, 4 (3) 1950, 277-298.
Especially pp. 291-292, 294, on prophets in traditional religion.

687. DECRAENE, Philippe. "Les incidences politiques des religions syncrétiques et des mouvements messianiques en Afrique noire," Afrique contemporaine, 17, Jan.-Feb. 1965, 19-22.
    The meaning of syncretistic and messianic; movements in the Congo from 17th century, especially Amicalism or Matswanism; growth of a pan-African religious consciousness.

688. DE JONGHE, Edward. "Formations récentes de sociétés secrètes au Congo belge," Africa (London), 9 (1) Jan. 1936, 56-63; Also in Congo (Brussels), 1, 1936, 233-242.
    Includes Kimbanguism, and Kitawala under the name of Mwana Lesa.

689. DE MOOR, Vincent. Leur combat: essais de missiologie. Paris: Beauchesne, 1937.
    Pp. 141-154, Watch Tower.

690. DENVIT, D. Le Congo d'aujourd'hui. Brussels: Collection Nationale, 1948. 94p.
    Includes discussion of Kimbanguism and Kitawala.

691. DIANGENGA, J. "Le Kimbanguisme," Courrier hebdomodaire (Centre de recherche et d'information sociopolitique, Paris), 60, 29 Jan. 1960, 16-17.
    By one of Kimbangu's sons.

692. DOUCY, Arthur. "Le mouvement des idées relatives à l'avenir politique du Congo belge," in L'avenir politique du Congo belge: Colloque du 22 Novembre 1958. Brussels: Librairie Encyclopédique S.P.R.L. 1959, 19-72.
    P. 19, place of "messianic movements" in the development of Congolese nationalism.

693. DOUGLAS, Mary. The Lele of the Kasai. London: O.U.P. for IAI, 1963. xiv + 286p.
    Pp. 241-258, seven witchfinding movements from 1900.

694. ____. "Techniques of sorcery control in Central Africa," in J. Middleton & E. H. Winter, item 155, 123-141.
    Witchfinding movements among the Lele.

695. DOUTRELOUX, Albert. "Prophétisme et culture kongo," Africa Kring. 10 (2), 1961, 169-174. (B.H.)
    Ngunzism as a phenomenon of social reorganization.

696. ____. "Magie Yombe: notes sur la fonction sociologique de forme 'parareligieuse'," Zaïre, 15 (1) 1961, 45-57.
    Concludes with reference to Kimbanguism as a development parallel to nationalism. (AA 14, 250).

697. ____. "Prophétisme et 'Leadership' dans la société Kongo," in Museum Lessianum, item 161, 67-81.

698. ____. "Mythe et réalité du colonialisme," Genève-Afrique (Geneva), 4 (1) 1965, 7-34.
    Pp. 25-26, the contribution of prophet movements (Kimbanguism) in the Congo to decolonisation.

698A. DUBUISSON, "La secte du Pinga et du Mama Okanga, crimes et superstitions indigènes," Bulletin des juridictions indigènes et du droit coutumier Congolais (Elizabethville), 4 (7), Jan.-Dec. 1936.
    A secret mutual protection society in Katanga in the 1930's.

699. DUFONTENEY, (Père). "Il 'Kibangismo' al Congo Belga," Le Mission Cattoliche (Milan), 53 (19) 1 Oct. 1924, 299-300; (20) 15 Oct. 1924, 313-315; (21) 1 Nov. 1924, 329-332; (22) 15 Nov. 1924, 346-347; (23) 1 Dec. 1924, 361-364; (24) 15 Dec. 1924, 371-373.
    An important early account by a Roman Catholic missionary.

700. FEHDERAU, Harold W. "Enthusiastic Christianity in an African church," Practical Anthropology (Tarrytown, N.Y.), 8 (6) Nov.-Dec. 1961, 279-280, 282.
    A description and defence of ecstatic behaviour in the worship of an unnamed African church.

701. _____. "Kimbanguism: prophetic Christianity in Congo," Practical Anthropology (Tarrytown, N.Y.), 9 (4) July-Aug. 1962, 157-178.
    Based on Andersson, item 598, together with reviews of subsequent literature - van Wing, item 772; Chomé, item 678; Raymaekers, item 748; and Gilis, item 707.

702. FLODÉN, S. A. 'Tata' Flodén berattar. Kongominnen 1 - 2. ('Father' Floden reports: Congo memories.) Stockholm: 1933. (E.A.)
    Pp. 147-167, on Kimbangu.

703. FOX, Renée C., DE CRAEMER, Willy, & RIBEAUCOURT, Jean-Marie. "La deuxième indépendance. Étude d'un cas: La Rebellion au Kwilu," Etudes congolaises (Brussels and Leopoldville), 8 (1) Jan.-Feb. 1965, and published separately. 35p. E.Tr., "The second independence: a case study of the Kwilu rebellion in Congo," Comparative Studies in Society and History, 8 (1) Oct. 1965, 78-109.
    The background of the Kwilu rebellion of Jan. 1964 as found in "messianic syncretist cults" in Kwilu area since the 1930's, often led by products of mission schools; fuller treatment of Mulélisme, a political form of messianism. (FA 1, 1191)

704. FRAMES, W. B. "'Prophets' in the Lower Congo," Congo Mission News (Leopoldville); Also in South African Outlook (Lovedale), 52 (615) 1 Feb. 1922, 36-38.
    Early articles on Kimbangu by a Protestant missionary.

705. FULLERTON, W. Y. The Christ of the Congo River. London: The Carey Press, n.d. (1928) 216p.
    Pp. 131-133, first hand account of Kimbangu's movement, by a Baptist missionary; other movements of 1924.

706. GEVAERTS, Frans. Vadé mecum à l'usage du service territorial. Brussels: Ministère des Colonies, 1953.
    Pp. 30-33, the banning of Kitawala in Congo provinces, 1937-1948.

707. GILIS, Charles-André. Kimbangu, fondateur d'église. Brussels: La Librairie encyclopédique, 1960, 126p.
    A sympathetic survey based on existing publications; questions whether any new material on Kimbangu remains to be found.

708. HAFFMANS, Rob. "Het Fenomeen van de Afrikaanse Sekten als aktueel missieprobleem in de Kongo" (The phenomenon of African sects as a current problem for missions in the Congo), Het Missiewerk (Nijmegen), 40 (1) 1961, 31-42.
     Includes brief accounts of Matswanism, Bougism, Dieudonnism, Tsakism, and Nzobism.

709. HOSKYNS, Catherine. The Congo since independence. London: O.U.P., 1965. xii + 518p.
     Pp. 78, 90, Charles Kisolo Kele (Kimbangu's eldest son, a minister of state in Lumumba's cabinet) and his part in releasing European hostages from Thysville in 1960.

710. HULT, Gustav Adolf. "Profetrörelsen" (Prophet Movements), in G. Palmaer (ed.), Mästaren på Kongos Stigar, Stockholm: 1941, 214-222. (K.S.)

711. JADIN, Louis. "Le Congo et la secte des Antoniens: restauration du royaume sous Pedro IV et la 'Sainte-Antoine' congolaise (1694-1718)," in Bulletin de l'Institut historique belge de Rome (Rome and Brussels), 33, 1961, 411-615.
     The Italian Capuchin mission and a 17th. c. prophetess, Béatrice, claiming to be a reincarnation of St. Anthony, and that Jesus was a Negro.

712. JAFFRÉ, C(ôme). "L'Afrique aux Africains ou le 'Ngounzisme' au Congo," Études (Paris), 218 (22) 5 Mar. 1934, 651-664.
     A Roman Catholic missionary on Kimbanguism.

712A. KIBANGI, R. Buana. "L'évolution du Kibangisme," Flambeau (Yaoundé), 10, Apr. 1966.

713. KISELEV, D. V. "Bel'gujskoye Kongo: ob'ekt imperialisticheskogo sopernichestva" (The Belgian Congo: the objective of imperialist rivalry), in Imperialisticheskaya bor'ba za Afriku. Moscow: 1953, 267-286.
     A Russian account of "Risings which date back to 1921" - i.e., Kimbangu?

714. KITWANGA, (Père?). "Belgisch Congo op een keerpunt van zijn geschiedenis" (Belgian Congo at a turning point in its history), Afrika-Christo (Lier, Belgium: Holy Ghost Fathers), 1 (1) 1946, 2-5. (B.Eth.)
     Kitawala, and revolts at Manono and Masisi.

715. KOPYTOFF, Igor. Suku religion: a study in internally induced re-interpretation. Unpublished Ph.D. dissertation (Anthropology), North-western University, 1960. (Mic. 60-6559)
     Pp. 141-167, three religious movements among the Basuku in the Congo: Mbiande 1924, Lupambula 1944-5, Holy Water 1954-9.

716. KROMER, Berthold. Vom Neuen Afrika (From the new Africa). Dusseldorf: Schwann, 1931, 159p. (K.S.)
     P. 74, Ngunzism.

717. LABRIQUE, J. "Étude du movement Kitawala," Belcopresse (Leopoldville), 3, 1956, 88-99.

718. LAMARCHAND, René. "The bases of nationalism among the Bakongo," Africa, 31 (4) Oct. 1961, 344-354.
      Pp. 345-6, role of Kimbangu. (AA 14, 102)

719. _____. "Congo (Leopoldville)," in J. S. Coleman & C. G. Rosberg Jr. (eds.), Political parties and national integration in tropical Africa. Berkeley: University of California Press, 1964.
      Pp. 567-568, messianic movements.

720. _____. Political awakening in the Belgian Congo. Berkeley: University of California Press, 1964. 357p. illus.
      Pp. 168-174, 186, 189, early nativistic and messianic movements, and Matswanism.

720A. LANTERNARI, Vittorio. "La religione della libertà dei populi del Congo" (The religion of independence of the people of the Congo), Ulisse (Rome), 6 (39) 1961, 60-69.

721. LEBEER, P. "L'est Africain et nous, Watch Tower et syndicalisme," Belcopresse (Leopoldville), 3, 1956, 87-88, 101-3.

722. _____. "Panorama du Kitawala au Congo," Belcopresse (Leopoldville), 4-5, 1956, 149-51, 169-70.

723. LERRIGO, P. H. J. "The 'prophet movement' in Congo, International Review of Missions, 11 (42) Apr. 1922, 270-277.
      A first-hand account of the genesis of Kimbanguism, especially the call of Kimbangu, and his healings, by a Baptist medical missionary.

724. LONGOLONGO. "Kitawala," Congo (weekly), 2 (16) 1946, 1 and 3. (B.Eth.)
      Kitawala: history, and account of revolts of 1941 and 1944.

725. MAQUET, Jean Noel. "Le kimbangisme à 38 ans.," Eurafrica (Brussels), 6, June 1959. (Sinda)

726. MAQUET-TOMBU, Jeanne. Le Siècle marche. Récit historique. Brussels: Office de Publicite, 1937. 230p. (E.A.)
      Includes Kimbanguism.

727. MASSON, J. "Simples réflexions sur des chants kibanguistes," in Museum Lessianum, item 161, pp. 82-90.
      Discussion of Raymaekers, item 749.

728. MAKENGERE. "Vigilance! Kitawala ou Watch-Tower," Revue coloniale belge (Brussels), 1 (8) Feb. 1946, 4-7.

729. MATAGNE, A. "Exploits du Kitawala," La Revue nationale, 30 (302) Oct. 1958, 311-313.

730. MBAMBI, A. "C'était en 1946 . . .," Liaison (Leopoldville), 75, 1960. (B.H.)
      A Congolese on Matswanism.

731. MERLIER, Michel. Le Congo de la colonisation belge à l'indépendance. Paris: F. Maspero, 1962. 332p.
      Pp. 231-249, secret societies and messianic movements in Congolese nationalism, including their role in the events leading to independence.

732. MINJAUW, Leon. Les redemptoristes belges cinquante ans au Bas-Congo 1899-1949. Louvain: Saint-Alphonse, 1949. 100p. (Sinda)
      Ch. vi, "Le Kibangisme."

733. MPANGI. "Het Kibangisme," Jezuitenmissies (Louvain), 9 (69) 1950, 218-228.

734. NEILS, M. Le prophétisme au Congo belge. Unpublished thesis, Protestant Theological Faculty, Aix, 1956. (mimeo.)

735. NEUFELD, Elmer. Kimbanguism: An African prophet movement. Nsukka, E. Nigeria: Department of Religion, University of Nigeria, 1963. 15p. (mimeo.)
      A sympathetic theological evaluation of the inception and persistence of Kimbanguism in Congo today, by a Mennonite missionary.

736. NIKLAUS, R. L. "Remodelled animism," The Alliance Witness (Christian and Missionary Alliance, U.S.A.), 27 Jan. 1960, 13.
      A missionary interpretation of Kimbanguism as anti-white.

737. NYRÉN, J. Bland skördeman i Kongo. (Among the harvesters in the Congo.) Stockholm: 1922. (E.A.)
      Pp. 226-229, Ethiopianism and Kimbanguism.

738. O'BRIEN, Conor Cruise. To Katanga and back: A U.N. case history. London: Hutchinson, 1962. F.Tr. Mission au Katanga. Paris: Plon, 1964. xiii + 442p.
      Pp. 118, 320-321, the association with Tshombe of the Apostles, a Katangese "revivalistic sect." Pp. 152, 163, violence fostered by Watchtower.

739. PAULUS, Jean-Pierre. "Le Kitawala au Congo belge (mouvement indigène à caractère politico-religieux)," Revue de l'Institut de sociologie Solvay (Brussels), 2 (3) 1956, 257-270, 288. (AA 9, 316.)
      The entry of Watch Tower from the Rhodesias via Katanga in 1951-52, prepared for by an earlier sect of Bereti Ambrasius; the anti-white and political nature varied in different areas of the Congo.

740. PETERS, Josef. "Kibangismus und allafrikanische Bewegung" (Kimbanguism and the pan-African movement), Die katholischen Missionen (Aachen), 53, Aug. 1925, 344-351.

741. PHILIPPART, Louis. Le Bas-Congo: État religieux et social. Louvain, Saint Alphonse, (1929) 1947. 203p.
      On the Manianga and Bandidu groups of the Kongo.

742. _____. "Notes sur le Kibangisme," Africa fraternae ephemerides romanae (Rome), 2, Apr. 1933, 99-111. (K.S.)
      By a Roman Catholic missionary.

743. PHILIPPE, René. "La Secte 'Nebele' chez les mangbetu," Africa-Tervuren, 8 (4) 1962, 98.
      An anti-European religious group dating from the first years of colonialization.

744.   _____. "La secte 'Ekitelakitela' des Budja (Congo-ex-belge)," in <u>Actes du VIe Congres international des Sciences anthropologiques et ethologiques, Paris, 1960</u>, Paris: Musée de l'Homme, Tome II, 2e vol., 1964, 459-464.
       An anti-sorcery sect founded by a woman, and largely confined to women; its hierarchy and rites. (FA 1, 666.)

745.   _____. "Les 'nganga nzambe' ou prêtres de Dieu?" <u>Africa-Tervuren</u>, 11 (1) 1965, 23-25.
       A neo-pagan movement described by a missionary. From the Boloma, it spread to the Boende in 1956 before being stopped on account of profiteering. (FA 1, 1199.)

746.   RAGOEN, J. "De Watch-Towers of Kitawala in Kongo," <u>Nieuw-Afrika</u> (Antwerp, White Fathers), 72 (7) 1956, 297-301. (B. Eth.)
       See also Ragoen, item 957, 1038.

747.   RAYMAEKERS, Paul. "Quelques notes dur le 'Bofomela' chez les mongo," <u>Bulletin de la Société royale belge de géographie</u> (Brussels), 3-4, 1927, 208-224. (B. Eth.)
       A reworking of the ancestor cult of the Mongo in the face of a high mortality rate.

748.   _____. "L'Église de Jésus-Christ sur la terre par le prophète Simon Kimbangu: contribution à l'étude des mouvements messianiques dans le Bas-Kongo," <u>Zaire</u> (Brussels), 13 (7) 1959, 675-756. Illus.
       A substantial study of the independent church which resulted from the Kimbangu movement.

749.   _____ (ed.) & BOKA, Simon (trans.). <u>250 Chants de l'Église de Jésus-Christ sur la terre par le prophète Simon Kimbangu. Première Série: 85 Chants de NSAMBU André</u>. Leopoldville: Institut de recherche économiques et sociales, Université Lovanium, 1960. 43p. (mimeo.)

750.   _____. (for RYCKMANS, André). "L'Église de Jésus-Christ sur la terre par le prophète Simon Kimbangu," in <u>Bouaké</u>, item 206.

751.   _____. <u>Hymnes de Liberation de l'E.J.C.S.K</u>. Paris: Archives de sociologie religieuse. Forthcoming.

752.   RÉUNION DES PASTEURS KIMBANGUISTES (ed.). <u>Nkanda Bisambu bia tata Simon Kimbangu/Office du prophète Simon Kimbangu</u>. Leopoldville: La réunion des pasteurs kimbanguistes, n.d. (1961?). 115p. illus.
       The liturgy of the "Church of Jesus Christ on earth through Prophet Simon Kimbangu," in French and Kokongo (lower Congo); with biography of Kimbangu in French, and prayers and hymns in Kikongo.

753.   RICHARDSON, Folke. "Profetrörelser i Nedre Kongo, deras uppkomst och framträdande drag," (Prophet movements in Lower Congo, their origin and continuing effect.), <u>Ymer</u> (Stockholm), 1, 1956, 25-42.
       A history of Kimbanguism and Matswanism, with notes on the role of the prophets and their origin. Reviews the literature in Swedish.

754.   RYCKMANS, André. "Les mouvements prophétiques Kongo en 1958," <u>Ngonge Kongo</u> (Leopoldville), 7, 1964, 29p.; and expected from Paris: Éditions du Seuil. (FA 2 (1))

755. SCHEBESTA, Paul. Vollblutneger und Halbzwerge (Full-blooded Negroes and
      Pygmies). Salzburg: Pustet, 1934. 263p. (K.S.)
            Pp. 77f., Ngunzism in Congo.

756. SCHEYVEN, R. Et le Congo? Brussels: Van Ruys, 1957. 111p.
            A collection of the author's articles "Congo 1956," in La libre
            belgique, 30 Nov.-16 Dec. 1956, including those on Kitawala and
            Kimbanguism.

757. SHAREVSKAYA, B. I. "Anticolonialnoe religiosno-politicheskoe dvizhenie v
      Nizhnem Congo" (The Anti-colonial politico-religious movement in the
      Lower Congo), Narody Azii i Afriki (Moscow) 6, 1962, 89-98.
            Kimbanguism and other messianic movements in the lower Congo as
            anti-colonial.

758. SINDA, Martial. "Ein unbekannter Aspekt des modernen Kongo: der religiose
      Synkretismus" (An unknown aspect of modern Congo: religious syncretism),
      Afrika (Hamburg), 3 (3), March 1961, 113-117. Illus.
            Matswanism, whose members await the return of Matswa, and the
            millennium in which they will rule. (AA 13, 380)

759. _____. Le messianisme congolais et ses incidences politiques depuis son
      apparition jusqu'à l'époque de l'independance, 1921-1961. Unpublished
      thesis, Paris, 1961.
            By a mu-Kongo; includes texts of many hymns and prayers, some in both
            French and vernacular.

760. SOBCHENKO, A. I. "Etnograficheskaia kharakteristika gorodskogo naselenia
      Belgiiskago Kongo" (Ethnographic analysis of the town population of the
      Belgian Congo), Sovetskaya Etnografia (Moscow), May-June 1957, 107-118.
            The waning of religious manifestations of the struggle for nationalism.
            (AA 9, 191.)

761. STONELAKE, Alfred R. Congo: Past and Present. London: World Dominion
      Press, 1937. 202p.
            Pp. 15, 56, 98, 134 on the "prophet" movements and Watch Tower.

762. SVENSKA MISSIONSFÖRBUNDETS ÅRSBOK. (Yearbook of the Swedish Missionary
      Society). 1921, 1922. (E.A.)
            1921: p. 114ff., Ngunza movement in the Congo, 1921.
            1922: p.87ff., Ngunza movement in Kingoye, Congo, 1922.

763. TALANOVA, E. V. "'Belyie' i 'Chernyie' v Belgiiskom Kongo," ('White' and
      'Black' in the Belgian Congo), Kratkiye Soobscheniye (Moscow), 21, 1954,
      44-50.
            "Mass struggle . . . sometimes takes Christian forms." (AA 7, 356)

764. TAS, F. "Profetisme bij Bayaka en Bakongo: 'Tonsi' of 'Tela' tijdens
      de oorlog van '40" (Prophetism in the Bayaka and Bakongo: The Tonsi or
      Tela during the war of 1940), Jezuitenmissies (Louvain), 13 (106)
      Apr. 1954, 168-175. Illus.

765. THIEL, V. "Le Kakinisme," Annales spiritaines (Paris), 59 (6) July 1949,
      91-92. (B.Eth.)
            A political-religious movement also called Matswanism.

72

766. TOUSSAINT, R. E. "Notes sur la secte 'Toni-Toni' en territoire de
      Kabongo," Bulletin de juridictions indigènes et du droit coutumier
      congolais (Elisabethville), 21 (5) Sept.-Oct. 1953, 99-104.
            An anti-witchcraft group founded in 1940 in Kasai Province. (AA5,
            617)

767. TSHIMBAYEKE,   . "Croyances superstitieuses des indigènes," Tam Tam
      (Paris), 3 (1-2) 1956, 23-24. (B.Eth.)
            The "sect" of Tutshilkele among the Tsokwe, 1948-1950, whose rites
            imitated the Europeans.

768. TURNBULL, Colin M. The lonely African. New York: Simon & Schuster,
      1962; Doubleday (Anchor), 1963. 223p.
            Pp. 53, 167-171, Kitawala, from the African viewpoint.

769. UBRUN, A. "Le mouvement kimbanguiste ou ngounziste au Bas-Congo,"
      Annales des Pères du Saint-Esprit, 51, Nov. 1935, 272-278.

770. Uppdrag in Afrika. Svenska missionsinsäter i de svärtas världsdel
      (Commission in Africa. Swedish missionary concerns in the blackest part
      of the world). Stockholm: 1927. (E.A.)
            Pp. 126ff., Ngunzism.

771. VAN WING, J. "Notes sur quelques problèmes congolais," Institut royal
      colonial belge, Bulletin des séances (Brussels), 21 (1) 1950, 176-95.
            Reference to Kimbanguism and Kitawala. (AA 2, 96)

772. _____. "Le Kibangisme vu par un témoin," Zaïre (Brussels), 12 (6) 1958,
      563-618.
            A historical assessment, critical of Kimbangu and Mpadism; claims
            Kimbangu became a Roman Catholic in 1951. (AA 11, 65)

773. _____. "Le kimbanguisme," Courrier hebdomadaire du Centre de recherche
      et d'information socio-politiques (Brussels), 8 Jan. 1960.

774. _____. "Les mouvements messianiques populaires dans le Bas-Congo.
      Notes marginales." Zaïre (Brussels), 14 (2-3) Feb.-Mar. 1960, 225-238.
            Detailed comment on E. Andersson, item 598.

775. VAN DER MEERSCH, W. J. Ganshof. Fin de la souverraineté belge au Congo:
      Documents et réflexions. Brussels: Institut royal des relations
      internationals, 1963. 676p.
            P. 79, brief political biography of C. Kisolokele, Kimbangu's son;
            pp. 154, 369, 390, role of religious movements in fomenting unrest
            and violence at independence; Kimbanguism in Bas-Congo; Mpere in
            Kwango-Kwilu and especially Kitawala in Maniema.

776. VAN LOCO, J. "Het kommunisme bij de Baloeba" (Communism among the
      Baluba), Nieuw-Afrika (Antwerp: White Fathers), 54, 1938, 374-376.

777. VANSINA, J(an). Les tribus Ba-Kuba et les peuplades apparentés. Tervuren:
      Musée royal du Congo belge; London: IAI., 1954.

778. _____. "Miko mi Yool, une association religieuse Kuba," Aequatoria
      (Coquilhatville), 22 (2) 1959, 7-20; (3) 1959, 81-92.
            An anti-sorcerer cult among the Kuba. (AA 11, 328.)

779. VERBEKEN, A. "À propos du Kimbanguisme et de son auteur," Revue congolaise (Brussels), 31 (3) Mar. 1959, 25-27.

780. VYSOTSKAYA, N. I. "O roli vozhdey u Rang i Bakongo" (The role of chiefs among the Fang and the Bakongo), Sovetskaya Etnografia (Moscow), Jan.-Feb. 1962.
    Pp. 71-76, includes Kimbanguism as a politico-religious movement which strengthened Bakongo consolidation. (AA 14, 408)

781. WAGRET, Jean-Michel. Histoire et sociologie politiques de la République du Congo. Paris: Pichon et Durand-Auzias, 1963. 250p. map.
    Pp. 39-50, 201-207: places religious movements in the context of the political development of Congo (Brazzaville); discusses Kimbangu, Mpadi and especially Matswa and Lassy; the role of the Matswa and Lassy movements in contemporary Congolese politics; mentions other movements such as "Mademoiselle of Zoka Zoka" from Gabon, Jehovah's Witnesses and Dieudonné.

782. WALDER, A. "Ngunzismen i Kongo" (Ngunzism in the Congo), Ansgarius. Illustrerad missionskalender utgiven av Svenska Missionsforbundet, 17 1922. 67-75.

783. WAUTHION, R. "Le mouvement Kitawala au Congo belge," Bulletin de l'association des ancients étudiants de l'institut universitaire des territoires d'outre-mer (Anvers), 3 (8) 1950, 3-10.
    A good account. (AA 2, 590.)

784. WEST CENTRAL AFRICAN REGIONAL CONFERENCE OF PROTESTANT MISSIONS. Report: Abundant Life in Changing Africa. Leopoldville: Regional Conference, 1946.
    P. 181, a motion for the Congo Protestant Council to set up a permanent commission on separatists.

785. WILLAME, J. C., & VERHAEGEN, B. "Les Provinces du Congo: structure et fonctionement. I. Swilu-Luluabourg Nord-Katanga-Ubangi," Cahiers économiques et sociaux (Leopoldville), 1, May 1964, 19-22.
    Syncretist movements in Kwilu province since 1933: the "talking-serpent" sect, Ngunzism, the Dieudonné and Mpeve sects, and Mulélisme.

786. YOUNG, Crawford. Politics in the Congo. Princeton: Princeton U.P. 1965, 659p.
    Pp. 247, 286, 391, Kimbanguism; pp. 252-253, "Messianic Sects and Ethnicity" (Kimbanguism, Kitawala); pp. 284-286, "Syncretist Religious Movements."

787. ZOLA, E. "A la recherche de la principale cause du Kibangisme," Pour Servir (Inkisi, Congo: Mayidi Seminary), 4 (2) Jan.-Feb. 1960, 6-11; 4 (7) 1960, 8-13. (mimeo.)

GABON

788. ADAM, (Pere). "Le Ngol," Annales Spiritaines (Paris), 58 (4) 1948, 57-59. (B.Eth.)
    A new religion whose name was derived from DeGaulle.

74

789. BALANDIER, Georges. "Les Fan, conquérants en disponibilité," Tropiques
      (Paris), 47 (316) Dec. 1949, 23-26.
          Includes discussion of the Bwiti cult as a politico-religious
          development among the Fang. (AA 1, 535)

790. _____. "Aspects de l'évolution sociale chez les Fang du Gabon (Afrique
      Equatorate from Caise)," Cahiers internationaux de Sociologie, 9, 1950,
      76-106.
          Pp. 79ff, Ngol and Bwiti as social regroupings of the Fang. (AA 3, 72)

791. _____. "L'utopie de Benoit Ogoula Igugua," Les Temps modernes (Paris),
      84-85, Oct.-Nov. 1952, 771-781.
          Messianism in Gabon. (AA 4, 480)

792. BRINDA, Matthieu (Prince). La Bible secrète des noirs selon le Bouity.
      Paris: Omnium Litterarum, n.d. (1952). 148p. illus.
          On the Bwiti movement, by a member.

793. FERNANDEZ, James (William), & BEKALE, P. "Christian acculturation and
      Fang witchcraft," Cahiers d'études africaines, 2 (6) Fall 1961, 244-270.
          Pp. 244-255, introduction and comment on Bekale's text, by Fernandez;
          pp. 256-270, text by Bekale, a Gabonese of Fang background; reference
          to Bwiti and other anti-witchcraft movements.

794. _____. "Redistributive acculturation and ritual reintegration in Fang
      culture," Unpublished Ph.D. dissertation (Anthropology), Northwestern
      University, (U.S.A.) 1963. (Mic. 64-2479)
          Bwiti in Gabon.

795. _____. "The Idea and the Symbol of the Saviour in a Gabon Syncretistic
      Cult (Basic Factors in the Mythology of Messianism)," International
      Review of Missions, 53 (211), July 1964, 281-289.
          Also résumé in X Internationaler Kongress für Religionsgeschichte,
          Marburg 1960. Marburg: N. G. Elwert, 1961, 84-85.

796. _____. "Symbolic consensus in a Fang reformative cult," American
      Anthropologist, 67 (4) Aug. 1965, 902-929.
          Analysis of Bwiti symbols.

797. _____. "Unbelievably subtle words: representation and integration in
      the sermons of an African reformative cult," in J. Middleton and V. W.
      Turner (eds.), item 156.

798. LASSERRE, Guy. Libreville la ville et sa région. Paris: Colin, 1958.
      347p.
          Pp. 313-317, Bwiti in Libreville; first-hand account of Nydeya Kanya,
          a combination of Catholicism and Bwiti, one of the "innumerable
          African churches."

799. OSCHWALD, P. "La Danse 'De Gaulle' à Lambaréné," Journal des missions
      évangéliques (Paris), 21, Feb. 1950, 7-13.
          The beginnings of the Ngol movement.

800. WALTER, R. "Le Bouite," Bulletin de la société des recherches congolaises
      (Brazzaville) 4, 1924, 3-7.

801. _____. "La statue du Bouiti," <u>Bulletin</u> <u>de</u> <u>la</u> <u>société</u> <u>des</u> <u>recherches</u> <u>congolais</u> (Brazzaville), 8, 1927, 142-143.

RUANDA

802. BUSHAYIJA, Stanislas. "Indifférence religieuse et néo-paganisme au Ruanda," <u>Rythmes</u> <u>du</u> <u>monde</u> (Bruges & Paris), 9 (1). 1961, 58-67.
    The neo-pagan attitudes and revivals that follow from superficial Catholicism. (AA 13, 402)

803. DE HEUSCH, Luc. "Un syncrétisme ancien, le Kubandwa (Rwanda)," in Bouaké, item 206.
    A fuller version is found in the next item.

804. _____. "Mythe et société féodale: le culte de kubandwa dans le Rwanda traditionnel," <u>Archives</u> <u>de</u> <u>sociologie</u> <u>des</u> <u>religions</u>, 9 (18) July-Dec. 1964. 133-146. (AA 16, 680)

805. GLUCKMAN, Max. <u>Politics,</u> <u>law</u> <u>and</u> <u>ritual</u> <u>in</u> <u>tribal</u> <u>society</u>. Oxford: Blackwell, 1965. xxxii + 339p.
    P. 157 mentions the Nyabingi "cult" as a periodic expression of Hutu against Tutsi in Ruanda.

806. PAUWELS, Marcel. "Le culte de Nyabingi (Ruanda)," <u>Anthropos</u> (Freiburg), 46 (3-4) 1951, 337-357. Illus. map.

807. PHILIPPS, J.E.T. "The Nabingi," <u>Congo</u> (Brussels), 9, Tome 1 (3) 1928, 310-321.
    A secret society in the Ruanda, the Ndowa, and the region of Kivu; anti-european, "popular," and anarchic, with a fanatic religious element; the account covers 1913-19.

808. SMITH, A. C. Stanley. <u>Road</u> <u>to</u> <u>revival:</u> <u>the</u> <u>story</u> <u>of</u> <u>the</u> <u>Ruanda</u> <u>Missions</u>. London: Church Missionary Society, 1946.
    On the East African revival movement in Ruanda.

SPANISH GUINEA

809. GONZALES DE PABLO, Aguilino. "La secta del 'Mbueti' o 'Mbiti'" (The sect of Bwiti), <u>Actas</u> <u>y</u> <u>memorias</u> <u>de</u> <u>la</u> <u>Sociedad</u> <u>Espanola</u> <u>de</u> <u>Antropología</u> <u>Etnografía</u> <u>y</u> <u>Prehistoria</u> (Madrid), 19, 1944, 70-84. (B.Eth.)

810. _____. "El Mbueti y sus doctrinas" (Bwiti and its doctrines), <u>Cuadernos</u> <u>de</u> <u>estudios</u> <u>africanos</u> (Madrid), 2, 1946, 69-92.
    The situation and role of Bwiti in Spanish Guinea; doctrines, a Bwiti vocabulary list, initiation rites and worship. (AA 9, 557.)

811. PERRAMON, Ramon. "Al habla con los buetis!" (Talking with the Bwitis), <u>Guinea</u> <u>Espanola</u> (Santa Isabel), 59, (1554) Mar. 1962, 72-73; (1555) April 1962, 109-10.
    Description of a Bwiti service and shrine in Spanish Guinea. (AA 15, 91)

812. PINILLOS DE CRUELIS, Manuel. "La secta del' Mhueti" (The Bwiti Sect),
      Africa (Madrid), 6 (86) Feb. 1949, 10-12.
          A syncretistic anti-white Gabon sect which has penetrated Spanish
          Guinea during the last sixty years.

EAST AFRICA

813. BAUMANN, Oswin. "Songo, der schwarze Prophet; Ein Beitrag zum Prophetentum
      in Ostafrika," (Songo, the black prophet: a contribution to the study
      of prophets in East Africa), Missionsbote (Olten, Switzerland), 30 (2)
      1950, 20-29. Illus.

814. GUTTMAN, B. "Sektenbildung und Rassenerlebnis in Ostafrica" (The develop-
      ment of sects and racial experience in E. Africa), Evangelisches Missions
      Magazin (Basel), ns, 78 (9) Sept. 1934, 277-292.

815. MINEAR, Paul S. "A glimpse of the situation in East Africa," Bulletin
      (Geneva: World Council of Churches Division of Studies), 8 (1) Spring
      1962.
          Pp. 10-11 on causes of separatism in East Africa.

816. PICH, V(ittorio) Merlo. "Si svolge su diversi fronti la battaglia per la
      conquista spirituale dell' Africa" (The battle for the spiritual
      conquest of Africa is waged on diverse fronts), Missioni Consolata
      (Turin), 60 (1) Jan. 1958, 14-17.

817. USHER-WILSON, L. C. "Dina ya Misambwa," Uganda Journal (Kampala), 16
      (2) Sept. 1952, 125-129.
          The "religion of the ancestors," a new religious group, anti-
          European, which manifested itself in Kenya and, to a lesser extent,
          in Uganda, from 1947. (AA 4, 524)

818. WARREN, Max. Revival: An enquiry. London: SCM Press, 1954. 123p.
          A theological analysis of the causes and meaning of the "revival"
          movement which affected mission church members in East Africa from
          1935, and remained within the mission churches without forming an
          independent church.

819. WELBOURN, F(rederick) B. "Separatism in East Africa," in Religion and
      social change in modern East Africa. Kampala: Makerere College, n.d.
      (1956), 68-82. (mimeo.)
          The Bamaliki, African Greek Orthodox Church, and Kikuyu movements.

820. _____. "Independency in East Africa," Ecumenical Review (Geneva), 11
      (4) July 1959, 430-436.
          An outline of his method of approach, and evaluation.

821. _____. East African rebels: A study of some independent churches.
      London: SCM Press, 1961. xii + 258p.
          Three independent churches in Uganda among the Baganda, and the
          Kikuyu independents in Kenya.

822. _____. East African Christian. London: O.U.P. 1965. vi + 226p.
          A general review of Christianity in East Africa; see especially
          chs. 12 and 13 on "spirit churches" and Ethiopian churches.

ETHIOPIA

823.   HABERLAND, Eike. "Besessenheitskulte in Süd-Äthiopien" (Possession cults
       in S. Ethiopia), Paideuma (Frankfurt), 7, 1960, 142-150.

824.   JENSEN, Adolf E. (ed.). Altvölker Süd-Äthiopiens (Ancient S. Ethiopian
       peoples). Stuttgart: Kohlhammer, 1959.
            P. 180, brief reference to prophetess Indo, or Akit-Galo, of the
            Ubamer in S. W. Ethiopia.

KENYA

825.   ANON. Report and constitution of the Kikuyu Independent Schools
       Association connected with the African Independent Pentecostal Church
       1938. Nyeri: (1935) 1938. (G.S.)
            In Kikuyu and English.

826.   _____. Uganda awake! an African calling. London: Highway Press, 1937.
       viii + 56p. illus. 2nd. rev. ed. Kampala, 1957.
            Inside account of the Revival movement largely based on material
            supplied by Dr. J. F. Church.

826A. _____. "Splinter Sects. Church and Africanism," Reporter (Nairobi),
       July 1964.

827.   _____. "Sect violence in Kenya also," East Africa and Rhodesia (London),
       40, (2079) 13 Aug. 1964, 931.
            Brief news item on the African Divine Church at Kapsengere.

828.   ASHTON-GWATKIN, F. "Dina ya maambwa (Cult of the Ancestors)," Spectator
       (London), 11 Aug. 1950, 173-174.
            A politico-religious movement connected with Mau Mau and the Kikuyu.

829.   BEECHER, Leonard J. "African Separatist Churches in Kenya," World
       Dominion (London), 31 (1) Jan.-Feb. 1953, 5-12. F. Tr., "Au Kenya:
       nationalisme et églises séparatistes africaines," Monde non-chrétien
       (Paris) n.s. 23, July-Sep. 1952, 324-336.
            A good general survey of various types.

830.   BELLAGAMBA, Antonio. "La Chiesa Kikuyu e fondata" (The Kikuyu Church is
       established), Missioni Consolata (Turin), 63 (15) Aug. 1961, 15-20.
            Reference to Mau Mau; by Roman Catholic missionary.

831.   BERNARDI, Bernardo. "Dopo la Mau Mau" (After Mau Mau), Missioni Consolata
       (Turin), 61 (9) May 1959, 9-12.

832.   BERTOLINO, Giovanni. "La nuova setta auche nel Meru" (The new sect also
       among the Meru), Missioni Consolata (Turin), 36 (6) June 1934, 86.
            On Mau Mau.

833.   BEWES, T. F. C. Kikuyu conflict. Mau Mau and the Christian witness.
       London: The Highway Press, 1953. 76p. (B. Eth.)

834.   _____. "Kikuyu religion, old and new," The African World (London),
       April 1953, 14, 16.
            African Christians' resistance to Mau Mau persecution, by an Anglican
            missionary.

835. _____. "The Christian revival in Kenya," World Dominion (London), 34 (2) April 1956, 110-114.

836. BROWN, John Cudd. The ghost dance of the Dakota Sioux and Mau Mau of the Kikuyu: A comparative study of colonial administration. Unpublished Ph.D. dissertation (Anthropology), Oregon (U.S.A.), 1956.

837. BUSTIN, E. La décentralisation administrative et l'évolution des structure politiques en Afrique orientale britannique. Eléments d'une étude comparative. Liège: Faculté de Droit, 1958.
    Pp. 372-373 on Dina ya Masamba from 1935 in North Nyanza; and Dini ya Jesu Cristo among Kikuyu and Kamba as precursers of Kenya resistance to colonial rule.

838. CAGNOLO, Constanzo. "Uno Schisma nella Chiesa protestante del Kikuyu" (A schism in the Kikuyu protestant church), Missioni Consolata (Turin), 46 (7) July 1944, 55-57; 46 (8) Aug. 1944, 69-72.
    The African Orthodox Church.

839. _____. "In memoria delle vittime dei Mau Mau" (In memory of the victims of Mau Mau), Missioni Consolata (Turin), 58 (15) Aug. 1956, 177-181.

840. _____. Kikuyu e Mau Mau (The Kikuyu and Mau Mau). Turin: Ed. Missioni Consolata (?), 1954.
    Includes account of Dina ya Msambwa or Cult of the Ancestors, by a Roman Catholic missionary.

841. CAVICCHI, Edmondo. "La Mau-Mau," Missioni Consolata (Turin), 54 (17) Sep. 1952, 198-208.
    A detailed account of forced oath-taking, Nyeri district, 1950.
    (AA 4, 232)

842. CORFIELD, F. D. Historical survey of the origins and growth of Mau Mau. Nairobi: Government Printer; London: Her Majesty's Stationery Office, 1960. 321p. map.
    The official "Corfield Report": pp. 41, 45, the African Orthodox Church, pp. 171-190, "Kikuyu Independent Schools" and various independent religious developments.

843. FARSON, Negley. Last chance in Africa. London: Gollancz, 1949. 384p.
    Pp. 127-130, Kikuyu independent schools and church; pp. 218-239, the Watu wa Mungu of the Kikuyu, and the Dina ya Msambwa and Elijah Maseidi of the Bantu Kavirondo.

844. FILESI, T. "Gli indigeni del Kenia ed il problema dei Mau Mau nei suoi rifflessi sulla vita del paese," (The natives of Kenya and the problem of Mau Mau: reflections on the life of the country), Universo (Florence), 36 (1) Jan.-Feb. 1956, 15-30.

845. FRANCOLINI, Bruno. "I Kikuyu e la Setta 'Mau Mau'" (The Kikuyu and the 'Mau Mau' Sect), Rivista di Etnografia (Naples), 6 (1-4) 1953, 1-12.

846. GHECIOHI, Gennaro. "Un sacerdote africano converte un gruppo di terror-isti Mau Mau condannati alla forca" (An African priest converts a group of Mau Mau terrorists condemned to the gallows), Missioni Consolata (Turin), 55 (9) May 1953, 110-111.

847. GLUCKMAN, Max. Order and rebellion in tribal Africa. London: Cohen and West, 1963. 273p.
  Ch. 4, "The Magic of Despair": on Mau-Mau as not neo-pagan; nativistic cults and separatist sects, based on Sundkler.

848. HUNTINGFORD, G. W. B. "The genealogy of the Orkoiik of Nandi," Man, 35, (art. 24) Feb. 1935, 22-23.
  Prophets in the Nandi tribes.

849. HUXLEY, Elspeth (Josceline). Red strangers. London: Chatto & Windus, 1939. 406p.
  Fiction: the Kikuyu of S. Nyeri; pp. 398-402, the Independent Orthodox Church.

850. _____. "The rise of the African zealot," Corona (London), 2 (5) May 1950, 163-166.
  The Watu wa Mungu of the Kikuyu, and the Dina ya Msambwa of the Bantu Kavirondo; the roots of such movements in secret societies.

851. _____. White man's country. Lord Delamare and the making of Kenya. London: Macmillan, 2 vols. 1935; Chatto & Windus, new edn. 1953.
  (1953) Vol. II, p. 14, brief reference to the Shiré rising; p. 123, Thuku and the young Kikuyu Association.

852. ISMAGILOVA, R. N. "Narody Kenii v usloviyah kolonial' nogo rezhima" (The peoples of Kenya under colonial regime), Afrikanskiy Ethnograficheskiy sbornik (Moscow), 1 (7) 1956, 118-220.
  Includes account of Mau Mau as a traditional secret society used as an excuse for suppression of a national - liberation movement.

853. KAMENYI, John. Prophets (Aroti): Turban People - Andu a Iremba. Nairobi: Christian Council of Kenya, n. d. (c. 1960), 5p. (mimeo.)
  A theological student's essay about his own people and the Kikuyu Independent Church.

854. KAUFMANN, Herbert. "Zwischen Zauberei und Christentum" (Between magic and Christianity), Frankfurter Allgemeine Zeitung, 134, 12 June 1965.
  A Roman Catholic secession, the "Legio Maria" in Kenya, with 60,000 members, led by "Cardinal" Simeon Ondeto, a Luo.

855. KENYATTA, Jomo. Facing Mount Kenya. London: Secker and Warburg, 1961.
  Pp. 269-279: attributes "new sects" to the blindness of missionaries, especially in opposing polygamy. Describes one Kikuyu group: Watu wa Mugu, or "People of God."

856. KILSON, Martin L. (Jr.) "Land and Kikuyu: A study of the relationship between land and Kikuyu political movements," Journal of Negro History, 40 (2) Apr. 1955, 103-153.
  Recognizes the religious aspect of the Thuku movement of 1921, and of the subsequent Kikuyu Central Association. (AA 7, 247.)

857. KITAGAWA, Daisuke. African independent church movements in Nyanza Province, Kenya. Nairobi: Christian Council of Kenya, 1962. (mimeo.)
  A private report to the council.

858. LAMBERT, H. E. "The background to Mau Mau. Widespread use of secret
      oaths in Kenya," Times British Colonies Review (London), 8, Winter 1952,
      21.
          (AA 5, 289)

859. LEAKEY, L(ouis) S(eymour) B(azett). Defeating Mau Mau. London: Methuen,
      1954. vii + 152p.
          Pp. 90-92, 113-114, documentation of the relation of the Kikuyu
          independent church to the political purposes of Mau Mau.

860. _____. "The religious element in Mau Mau," African Music (Roodepoort,
      Transvaal), 1 (1) 1954, 77.
          Extracted from The Manchester Guardian Weekly, 1 July 1954. Mau
          Mau hymn books setting new words to Christian tunes.

861. LEIGH, Ione. In the shadow of the Mau Mau. London: W. H. Allen, 1954.
      224p. illus.
          Especially pp. 23, 28-29, 216, on "Dini ya Masambwa" and "Dina ya
          Jesu Christo."

862. LEVINE, Robert A. "An attempt to change the Gusii initiation cycle,"
      Man, 59, art. 179, July 1959, 117-120.
          An abortive movement among the Gusii in 1957, reminiscent of the
          cult of Mumbo in the same area.

863. LEYS, Norman (Maclean). A last chance in Kenya. London: Hogarth Press,
      1931, 173p.
          Pp. 71-72, secessions due to prohibition of clitoridectomy.

864. LONSDALE, J. M. A political history of Nyanza Province. London: O.U.P.,
      forthcoming.
          References to the cult of Mumbo and other independent churches.

865. MARINO, Nicola. "Apostolato tra i carcerati Mau Mau" (The apostolate
      among imprisoned Mau Mau), Missioni Consolata (Turin), 57 (17) Sept.
      1955, 202-203.

866. MASEMBE, J. and OKUNGA, D. N. "Paganism - old and new," in Religion and
      social change in modern East Africa. Kampala: Makerere College, n.d.
      (1956), 83-94. (mimeo.)
          Mau Mau and Dini ya Msambwa.

867. MATHESON, A. "Na de Mau Mau een nieuwe toekomst voor de Kikuyu's Meded"
      (After Mau Mau - a new future for the Kikuyu). Afrika-instituut
      (Rotterdam), 10 (9) Sept. 1956, 258-62.

868. McCARTHY, John J. "Pastoral letter on secret societies," in The church
      to Africa. London: Africa Office, Sword of the Spirit, n.d. (1959),
      pp. 130-136.
          The vicar-apostolic of Zanzibar on Mau Mau, in 1952.

869. MERLO, Mario. "Il terrorismo Mau Mau" (Mau Mau terrorism), Missioni
      Consolata (Turin), 57 (5) Mar. 1955, 62-65.

870.   MIDDLETON, John. "Kenya: Administration and changes in African life,
       1912-1945," in V. Harlow & E. M. Chilver (eds.) History of East Africa,
       Oxford: Clarendon Press, 1965, vol. II.
            Includes a short summary of the literature on independent churches
       in Kenya.

871.   _____. Lugbara religion: Ritual and authority among an East African
       people. London: OUP for IAI, 1960. xii + 276p.
            Pp. 258-269, prophets and the Yakan cult from 1883 until today.

872.   _____ & KERSHAW, Greet. The Kikuyu and Kamba of Kenya. London: IAI
       (1953), revised edn. 1965.
            P. 64, brief account of "modern religious movements" among the
       Kikuyu; p. 87, spirit-possession among the Kamba; pp. 28, 64, the
       Mau Mau.

873.   MINA, Gian Paola. "Hanno ucciso la nostra mamma" (They have killed our
       mother), Missioni Consolata (Turin), 55 (23) Dec. 1953, 250-253.
            On Mau Mau.

874.   MOMBASA, Leonard. (BEECHER, L. J.) "After Mau Mau - What?" Inter-
       national Review of Missions, 44 (174) Apr. 1955, 205-211.
            Review article on Leakey, item 859, by an Anglican archbishop.

875.   MORIONDO, B(artolomeo). "Come conobbi l'Archivescovo ortodosso" (How I
       knew the Orthodox Archbishop), Missioni Consolata (Turin), 46 (8-9)
       Sept.-Oct. 1944, 92-94.
            On the African Orthodox Church.

876.   MÜHLMANN, Wilhelm E. "Zwischen Erweckung und Terror: Der Mau-mau-aufstand
       in Kenya" (Between the revival and the terror: the Mau Mau rebellion
       in Kenya), in W. E. MÜHLMANN (ed.), item 160, 105-149. Bibl.

877.   MURIU, N. & NJAGA, W. "Revival in Kikuyuland," in Religion and social
       change in modern east Africa, Kampala: Makerere College, n.d. (1956),
       pp. 9-19. (mimeo.)

878.   NORBECK, Edward. Religion in primitive society. New York: Harper &
       Brothers, 1961. Bibl.
            Pp. 229-266, a general treatment of religious movements including a
       discussion of the "Mau Mau Religion."

879.   NOTTINGHAM, J. C. "Sorcery among the Akamba in Kenya," Journal of African
       Administration (London), 11 (1) Jan. 1959, 2-14.
            An administrative officer describes an anti-witchcraft campaign that
       was assisted by government in 1954-1955.

880.   "NYANGWESO." "The cult of Mumbo in Central and South Kavirondo,"
       Journal of the East Africa and Uganda Natural History Society (Nairobi),
       38-39, May-Aug. 1930, 13-17.
            An anti-European movement among the Luo and Gusii of S. W. Kenya,
       from 1914.

881.   OGOT, Bethwell A. "British administration in the Central Nyanza District,
       1900-60," Journal of African History, 4 (2) 1963, 249-273.
            Pp. 256-257, 262, John Owalo's Nomia Luo Mission, from 1907;
       p. 257, the cult of Mumbo, in S. Nyanza, from 1913; pp. 261; 263,
       Thuku.

882.   _____ & WELBOURN, F. B. A place to feel at home. London: O.U.P.,
        1966. Illus.
            The Luo people of W. Kenya: the secession of the "Church of Christ
        in Africa" from Kenya Anglican church in 1957, and Zayako Kivuli's
        "African Israel Church, Nineveh," from 1942.

883.   PICH, V(ittorio) Merlo. "I falsi profeti al Kenya" (False prophets in
        Kenya), Missioni Consolata (Turin), 36 (6) June 1934, 84-86.

884.   _____. "Disarmano i Mau Mau" (The Mau Mau are disarmed), Missioni
        Consolata (Turin), 55 (15) Aug. 1953, 180-182.

885.   _____. "Che cosa significa Mau Mau" (What does Mau Mau mean?), Missioni
        Consolata (Turin), 56 (17) Sept. 1954, 209.

886.   _____. "La Fine dei Mau Mau" (The end of Mau Mau), Africa (Rome), 15
        (2) Mar.-Apr. 1960, 79-80. Illus.

887.   _____. "Les aspects religieux du mouvement Mau Mau," in Museum Lessianum,
        item 161, 125-139.
            A comprehensive article by a Roman Catholic Missionary in Kenya.

888.   RATH, J. T. "Mau Mau: das warnende Zeichen" (Mau Mau: the warning
        signs), Zeitschrift fur Missionswissenschaft und Religionswissenschaft
        (Munster), 39 (4) 1955, 297-316.

889.   RAWCLIFFE, D. H. The struggle for Kenya. London: Gollancz, 1954.
        189p.
            On Mau Mau: especially ch. 2, the Kikuyu Central Association, and
        independent churches (pp. 24-25); ch. 3, "The Dinis" - Dini ya Roho,
        Dini ya Msambwa, Watu wa Mungu (arathi), Dini ya Jesu Kristo, etc.

890.   RAWSON, D. C. "Background of the Mau-Mau," Natural History (New York),
        58 (7) Sept. 1954, 296-302.

891.   RAYT, M. "Narod Kiku'yu," (The Kikuyu People), Sovetskaya Etnografia
        (Moscow), 3, 1953, 170-173.
            The invented activities of a small religious anti-imperialist sect,
        "Mau Mau," as explanation given by imperialists for their reign of
        terror in 1952.

892.   ROSANO, Lorenzo. "Ho incontrato Kenyatta" (I have met Kenyatta), Missioni
        Consolata (Turin), 63 (15) Aug. 1961, 14.

893.   ROSBERG, Carl & NOTTINGHAM, John. Nationalism and the myth of "Mau-Mau."
        Forthcoming, 1966.
            See chapter on "control nationalism" which is specifically concerned
        with the Kikuyu independent churches.

894.   ROSENSTIEL, Annette. "An anthropological approach to the Mau Mau problem,"
        Political Science Quarterly (New York), 68 (3) Sept. 1953, 419-32.
            Relates Mau Mau to nativism and cargo cults.

895.   SANGREE, Walter H. Structural continuity and change in a Bantu tribe:
        the nature and development of contemporary Tiriki social organization.
        Unpublished Ph.D. dissertation (Anthropology), Chicago, 1959. (Mic.
        60-7295)

896.   _____. The Dynamics of the Separatist Churches. Chicago: Unpublished
         paper, 17 Feb. 1960, 25p. (mimeo.)
             Tests Sundkler's "repressed leadership" theory on the Church of
             Israel, Tiriki tribe.

897.   _____. Age, prayer and politics in Tiriki, Kenya. London: O.U.P. for
         East African Institute for Social Research. Forthcoming.
             Includes account of independency among the Tiriki.

898.   SESTERO, Ottavio. "L'eccidio dei maestri di Gethi" (The massacre of the
         teachers of Gethi), Missioni Consolata (Turin), 59 (9) May 1957, 108-109.

899.   SMITH, N. Langford, in The Church in the world (Bulletin of the British
         Council of Churches), London, 53, Dec. 1953, pp. 7-8.
             The revival in Kenya.

900.   WATHIOMO MUKINYA. (Nyeri: Roman Catholic, Missioni Consolata).
             Articles in monthly issues of Mar. 1922, Sept. 1928, Apr. & May
             1952, are reported to be relevant. In Kikuyu, and with possible
             variations in title.

901.   WEATHERBY, J. M. "Inter-tribal warfare on Mount Elgon in the 19th and
         20th centuries," Uganda Journal (Kampala), 26 (2) 1962, 200-212.
             Refers to the role of prophets among the Sabei and Nandi.

902.   _____. "The Sabei 'Prophets'," Man, 63 (art. 223) Nov. 1963, 178-179.
             19th. c. prophets among the Sabei-speaking peoples of Mt. Elgon.

903.   WHISSON, M. G. The will of God and the wiles of men. Kampala: E.
         African Institute of Social Research, n.d. (1962?), 34p. (mimeo.)
             Pp. 19-26, causes of separatism among the Luo; the Nomiya Luo Mis-
             sion Church of prophet John; pp. 26-31, the Revival.

904.   WIPPER, Audrey. The Cult of Mumbo. Kampala: East Africa Institute of
         Social Research, 1966. 31p. (mimeo.)
             Historical study of an anti-European movement with a new god,
             Mumbo, among the Luo and Gusii of S. W. Kenya from 1914 until today.

905.   WISTE, Marcel. "La révolte des Mau-Mau au Kenya," Problèmes d'Afrique
         centrale (Anvers), 6 (21) 1953, 190-199.
             Treats Mau Mau as a "politico-religious sect." (AA 5, 631.)

SUDAN

906.   EVANS-PRITCHARD, E. E. The Nuer: A description of the modes of liveli-
         hood and political institutions of a Nilotic people. Oxford: Clarendon
         Press, 1940. viii + 271p.
             Pp. 184-189, Nuer prophets.

907.   _____. Nuer religion. Oxford: Clarendon Press, 1956.
             Pp. 305-310, Nuer prophets as response to social and political change.

908.   JACKSON, H. C. "The Nuer of the Upper Nile province," Sudan Notes and
         Records (Khartoum), 6 (1) 1923, 59-107; (2) 123-189.
             Nuer prophets as influenced by the Mahdism.

909. SELIGMAN, C(harles) G(abriel), & Brenda Z(ara). <u>Pagan tribes of the Nilotic Sudan</u>. London: Routledge & Kegan Paul (1932), 1965. 592p. illus.
      Pp. 188-190, Wal, a prophet possessed by the Deng divinity in 1907; pp. 231-233 on Ngundeng and Dwek.

TANZANIA

910. BELL, R. M. "The Majimaji Rebellion in the Luvale District," <u>Tanganyika Notes and Records</u> (Dar es Salaam), 28, Jan. 1950, 38-57.
      Especially pp. 40-42, and <u>passim</u>, on Ngameya and his holy water. (AA 2, 118)

911. CROSSE-UPCOTT, A. R. W. "The Origin of the Majimaji Revolt," <u>Man</u>, 60, (art. 98) May 1960, 71-73.
      Traditional water cults behind the Tanganyika rising of 1905. (AA 12, 101)

912. KLAMROTH, M. "Beiträge zum Verständnis der religiösen Vorstellungen der Saramo im Bezirk Dares-salam (Deutsch Ostafrika)," (A Contribution to the understanding of the religious ideas of the Saramo in the area of Dar-es-Salaam). <u>Zeitschrift für Kolonialsprachen</u> (Hamburg), 1, 1910-1911.
      Pp. 141-143, on Zaramo prophets.

913. KOOTZ-KRETSCHMER, Elise. <u>Die Safwa, II</u> (The Safwa). Berlin: Reimer, 1929.
      P. 192 on prophets.

914. MOFFETT, J. P. <u>Handbook of Tanganyika</u> (2nd. edn.). Dar-es-Salaam: Government Printer, 1958. 703p. illus. maps.
      Pp. 71-76, the Majimaji rising, 1905-1907. See also Sayers, item 916.

915. NORDFELT, M. <u>I degeln</u> (In the struggle). Stockholm: 1945. (E.A.)
      Pp. 10 ff., prophet Mwakipesile in South Tanganyika.

916. SAYERS, Gerald F. <u>The handbook of Tanganyika</u>. London: Macmillan, 1930. 636p.
      Pp. 72-75, the Majimaji rebellion, 1905-1906. See also Moffett, item 914.

917. VON GOETZEN, Gustav Adolf Graf. <u>Deutsch-Ostafrika im Aufstand 1905-6</u> (German East Africa in the 1905-6 uprising). Berlin: O. Reimer, 1909. xiii + 234p.
      A principal German source on the Majimaji uprising, by the colony's Governor.

918. WILSON, Monica. "To whom do they pray?" <u>Listener</u> (London), 56 (1440) 1 Nov. 1956, 692-693.
      Includes reference to proliferation of "sects" as the Nyakyusa become more Christianized. (AA 8, 249.)

919. _____. <u>Communal rituals of the Nyakyusa</u>. London: O.U.P., 1959. 228p.
      Pp. 167, 171-173, 219-220, the African National Church and the Last Church of God and of His Christ; the relation of independency to nationalism.

UGANDA

920. ANON, "Notes of the month," Church Missionary Review (London), 66 (790)
     Feb. 1915, 122-123.
          Mugema and Malaki in Uganda.

921. BESSELL, M. J. "Nyabingi," Uganda Journal (Kampala), 6 (2) 1938, 73-86.
          The Nyabingi movement in Uganda and Ruanda.

922. CHURCH MISSIONARY SOCIETY (Anglican), Proceedings. London: 1915, 65-67;
     1916, 56-57, 59; 1917, 36.
          The "Malaki movement or sect."

923. COOK, Albert R. Uganda memories (1897-1940). Kampala: Uganda Society,
     1945. xv + 415p.
          Pp. 323-324, the Malakites.

924. DRIBERG, J. H. "Yakan," The Journal of the Royal Anthropological Insti-
     tute, 61, July-Dec. 1931, 413-420.
          A secret society, also known as the Allah water cult, among the
          Lugbara of Uganda from 1918, and elsewhere; its connections with
          the Nebeli and other cults, and the earlier Mahdist movement.

925. HOPKINS, Elizabeth. "The Nyabingi cult in southwestern Uganda," in J.
     Middleton and V. W. Turner (eds.), item 156.

926. MAIR, Lucy P. An African people in the twentieth century. London:
     Routledge & Kegan Paul (1934) 1965. 300p. illus.
          Pp. 230-233, 241-246, 266-272, et passim, prophets in traditional
          religion.

927. MIDDLETON, John. "The yakan cult among the Lugbara," Man 58, (art. 156)
     July 1958, 112.
          A water-drinking cult from c. 1900 to the 1920's, as a reaction to
          imposed social changes under European administration. (AA 10, 409)

928. _____. Lugbara religion. London: O.U.P. 1960. xii + 276p.
          Pp. 258-264, "Prophets and the yakan cult," from 1883 till today.

929. _____. "Witchcraft and sorcery in Lugbara," in J. Middleton & E. H.
     Winter, item 155, 257-275. 7.
          Pp. 274-275, current status of witch finding movements among the
          Lugbara.

930. _____. "The Yakan or Allah water cult among the Lugbara," The Journal of
     the Royal Anthropological Institute, 93 (1) Jan.-June 1963, 80-108.
          A neo-pagan cult in Uganda and adjacent areas, from the 1880's.
          (AA 15, 259.)

931. _____. "Two prophetic movements among the Lugbara of Uganda," in J.
     Middleton and V. W. Turner (eds.), item 156.

932. ROSCOE, John. The soul of Central Africa. London: Cassell, 1922. 336p.
          Pp. 47, 262-265, the Bamaliki, and Semei Kakunguru's "church of the
          Almighty," in Uganda.

933. STENNING, D(errick) J. Preliminary observations on the Balokole movement,
      particularly among Bahima in Ankole District. Kampala: E. African
      Institute of Social Research, 1958. 18p. (mimeo.) (Privately circulated)
            Origins of the revival movement in independent churches.

934. _____. "Salvation in Ankole," in M. Fortes & G. Dieterlin (eds.), item
      87, pp. 269-275.
            The Balokole, revival in E. Africa.

935. TAYLOR, John Vernon. The growth of the church in Buganda. London:
      SCM Press, 1958.
            Pp. 97-105, Church of the One Almighty God and the African Orthodox
      Church with comments on the general failure of independents to grow
      in Buganda.

936. THOMAS, H. B. "Capax Imperii - the story of Semei Kakungulu," Uganda
      Journal (Kampala), 6 (3) Jan. 1939, 125-136.
            A Christian chief, d. 1928: pp. 135-136, his early support of
      Malaki, and founding of his own "Christian Jew" religion.

937. UGANDA, Commission of Enquiry. Report of the Commission of Enquiry into
      the disturbances in Uganda, during August 1949. Entebbe: Government
      Printer, 1950. (S. & P.)
            On Reuben Spartas of the African Orthodox Church.

938. WELBOURN, F(rederick) B. "Abamaliki in Buganda, 1914-1919," Uganda
      Journal (Kampala), 21 (2) Sept. 1957, 150-161.
            An early 20th. c. secession from the Church Missionary Society, the
      Society of the One Almighty God, which is now in decline. (AA 10,
      569.)

939. _____. "The importance of ghosts," in V. E. W. Hayward (ed.), item 110,
      pp. 16-26.
            Pp. 15-26, mention of Reuben Spartas' Orthodox Church, J. K. Mugema,
      and the African Israel Church.

CENTRAL AFRICA

940. ANON. The watchtower story. New York: Watchtower Press, 1948. (G.S.)
            The American Watchtower side of the Central Africa story.

941. BLOOD, A. G. B. The history of the Universities Mission to Central Africa.
      London: 1957. Vol. II, pp. 195-197, 285, on Kitawala.

942. CAVERHILL, A. M. "Ethiopianism," Life and Work (Edinburgh), 33, 1911,
      p. 383; 34, 1912, p. 30; and earlier, in briefer form, in Life and Work
      in Nyasaland, 2, Apr.-May 1911, 18. (S. & P.)
            An important article on Nyasaland and Central Africa.

943. CUNNISON, Ian. "Jehovah's Witnesses at work: expansion in Central
      Africa," The Times British Colonies Review (London), 29 (1) 1958,
      p. 13. Illus. (AA 10, 269.)

944. FRAENKEL, Peter. Wayaleshi. London: Weidenfeld and Nicholson, 1959.
            Pp. 124-130, a Watchtower member in Southern Rhodesia; pp. 63-64,
      Lenshina in Zambia.

945. GRAY, Richard. The two nations. Aspects of the development of race relations in the Rhodesias and Nyasaland. London: O.U.P. for Institute of Race Relations, 1960. 373p. Maps.
     Pp. 145-149, Ethiopianism (African Methodist Episcopal Church); Zionism (Last Church of God and His Christ, Nyasaland); Watch Tower.

946. GRESCHAT, Hans-Jürgen. "'Witchcraft' und kirchlicher Separatismus in Zentral-Afrika," (Witchcraft and Church separatism in Central Africa), in E. Benz (ed.), item 41, 90-104, 104.

947. HOOKER, J. R. "Witnesses and Watchtower in the Rhodesias and Nyasaland," Journal of African History, 6 (1) 1965, 91-106.
     A general review of the spread of Watchtower and related movements; from local sources. (FA 2, 1966) (AA 17, 102)

948. JAMES, C(yril) L(ionel) R. A history of Negro revolt. Fact (London), 18, Sept. 1938, 97p.
     Pp. 47-52, Chilembwe, Kimbangu, Thuku; pp. 82-85, Rhodesian miners' revolt of 1935 and Watch Tower society.

949. JEFFREYS, M. D. W. "Role of the native prophet in a vanishing culture," Forum (Johannesburg), 5 (6) Sept. 1956, 17-18.
     Rhodesian prophetesses and their "rites of passage"; nativistic movements - revivalist and passive types.

950. JOSSE, (Père?). "De l'hérésie a l'émeute. Les méfaits du Kitawala," Grand Lacs (Namur: White Fathers), 61, n.s. 82-83-84, 1 Feb. 1946, 71-76.

951. KARSTEDT, (Franz) Oskar. Deutschland in Afrika (30 Jahre dt. Kolonial-arbeit) (Germany in Africa; 30 years of German colonial rule). Berlin: O. Stollberg, 1937. (K.S.)
     P. 141, Thuku in Kenya; pp. 231f., Ethiopianism and Chilembwe.

952. _____. Probleme afrikanischer eingeborenpolitik (Problems of African native politics). Berlin: Mittler, 1942.
     Pp. 95-101, Watch Tower movement, by an extreme German nationalist who was also sympathetic to missions ("German" ones).

953. KINGSNORTH, J. "Letter from Central Africa," Theology (London), 61 (456) June 1958, 239-243.
     P. 240 on Jehovah's Witnesses.

954. MacKENZIE, D. R. The spirit-ridden Konde: a Record of . . . residence among . . . inhabitants of the Lake Nyasa region. London: Seeley Service, 1925. 318p. map. illus.
     Pp. 22, 217f., 220f., prophets, and predictions concerning the whites.

955. MacMINN, R. D., "The first wave of Ethiopianism in Central Africa," The Livingstone News (Livingstonia), (4), 1909, 56-59, passim to no. 2, April 1911. (G.S.)

956. MOORE, N. O. & WILCOX, Wayland D. "The report of the visit to South and Central Africa by N. O. Moore and Wayland D. Wilcox," The Sabbath Recorder (Plainfield, N. J.: Seventh Day Baptist Journal), 73 (22) 25 Nov. 1912, 695-735. (S. & P.)
     A basic source for the history of independent churches in Central Africa.

88

957. RAGOEN, J. "De Watch-Towers of Getuigen van Jehova in Midden-Afrika"
      (The Watch Tower, Jehovah's Witnesses in Central Africa), Nieuw-Afrika
      (Antwerp: White Fathers), 72 (3) 1956, 111-115. (B.Eth.)
          See also Ragoen, items 746, 1038.

958. RAWLINSON, G. C. "Some lessons of the Chilembwe rebellion," Central
      Africa (London: Universities Mission to Central Africa), 35 (411)
      Mar. 1917, 61.
          An Anglican missionary's reactions to the report of the government
      commission.

959. RICHARDS, Audrey I. "A modern movement of witchfinders," Africa (London),
      8 (4) Oct. 1935, 448-461. F.Tr. "Un mouvement modern pour déceler les
      sorciers les Bamucapi," Bulletin des juridictions indigènes et du droit
      coutumier congolais (Elisabethville), 5 (3) May-June 1947, 82-90.
          An anti-mission movement which swept Central Africa to the Congo
      c. 1934.

960. ROTBERG, Robert I. The rise of nationalism in Central Africa. The making
      of Malawi and Zambia 1873-1964. Cambridge, Mass.: Harvard U.P., 1965.
          Pp. 64-72, Chilembwe, Kamwana, Domingo; pp. 135-155, Watch Tower,
      Mwana Lesa, "The Schismatic Sects, Wilfred Good and the ana mulungu."

961. ROWLEY, Henry. The story of the Universities' Mission to Central Africa.
      London: Saunders, Otley, 1866. 493p.
          P. 113-116, Chibisa, a prophet among the Nungwi on the R. Shiré.

962. SHEPPERSON, George. "The politics of African church separatist movements
      in British Central Africa, 1892-1916," Africa (London) 24 (3) July 1954,
      233-246.
          Joseph Booth; American influences; Watch Tower Society. (AA 6, 599)

963. _____. "The literature of British Central Africa," Rhodes-Livingstone
      Journal, 23 (42) June 1958, 12-46. Illus.
          Pp. 40-43, "The role of the smaller, less orthodox missions," and
      independents. (AA 10, 271)

964. _____. "Notes on Negro American influences on the emergence of African
      nationalism," Journal of African History, 1 (2) 1960, 299-312; also in
      W. J. Hanna (ed.) Independent black Africa, the politics of freedom.
      Chicago: Rand McNally, 1964, 192-207.
          Pp. 304-7 on Ethiopianism in South and Central Africa; 309-10 on
      the African Church of Majola Agbebi in Nigeria.

965. _____. "Religion in British Central Africa," in W. M. Watt, item 233,
      pp. 47-51.

966. WILKINSON, F. O. Green. "Christianity in Central Africa," African
      Affairs (London), 62 (247) Apr. 1963, 114-124.
          P. 121, "the new sects" as unlikely to have lasting effects; by an
      Anglican missionary.

967. WILLS, A. J. An introduction to the history of Central Africa. London:
      O.U.P., 1964. 386p.
          Pp. 230-233, 286, mainly on Chilembwe and the 1915 rising, and
      Watch Tower.

MALAWI

968. ANON. "Sinners are saints in 'Do what you like church'," The Sunday Mail (Salisbury), 19 Feb. 1961.
   The Church of the Ancestors, called "Do Bad Things Church" by its critics for allowing polygamy.

969. CHURCH OF SCOTLAND. Reports of the Foreign Missions Committee. Edinburgh: Church of Scotland, annually.
   See 1958 Report, pp. 35-37 on independency, especially in Nyasaland; 1960 Report, p. 13 mentions Jehovah's Witnesses, and influence of "Ras Tafari sect"; p. 14, a brief account of an anti-witchcraft exorcist, Chikanga, with political associations and Christian forms, active in Nyasaland in 1960.

970. DUFF, Sir Hector. African small chop. London: Hodder and Stoughton, 1932. 223p.
   Pp. 49-52, colonialist view of Chilembwe.

971. DU PLESSIS, Johannes C. Through the dark continent. A record of a journey across Africa during the years 1913-1916. London: Longmans, Green, 1917.
   Pp. 347-349, Chilembwe.

972. FRASER, Donald. The new Africa. New York: Missionary Education Movement of the United States and Canada, 1928. (S. & P.)
   P. 89, Chilembwe.

973. JONER, Griff. Britain and Nyasaland. London: Allen & Unwin, 1964. 315p.
   Pp. 95-96, 215-221, etc., on Chilembwe's role in the development of nationalism in Nyasaland.

974. LIVINGSTONE, W(illiam) P(ringle). Laws of Livingstonia: A narrative of missionary adventure and achievement. London: Hodder and Stoughton, n.d. (1922). x + 385p.
   Pp. 259, 339, 352-355, on Chilembwe's uprising and Law's reaction.

975. _____. A prince of missionaries: the Rev. Alexander Hetherwick of Blantyre, Central Africa. London: J. Clark, n.d., (1931). 205p.
   Pp. 154-155, Chilembwe.

976. LUCAS, C(harles) P(restwood) (ed.). The empire at war. London: Royal Commonwealth Society, 1921-1926.
   Vol. IV, pp. 258-259, Chilembwe and the Shiré rising of 1915.

977. MARCOSSON, Isaac F. An african adventure. New York: John Lane, 1921. 288p. (S. & P.)
   P. 94, Chilembwe.

978. MARWICK, M(ax) G. "Another modern anti-witch movement in East Central Africa," Africa (London), 20 (2) April 1950, 100-112.
   The Bwanali-Mpulumutsi movement of 1947, in S. Nyasaland. (AA 2, 126)

979. MAUGHAM, R(eginald) C(harles) F(ulke). Nyasaland in the nineties and other recollections. London: Lincoln Williams, 1935.
   P. 55, Chilembwe.

980. NORMAN, L. S. "Rebellion," Blackwood's Magazine, 230 (794) Dec. 1931, 862-873.
    A first hand account of Chilembwe's rebellion.

981. RANGELEY, W. H. J. "'Nyau' in Kota-Kota District," Nyasaland Journal (Blantyre), 2 (2) July 1949, 35-49; 3 (2) July 1950, 19-33.
    A Chewa secret society with Christian aspects.

982. READ, Margaret. The Ngoni of Nyasaland. London: O.U.P. for IAI, 1956. 212p.
    Pp. 179-182, 187, indigenous prophets among the Ngoni.

983. Report of the Commission . . . to inquire into . . . the native rising within the Nyasaland Protectorate. Zomba: 1916 (Cmd 6819) (S. & P.) Chilembwe.

984. SHEPPERSON, George. "Education sponsors freedom--the story of African native John Chilembwe," The Negro History Bulletin (Washington, D.C.), 15 (4) Jan. 1952, 69-73.
    An early presentation by Shepperson of Chilembwe's biography.

985. _____. "The politics of African church separatist movements in British Central Africa 1892-1916," Africa, 24 (3) July 1954, 233-246.
    Excellent summary discussion of Charles Booth, Elliott Kamwana and John Chilembwe, and their relationship to early Nyasaland nationalism.

986. _____ & PRICE, Thomas. Independent African: John Chilembwe and the origins, setting, and significance of the Nyasaland native rising of 1915. Edinburgh: Edinburgh U.P., 1958. 564p. bibl. illus.
    Ethiopianism in Central Africa, the Watchtower Movement of Elliott Kamwana, and in great detail the Chilembwe rebellion from the historical point of view.

987. _____. "Nyasaland and the millennium," in Sylvia Thrupp (ed.), item 14, pp. 144-59.
    Traces the sources of millennial ideas in Central and South Africa, particularly the role of the Jehovah's Witnesses.

988. WILSON, George Herbert. The history of the Universities' Mission to Central Africa. London: Universities' Mission to Central Africa, 1936. xvi + 228p.
    Pp. 164-166 on Chilembwe uprising.

989. WISHLADE, R. L. "Chiefship and politics in the Melanje district of Southern Nyasaland," Africa (London), 31 (1) Jan. 1961, 36-45.
    Pp. 44-5, the Church of the Ancestors. (AA 12, 512.)

990. _____. Sectarianism in Southern Nyasaland. London: O.U.P. for IAI, 1965. 162p. illus. map. bibl.
    A comprehensive survey, including doctrine, ritual, officers, role in society, etc., with special attention to the Ethiopian Church and the Faithful Church of Christ.

991. WORSLEY, Peter M. "Religion and politics in Central Africa," Past and Present (Oxford), 15, Apr. 1959, 73-81.
    Review article of Shepperson and Price, item 986.

MADAGASCAR

992. DELORD, Raymond. "Messianisme à Madagascar," *Monde* *non-chrétien*.
      (Paris), n.s., 8, Oct.-Dec. 1948, 975-981.
          A syncretist religion founded by a prophetic leader, Andrian-
          ampoinimerina. (AA 1, 440)

MOZAMBIQUE

993. DE FREITAS, Afonso I. Ferraz. "Seitas religiosas gentilicas de Moçambique"
      (Heathen religious sects in Mozambique), *Estudos* *ultramarinos* (Lisbon),
      1, 1961, 91-122.
          "Ethiopian sects" in Southern Africa sympathetically considered;
          their religious and social contributions; special reference to 13
          principal Ethiopian sects in Mozambique, and the assistance given
          them by American Protestantism. (AA 14, 136)

994. GUYE, M. H. "Le culte de Mourimi," *Bulletin* *de* *la* *mission* *romande*
      (Lausanne), 362, 1916.
          The Murimi pagan revival, about 1916.

995. JUNOD, Henri A. "Le mouvement de mourimi: un reveil au sein de l'ani-
      misme thonga," *Le* *Journal* *de* *psychologie* *normale* *et* *pathologique* (Paris),
      21 (10) 15 Dec. 1924, 55-69.
          On the Murimi witchfinding movement in Mozambique, by a missionary.

996. _____. "Le culte de Montchapi," *Bulletin* *de* *la* *Mission* *suisse.* (Lausanne),
      538, 1935.
          In Mozambique, anti-white.

997. _____. *The* *life* *of* *a* *South* *African* *tribe.* New Hyde Park, N.Y.:
      University Books, 1962, 2 vols. (reprint).
          Vol. I, pp. 597-602, the Murimi movement, a chiliastic neo-pagan
          movement which abolished charms.

RHODESIA

998. MURPHREE, Marshall W. "The Budjga Vapostori: a study in religious inter-
      dependence," in J. Middleton and V. W. Turner (eds.), item 156.

999. RANGER, Terence O. *State* *and* *church* *in* *Southern* *Rhodesia,* *1919-1939.*
      Salisbury: Historical Association of Rhodesia and Nyasaland (Local
      Series, 4), n.d. (1961). 28p. (mimeo.)
          Pp. 3ff. government opposition to American fundamentalist and
          pentecostal missions and their African offshoots; pp. 26-28, the
          vision of an independent African church.

1000. _____. "The early history of independency in Southern Rhodesia," in W.
       M. Watt (chairman), item 233, 52-74.
          The relation of Ethiopianism, Zionism and Watchtower to politics.

1001. _____. "Traditional authorities and the rise of modern politics in Southern Rhodesia 1898 to 1930," in E. T. Stokes and R. Brown (eds.), Zambesian Historical Studies, Manchester: Manchester U.P., forthcoming, 1966.
        Nyamanda movement; Ethiopian influence on early nationalism.

1002. ROUMEGUÈRE, Jacqueline (née Eberhardt). "Exorcisme des demons et phenomènes de possession chez les Karanga de la Rhodésie du Sud," in item 206.

1003. SITHOLE, N(dabaningi). African nationalism. Cape Town: O.U.P., 1959. 174p.
        Pp. 60, brief reference to Nemapare's Methodist secession in Southern Rhodesia; by an African clergyman and nationalist leader.

ZAMBIA

1004. ANON. "Lumpa church," Notes et Documents (Rome: White Fathers), 19, Aug.-Sept. 1961, 401-410.
        The origins, aims, doctrine, and organization.

1004A. _____. "Suicide of the Lumpa?" Economist (London), 212, Aug. 8, 1964, 538p.
        The conflict with government in 1964.

1005. _____ in Illustrated London News, 245 (6523), 8 Aug. 1964, p. 186; (6524) 15 Aug. pp. 226-227; (6525) 22 Aug. p. 256.
        Photographs and news items about the Lumpa church troubles in Zambia, 1964.

1006. _____. "Lenshina," Nigrizia (Verona), 83 (9) Sept. 1964, 20-23, Illus.
        A syncretism of Roman Catholic, Protestant, and traditional elements. (FA 1, 132).

1007. _____. "Postscript on the Lumpa movement," Newsletter (London: Institute of Race Relations), Sept. 1964, 25-28.

1008. _____. "À la veille de son indépendance la Rhodésie du Nord fait face au fanatisme lumpa," Afrique Contemporaine (Paris), 15, Sept.-Oct. 1964, 18.

1009. _____. "Rodesia: Alicia, la profetisa" (Rhodesia: the prophetess Alice), El Siglo de las Misiones (Bilbao), 586, Nov. 1964, 385.
        Also in Le Missioni Cattoliche (Milan), 8-9, 1964.

1010. _____. "La secta Lumpa" (The Lumpa Church), Actualidad Africana (Madrid), 151, Jan. 1965, 10f.

1011. _____. "Lumpa prophetess seeks to join United Church," Ministry (Morija, Basutoland), 5 (4) July 1965, 200.
        A news item on Alice Lenshina's request in 1965 to the United Church of Zambia, and on her position after the 1964 troubles.

1012. _____. "Official description of development of Lumpa church, Lenshina opposition to witchcraft and political parties," East Africa and Rhodesia (London), 40 (2080) 20 Aug. 1964, 941-942, 950.
        By the information department of Zambia.

1013.   ____. "Lumpa sect uprising," Africa Diary (New Delhi), 4 (37) 5-11 Sep. 1965. Illus.
      A useful comprehensive news survey culled from five newspapers, some African.

1014.   BRADLEY, Kenneth Granville. The story of Northern Rhodesia. London: Longmans, 1941.
      P. 71, Kitawala.

1015.   CAVE, Sigrid. "Von der Lumpa-Sekte in Zambia" (On the Lumpa sect in Zambia), Mittellungen der Norddeutchen Mission (Bremen), 1, Feb. 1965, 1-2.
      A first-hand account by a missionary's wife.

1016.   CHÉRY, H. - Ch. "Les sectes en Rhodésie du Nord," Parole et Mission (Paris), 2 (7) Oct. 1959, 578-594.
      Independent movements, from p. 584, with longer sections on the Lumpa Church (pp. 589-593), and the Church of the Sacred Heart (pp. 585-589); based on information from the White Fathers, Abercorn district.

1017.   COLSON, Elizabeth. "Social change and the Gwembe Tonga," Rhodes-Livingstone Journal, 23, June 1964, 1-13.
      P. 7, a new prophet; p. 13, reaction of young men in questioning ancestor cult and joining a "small embryo church." (AA 17, 116)

1018.   ____. "Converts and tradition: the impact of Christianity on Valley Tonga religion," in J. Middleton and V. W. Turner (eds.), item 156.

1019.   COPPER BELT, Commission of Enquiry. Report of the Commission to enquire into the disturbances on the Copper Belt, Northern Rhodesia. London: His Majesty's Stationery Office, Cmd. 5009, Oct. 1935.
      Pp. 42-51, on the Watch Tower movement.

1020.   CUNNISON, Ian. "A Watch Tower assembly in Central Africa," International Review of Missions, 40 (160) Oct. 1951, 456-468.

1021.   ____. The Luapula peoples of Northern Rhodesia: custom and history in tribal politics. Manchester: Manchester U.P. for Rhodes-Livingstone Institute, 1960. xiii + 258p.
      Pp. 204-208, Watchtower in Zambia.

1022.   DOKE, Clement M. The Lambas of Northern Rhodesia. London: George G. Harrap, 1931.
      Pp. 258-268 on indigenous prophets, possessed by the spirits of chiefs.

1023.   FERNANDEZ, James W. "The Lumpa uprising WHY?" Africa Report (Washington, D.C.) 9 (10) Nov. 1964, 30-32.
      The uprising as reaction to a situation of uncertainty in the face of growing mission and political hostility. (FA 1, 1065)

1023A.   FRANKLIN, H. "Zambia's Holy War," Spectator (London), 213, Aug. 7, 1964, 173.
      The Lumpa conflict of 1964.

1024. FRIEDRICH, Adolf. Afrikanische Priestertumer (African priesthoods). Stuttgart: Strecker & Schroder, 1939. 289p.
Pp. 296-299, Ila prophets; based on Smith and Dale, item 1043.

1025. GANN, L. H. The birth of a plural society: The development of Northern Rhodesia under the British South Africa Company, 1894-1914. Manchester: Manchester U.P. for Rhodes-Livingstone Institute, 1958. xxi + 230p. illus.
Pp. 32-33, the Barotseland Ethiopian Church.

1026. _____. A history of Northern Rhodesia, early days to 1953. London: Chatto & Windus, 1964. xvi + 478p. map.
Pp. 231-236, discontent in 1920's expressed in religious and magical forms; Tomo Nyenawa (Mwana Lesa) and Watch Tower groups; cargo cult ideas; p. 456, statistics.

1026A. HATCH, John. "Prophetess," New Statesman (London), 68, Aug. 7, 1964, 176.
On Alice Lenshina and the 1964 conflict.

1027. HÉLÈNE-MARIE, (Mère). "Sectes politico-religieuses," Trait d'union (Antwerp: The White Sisters), 37 (3) 1956, 19.
Kitawala; and the "Regina" or Lumpa movement.

1028. HEWARD, Christine. "The rise of Alice Lenshina," New Society (London), 4 (98) 13 Aug. 1964, 6-8.
General background article to the Lenshina revolt of 1964.

1029. LALONDE, Leopold. "The Mwakalenga: African National Church," Notes et Documents (Rome: White Fathers), 40, Sept.-Oct. 1963, 385-386.
George Nyasulo and the "Mwkalenga sect."

1030. MACPHERSON, Fergus. "Notes on the beginning of the (Alice) movement," Occasional Papers (London, International Missionary Council), 1, 1958, 2-5.
A first-hand account by the missionary most concerned.

1031. MARTIN, Marie-Louise. "The conflict between the Lumpa Church and the government in Zambia (Northern Rhodesia)," Ministry (Morija, Basutoland), 5 (1) Oct. 1964, 46-48.
Based on Taylor and Lehmann, and the Mindolo Report, with further thoughts on messianism, religious and political.

1032. MARWICK, M. G. Sorcery in its social setting. Manchester: Manchester U.P., 1965. xxii + 339p.
Pp. 59, 79, 93-4, 105, 257-8. The Mcape and Bwanali-Mpulu witch-finding movements, which differ from traditional sorcery beliefs in that they "rearrange and synthesize the old and the new."

1033. MURRAY, J. P. "Zambia and the future," African Affairs (London), 64 (254) Jan. 1965, 19.
A brief discussion of Lenshina riots as compared with earlier Watchtower troubles.

1033A. NORTHERN RHODESIA. Northern Rhodesia annual report on African affairs, 1955. Lusaka: 1956.
   Pp. 23-28, et passim, the Lumpa Church.

1034. NORTHERN RHODESIA, (Anglican) Bishop of. "The Watch Tower," Central Africa (London: U.M.C.A.), 43, June 1925, 120-122.
   A description of the renewed appearance in 1924.

1035. OGER, Louis. "Le mouvement Lenshina en Rhodésie du Nord," Église vivante (Paris-Louvain), 14 (2) Mar.-Apr. 1962, 128-138.
   A sympathetic description of Alice Leshina.

1036. _____. "L'Église du Sacré-Coeur," Notes et Documents (Rome: White Fathers), 51, Nov. 1964, 421-430. Also S.Tr., "La Iglesia de Sagrado Corazon: una secta sincretista nacida de la Iglesia Católica" (The Church of the Sacred Heart: a syncretistic sect derived from the Catholic Church), Actualidad Africana (Madrid), 151, Jan. 1965, 8ff.
   Emilio Mulolani, and the origins and development of his secession from the Roman Catholic Church; by a White Father.

1037. QUICK, Griffith. "Some aspects of the African Watch Tower movement in Northern Rhodesia," International Review of Missions, 29 (114) Apr. 1940, 216-225.

1038. RAGOEN, J. "De Watch-Towers in Noord-Rhodesia," Nieuw Afrika (Antwerp: White Fathers) 72 (4) 1956, 157-161. (B. Eth.)
   See also Ragoen, items 746, 957.

1039. RANGER, Terence O. "The 'Ethiopian' episode in Barotseland, 1900-1905," Rhodes-Livingstone Journal, 37, June 1965, 26-41.
   The African Methodist Episcopal church mission from South Africa.
   (AA 17, 121)

1040. REYNOLDS, Barrie. Magic, divination and witchcraft among the Barotse of Northern Rhodesia. Berkeley: University of California Press, 1963. xix + 181p. Illus.
   Pp. 133-138, "The Twelve Society" from 1944, a healing society combining traditional elements and borrowings from the Seventh Day Adventists, and organized like a church.

1041. ROTBERG, Robert. The Lenshina movement of Northern Rhodesia," Rhodes-Livingstone Journal (Lusaka), 29, June 1961, 63-78.
   The history and character of the movement, particularly its xenophobic character. (AA 13, 124)

1042. RUKAVINA, Kathaleen (Stevens). Jungle pathfinder: Central Africa's most fabulous adventurer. London: Hutchinson, 1951. 255p.
   Pp. 184, 195, on "Mwana Lesa affair" of 1925.

1043. SMITH, E(dwin) W. & DALE, A(ndrew) M(urray). The Ila-speaking peoples of Northern Rhodesia. London: Macmillan, 2 vols., 1920. 423, 433p.
   Vol. I: pp. 345-346, a local prophet. Vol. II: pp. 136-152, Chilenga, Mwana Lesa, Mupumani, prophets among the Ila; pp. 197-212, the Mwana Lesa movement.

1044. STONE, W. V. "The 'Alice Movement' in 1958," <u>Occasional Papers</u> (London, International Missionary Council), 1, 1958, 5-10.
      A first-hand account of Lenshina by a missionary of the Church of Scotland. See also his later comments in <u>Ministry</u>, 3, Apr. 1965, 148.

1045. TAYLOR, John V. & LEHMANN, Dorothea A. <u>Christians of the Copperbelt</u>. London: S.C.M. Press, 1961. 308p.
      Part IV describes some independent churches including the "Alice Movement," Jehovah's Witnesses, and the African Methodist Episcopal Church.

1046. TAYLOR, S. "Watch Tower movement. Bishop of Northern Rhodesia's views," <u>East Africa and Rhodesia</u> (London), 1350, 1950, p. 1530.

1047. TORREND, J. "A mysterious visitor to Tongaland," <u>Zambesi Mission Record</u> (Leyland, England), 3 (44) 1909, 548-550.
      A prophetess from the Soli.

1048. WATSON, William. <u>Tribal cohesion in a money economy</u>. Manchester: Manchester U.P. for Rhodes Livingstone Institute, 1958. 246p. bibl. Illus.
      P. 197-203, <u>et passim</u>, Jehovah's Witnesses among the Mambwela, and in Zambia.

1049. WELBOURN, F(rederick) B. "Lumpa and Zambia," <u>Venture</u> (London), 16 (9-10) Sept. 1964, 41.
      Background of, and comment on, the Lumpa Church troubles, 1964.

1050. VON HOFFMAN, Carl (Eugene Lohrke, ed.). <u>Jungle Gods</u>. London: Constable & Co., 1929. Illus.
      Pp. 42-74, account of Mwana Lesa based on District Office files; pp. 283-284, Chilembwe, Watchtower (after Buell).

SOUTHERN AFRICA

1051. KNOOB, Willi J. "Ethnologische Aspekte der religiösen Bewegungen im südlichen Afrika" (Ethnological aspects of religious movements in Southern Africa), in W. E. Mühlmann (ed.), item 160, 87-103.

1052. LEUTWEIN, Paul. <u>Afrikanerschicksal</u> (African destiny). Stuttgart: Union, 1929. (K.S.)
      Chs. 1, 8, 9, Witbooi; pp. 24, 148, Stürmann.

1053. LEUTWEIN, Theodor. <u>Elf Jahre Gouverneur in Deutsch Südwestafrika</u>, (Eleven years as Governor in German S. W. Africa). Berlin: Mittler & Sohn, 1906. x + 589p. (K.S.)
      Pp. 298-306, 454-464, Witbooi and Stürmann.

1054. LIVINGSTONE, David. <u>Missionary travels and researches in South Africa</u>. London: John Murray, 1857. 687p. Maps.
      Pp. 86-87, reference to a Kololo prophet, Tlapáne, near Victoria Falls.

1055.   MARTIN, Marie-Louise. "Face aux mouvements prophétiques et messianiques
        en Afrique méridionale," Monde non-chrétien, n.s. 64, Oct.-Dec. 1962,
        226-255.   Also E. Tr. and abbreviation, "The church facing prophetic
        and messianic movements," Ministry (Morija, Basutoland), 3 (2) Jan. 1963,
        49-61.
                A general survey of origins and causes; discussion of attitudes to
                be adopted by the older churches. (AA 15, 119)

1056.   _____. The biblical concept of messianism, and messianism in Southern
        Africa. Morija (Basutoland): Sesuto Book Depot, 1964. 207p.
                Parts 1 and 2, biblical; part 3, pp. 89-187, on messianism in Africa,
                especially Southern Africa; a theological treatment, which includes
                Xhosa and Tswana prophets, Witbooi, Mgijima, Shembe, LeKganyane,
                Zionism, and a typology of messianism.

1058.   MIRBT, Carl (J. C.) "Äthiopische Bewegung," (The Ethiopian Movement),
        in Deutsches Koloniallexikon. Leipzig: Quelle & Meyer, 1920, Vol.
        I, p. 93. (K.S.)

1059.   ROSENTHAL, Eric (ed.). Encyclopaedia of Southern Africa. London:
        F. Warne, 1964. 604p.
                P. 164, "Ethiopianism," a brief article.

1060.   SCHLOSSER, Katesa. Eingeborenenkirchen in Süd-und Südwestafrika: ihre
        Geschichte und Sozialstruktur. (Native churches in S. and S. W. Africa:
        their history and social structure). Kiel: W. G. Mühlau, 1958. 355p.
        illus. bibl.
                Chapters on Nicholas B. H. Bhengu, Cecil Hector of Independent
                Lutheran Mission Church of South Africa; Prophets Mgijima, Lekganyane,
                and Shembe.

1061.   _____. "Die Sekten der Eingeborenen in Süd-und Südwestafrika als
        Manifestationen des Gegensatzes zwischen Weissen und Nichtweissen"
        (The sects of S. and S. W. African natives as manifestations of con-
        flict between whites and non-whites), Afrikanischer Heimatkalender
        (Windhoek), 1962, 101-107.

1062.   _____. "Les sectes d'Afrique du Sud en tant que manifestation de la
        tension raciale," in Bouaké, item 206.
                Probably similar to previous article.

1063.   _____. "Profane Ursachen des Anschlusses an Separististenkirchen in Süd-
        und Südwestafrika" (Non-religious reasons for joining separatist churches
        in S. & S. W. Africa), in E. Benz (ed.), item 41, 24-45.

1064.   SOGA, J. H. The South-Eastern Bantu. Johannesburg, 1930.
                Pp. 241-247 on prophets.

BASUTOLAND

1065.   CASALIS, A. (ed.). "Condemnation of W. Matita," Leselinyana (Morija,
        Lesotho Evangelical Church), (19), 1922; repeated in next issue (20).
                An official statement of the Synod of the (then) Paris Mission.

1066. ELLENBERGER, Victor. A century of mission work in Basutoland, 1833-1933.
       Morija: Sesuto Book Depot, 1938. 382p. F. Tr. Un Siècle de Mission au
       Lessouto (1833-1933). Paris: Société des Missions évangéliques, 1933.
       447p.
           Pp. 322, 349, on Matita's church, from 1910; also on a late 19th.
           century secession from the Paris Mission Society, and subsequent
           reunion, at Hermon.

1067. SHEDDICK, V. G. J. The Southern Sotho. London: IAI, 1953.
           P. 67, brief reference to appearance of separatist churches in
           Basutoland.

BECHUANALAND

1068. GROSSER GENERALSTAB. Die Kämpfe der deutschen Truppen in Südwestafrika
       (The struggle of the German troops in S. W. Africa). Berlin: vol. II,
       1917. (K.S.)
           Pp. 20, 47, 56, 64f., 82f., 161, Stürmann, a Bechuana prophet,
           early 20th. c.

1069. SCHAPERA, I(saac) (ed.). Ditirafalô tsa Merafe ya Batswana. Lovedale:
       Lovedale Press, 1940.
           Pp. 146-149, suppression of the Ethiopian developments in the
           BaNgwaketse Free Church in 1911.

1070. _____. "A short history of the Bangwaketse," African Studies (Johannes-
       burg), 1 (1) Mar. 1942, 1-26; and republished separately.
           Pp. 20-22, secession of the King Edward BaNgwaketse Free Church in
           1902 from the London Missionary Society.

1071. _____. (tr. and ed.). The political annals of a Tswana tribe. Minutes
       of Ngwaketse public assemblies 1910-1917. Cape Town: the University,
       1947. (mimeo.)
           Pp. 47, 57, 62f., "attempts to introduce new sects."

1072. SCHWABE, Kurd. Der krieg in Deutsch-Südwestafrika 1904-1906. (The War
       in German S. W. Africa). Berlin: .Weller, 1907. vii + 247p. (K.S.)
           Pp. 21, 315, Stürmann, a Bechuana prophet.

SOUTH AFRICA

1073. ANON. "Bischof Turner und die äthiopische Kirche," (Bishop Turner and
       the Ethiopian Church), Die Evangelischen Missionen (Gutersloh), 4, 1898,
       214.

1074. _____. "Christmas with the Ethiopians at Zalaze," The Mission Field
       (London: S.P.G.), 49 (579) Mar. 1904, 86-89. Illus.
           Dwane and the Order of Ethiopia, by E. C. West, an Anglican
           missionary.

1075. _____. A question of colour: a study of South Africa. London: Black-
       wood, 1906.
           Pp. 249-265, the origin and history of Ethiopianism.

1076.   _____.   "The Israelites," <u>South African Outlook</u> (Lovedale), 1922, 9-11.
         On Enoch Mgijima, and the legal aftermath of the Bulhoek incident.

1077.   "1300 Baptized on one Sunday in South Africa," <u>Pentecost</u> (London), 22,
         Dec. 1952, 7. (K.S.)
         N.B.H. Bhengu's church in E. London.

1078.   _____.   "Zion Christian Church," <u>Drum</u> (Johannesburg), 4 (7) July 1954.
         (pp. 7-9). Illus.
         Edward Lekganyane's church at "Zion City Moria," N. Transvaal.

1079.   _____.   "Rev. N. Bhengu," <u>Bantoe</u>/<u>Bantu</u> (Pretoria), 6, June 1957, 33-34.
         Illus.
         Report of effects of Bhengu's preaching at Clermont, Natal.

1080.   _____.   "Government recognition of Bantu churches and allocation of sites
         in Bantu areas and Bantu urban townships," <u>Bantoe</u>/<u>Bantu</u> (Pretoria), 9,
         Sept. 1959, 101-108.
         Historical summary: the 1925 conditions for recognition as a church;
         the 1905, 1956, and 1957 regulations for allocation of church sites.

1081.   _____.   "South African preaches to white and blacks," <u>African Challenge</u>
         (Lagos), Jan. 1962, 3. Illus.
         An interview with N.B.H. Bhengu.

1082.   _____.   "Black women and God," <u>Hibbert Journal</u>, 64 (243) July 1963,
         166-169. Illus.
         A sympathetic presentation of the material in Brandel-Syrier, item
         1105, on <u>Manyano</u>, women's movements in S. African churches.

1083.   _____.   "A Dream becomes Reality," <u>BaNtu</u> (Pretoria), 12 (3) Mar. 1965,
         140-142. Illus.
         A new church built for St. John's Apostolic Faith Mission near Ger-
         miston; general account of the Church, and its Bishop Masenga.

1084.   _____.   "Bantu multitude thanks minister de Wet Nel," <u>BaNtu</u> (Pretoria),
         12 (6) June 1965, 238-241. Illus.
         The welcome at Moria by Bishop Len-Kganyame and some 40,000 members
         of the Zion Christian Church to the Government Minister of Bantu
         Development.

1085.   _____.   "Pilgrimage to Mecca of Northern Transvaal," <u>BaNtu</u> (Pretoria),
         12 (6) June 1965, 244-247. Illus.
         50,000 members of Zion Christian Church gather at Moria, N. Transvaal,
         for Easter.

1086.   _____.   "Independent churches in South Africa offered aid by Christian
         Institute," <u>Ministry</u> (Morija, Basutoland), 5 (4) July 1965, 200.
         A news item from the director of the Christian Institute of South
         Africa.

1087.   ARNETT, Benjamin William. <u>Episcopal handbook A.M.E. Church</u>. 1900. (G.S.)
         Pp. 8-17, reference to James Dwane.

1088.   ASHTON, Hugh. <u>The Basuto</u>. London: O.U.P. for IAI, 1952. 355p. illus.
         P. 118, Edward Motaung's Apostolic Church among the Tlokwa.

1089.   ASMUS, Gustav. Die Zulu. Essen: Essener Verlagsanstalt, 1939.
            Pp. 99-100 on prophets.

1090.   AXENFELD, Karl. "Die allegemeine südafrikanische Missionskonferenz zu
            Johannesburg vom 13 bis 20 Juli 1904" (The General Missionary Conference
            of S. Africa at Johannesburg . . .), Allegemeine Missions-zeitschrift
            (Berlin), 32 (1) 1905, 13-29.
            Ethiopianism as discussed at the conference.

1091.   _____. "Nachwirkungen der Johannesburger Missionskonferenz" (Aftermath of
            the Johannesburg Missionary Conference), Allegemeine Missions-zeitschrift
            (Berlin), 32 (7) 1905, 332-342.
            Bishop Turner and the African Methodist Episcopal Church.

1092.   _____. "Die Schlange im Grase," (The snake in the grass), Die Evangelischen
            Missionen (Gütersloh), 11, 1905. 56-62.
            Early Ethiopianism in South Africa.

1093.   _____. "Der Aethiopismus in Süd-Afrika," (Ethiopianism in South Africa)
            Koloniale Abhandlungen (Berlin), 6 (1906). 13p.
            A short monograph in a series.

1094.   BAER, G. F. A. "Missionary endeavour in Pondoland," International Review
            of Missions, 42 (168) Oct. 1953, 413-20.
            Reference to separatist churches in South Africa being caused by
            dissatisfaction with European Christianity.

1095.   BARNES, J. A. "African separatist churches," Rhodes-Livingstone Journal,
            9, 1950, 26-30.
            A review-article on Sundkler, item 1262.

1096.   BECHLER, Theodor. "Unabhängigkeitsbewegungen der Farbigen in Südafrika"
            (Independence movements among native peoples of S. Africa), Evangelisches
            Missions-Magazin (Basel), n.s. 47, 1903, 265-280, 324-341.
            Republished separately, Basel: Basler Missionsbuchhandlung, 1903,
            40p. (B.S.)

1097.   BENSON, Mary. The African patriots. London: Faber, 1963. 296p. illus.
            Pp. 26-27, 51, 77: side references to separatists or ethiopianism
            as background to the history of the African National Congress.

1098.   BERRY, Llwellyn L. A century of missions of the African Methodist
            Episcopal Church, 1840-1940. New York: Gutenberg, 1942. 336p. (S.&P.)

1099.   BERTHOUD, Alex. L. "The Missionary situation in South Africa," Inter-
            national Review of Missions, 49 (193) Jan. 1960, 83-90.
            Suggestion for an ecumenical evangelical centre open to "separatist
            churches" for training leaders.

1100.   BEYERHAUS, P(eter). "Prize winning contest," Ministry (Morija, Basutoland),
            5 (4) July 1965, 194.
            The announcement of an essay competition on "Zionism: Indigenous
            Christianity or Renascent Paganism?"

1101. BHENGU, Nicholas B. H. Revival fire in South Africa. Philadelphia: Afro-American Missionary Crusade Inc., 1950.
By the leader of Bhengu's Church, a pentecostal evangelical church in East London.

1102. _____. (ed.). Back to God. South African Church Magazine (East London), 1 (2) July 1955. (K.S.)
Various articles concerning Bhengu's church.

1103. Blue Books on Native Affairs. Cape of Good Hope.
Cited by Shepperson & Price, item 986, as an important source on Ethiopianism. Especially 1898, 34, 44-45; 1899, 16, 118; 1900, 4, 25, 49; 1902, 24, 54, 84; 1903, 34, 44-45; 1904, 30, 123; 1905, 22, 76; 1906, 7, 22, 32, 53-54; 1907, 17, 37; 1908, 30, 40. (S. & P.)

1104. BOURQUIN, W. "Irrungen und Wirrungen in Silo" (Confusion upon confusion in Shiloh), Missions-blatt der Brudergemeinde (Herrnhut), 87 (4) Apr. 1913, 73-80. (K.S.)
On Enoch Mgijima.

1105. BRANDEL-SYRIER, Mia. Black woman in search of God. London: Lutterworth, 1962. 251p. Illus.
The "Manyanos," semi-independent women's church organizations in South Africa.

1106. BRIDGMAN, Frederick B. "The Ethiopian Movement and other independent factors characterized by a national spirit," in Report of proceedings, First General Missionary Conference for South Africa, Johannesburg, 1904. Johannesburg: Argus, 1904, 162-177.
An American missionary on the origins of independent churches and in criticism of their activities. Pp. 177-183, the Conference discussion and resolutions.

1107. _____. "The Ethiopian movements in South Africa," Christian Express (Lovedale), 1903. Also in The Missionary Review of the World (Princeton, N. J.), 17 (6) June 1904, 434-445. (G.S.)

1108. BROOKES, Edgar H(arry). The colour problems of South Africa. Lovedale (C.P.): Lovedale Press, 1934. viii + 237p.
Pp. 34-35, 161-162, 170, "separatist church movement"; Appendix I: list of 323 native separatist churches as at 4 Aug. 1932.

1109. _____. A century of missions in Natal and Zululand. (Durban): n. pub., n.d. (1927). 60p.
Pp. 32-33, 54, the "separatist churches" and their causes.

1110. BROWN, Kenneth I. "An African experiment in Christian union," The Christian (Disciples of Christ), 103 (4) 24 Jan. 1965, pp. 4-5; 103, (5) 31 Jan. 1965, pp. 8-9, 24.
A union between the Holy Catholic Apostolic Church in Zion, and the Disciples of Christ, in S. Africa, under the United Christian Missionary Society, 1961.

1111. BRULS, J. "Prophètes bantous en Afrique du Sud," Église vivante (Paris-Louvain), 1 (3) 1949, 341-353.

1112. BUCHAN, John. Prester John. New York: Nelson, 1910. vi + 376p.
A widely read novel portraying an Ethiopian led rebellion in South
Africa which was cited as a prediction of the Chilembwe rebellion
in Nyasaland.

1113. BUDAZA, G. S. The native separatist church movement. Unpublished M. A.
dissertation, University of S. Africa, 1948.
By a Bantu; mainly on Limba's Church of Christ.

1114. BURCKHARDT, G. "Die tembukirche des kaffernhaüptlings Dalindyebo" (The
Tembu Church of the Kafir leader Dalindyebo), Die Evangelischen Missionen
(Gütersloh), 2, 1896, 235-7.
Nehemiah Tile's church.

1115. BURNET, Amos. "Ethiopianism," Church Missionary Review (London), 73
(837) March 1922, 29-34.

1116. BURROWS, H. R. (ed.). Baumannville: a study of an urban African community.
Capetown: O.U.P., 1959. viii + 79p.
Pp. 58-63, the place of independent churches in a small community
near Durban.

1117. CAMERON, J. & FLETCHER, G. C. "The Ethiopian movement in South Africa,"
The Mission Field (London: S.P.G.), 48 (574) Oct. 1903, 309-313.
Letters from two English missionaries working with the Order of
Ethiopia.

1118. CAMERON, W. M. "The Ethiopian movement and the Order of Ethiopia,"
The East and the West (London: S.P.G.), 2 (8) Oct. 1904, 375-397.
Relations with the Anglican Church in S. Africa.

1119. CAPETOWN, Archbishop of. "The Ethiopian movement," The Mission Field
(S.P.G., London:), 45 (539) Nov. 1900, 401-405.
A description of the reception of Dwane and the Ethiopian Order,
with the Anglican Synod resolutions.

1120. CAWOOL, Lesley. The churches and race relations in South Africa.
Johannesburg: African Institute of Race Relations, 1964. 140p.
Pp. 59-60, the Order of Ethiopia; pp. 139-140, appendix on indepen-
dent or separatist churches.

1121. COAN, J. R. Expansion of missions of the African Methodist Church in
South Africa, 1896-1908. Unpublished Ph.D. dissertation, Hartford
Seminary Foundation, Connecticut, 1961.

1122. COPE, Jack. The fair house. London: MacGibbon and Kee, 1955. (G.S.)
Fiction: "the most important treatment by a S. African novelist of
the Ethiopian scare."

1123. COPPIN, Levi Jenkins. Observations of persons and things in South Africa
1900-1904. Philadelphia: A.M.E. Book Concern, n.d. 210p.
Pp. 8-18, Bishop Turner's visit to South Africa; Ethiopianism.

1124. CRAD, Joseph. (Pseudonym of E.C.T. Ansell.) African Odyssey. London:
J. Gifford, 1939. 285p.
"Ethiopian" leaders in the Zulu war of 1906 who claimed religious
sanctions: Dinizulu, pp. 203ff; Makanda, pp. 215f.

1125. DAVIDSON, A. B. "Sozdaniye Afrikanskogo Nationalnogo Kongressa" (The establishment of the African National Congress), Narody Azii i Afriki (Moscow), 6, 1962, 78-88.
    The independent Bantu churches in S. Africa as having prepared the way for this Congress, and supplied some officers. (AA 15, 116.)

1126. DAVIES, Morton & SHEPHERD, R. H. W. (eds.). South African missions, 1800-1950. London: Nelson, 1954. xxiv + 232p.
    Pp. 181-186, several short selections about independent churches from Sundkler, Lea and Johnson.

1127. DE RIDDER, J. C. The personality of the urban African in South Africa: A thematic apperception test study. London: Routledge & Kegan Paul, 1961.
    Pp. 103-106, 161-164, reference to role of "sects"; Johannesburg.

1128. DIETEL, R. W. & PAUL, C. Die schwarzen Juden (The Black Jews). Leipzig: Richter, 1901. (K.S.)
    Pp. 109f., Mlandscheni, pp. 112-114, Mchlakaza and Nonquas - mid-19th. c. Bantu prophets.

1129. DLEPU, B. S. "Native separatist church movements," in Report, Sixth General Missionary Conference of South Africa, 1925, Cape Town: Nasionale Pers, 1925, pp. 110-118.

1130. DUBB, A. A. The role of the church in an urban African society. Unpublished M.A. thesis (Anthropology), Rhodes University, 1962. Publication expected - Cape Town: O.U.P.
    Includes Bhengu's semi-independent Church in East London.

1131. _____. "Tribalism in the African church," in A. A. Dubb (ed.), The Multitribal Society. Lusaka: Rhodes-Livingstone Institute, 1962, pp. 111-119.
    Pp. 115-119 on S. African "separatist churches."

1132. DUBE, J(ohn) L(angalibalele). "Ethiopianism," Die Basuin, 1 (5) 1930, 7-8.
    By a Zulu, first president of the African National Congress.

1133. _____. U-Shembe. Pietermaritzburg: Shooter & Shuter, 1936. 117p. (B. Eth.)
    A life of Shembe, in Zulu.

1134. DU PLESSIS, Johannes. A History of Christian missions in South Africa. London: Longmans Green, 1911; reissued Cape Town: C. Struik, 1965. 494p. illus.
    Pp. 302, 305, 453, the Ethiopian movement; pp. 358, 455, the Ethiopian Order.

1135. _____. The life of Andrew Murray of South Africa. London: Marshall Brothers, 1919. 553p.
    Pp. 103, 123, 497, Jerusalem trekkers or Marico Boers, an independent millennial movement among the Boers during the time of the Great Trek.

1136. _____. "Die oorsprong van die Ethiopiese Kerkbeweging in Suid-Afrika" (The origin of the Ethiopian Church movement in South Africa), Het zoeklicht, 2, 1924, 196-201, 232-238, 274-279.
    The origin and growth of independent churches; the basic cause found in factors encouraging individualism. In Afrikaans.

1137. _____. "Ethiopianisme," Die Basuin, 2 (3) July 1931, 5-7; (4) Sep. 1931, 18-19; (5) Nov. 1931, 17-20; 3 (2) May 1932, 15-16; (3) July 1932, 21-22; (5) Nov. 1932, 9-11.

1138. _____. "Hoe die Ethiopische Beweging in Suid-Africa begin het" (How the Ethiopian Movement began in S. Africa), Die Sending Instituut Jaarblad (Wellington, South Africa), 1937, 14-17.

1139. _____. "Die oorsake van Separatisme in die Sendingvelde van Suid-Africa" (The causes of separatism in the South African mission field), Op die Horison (Stellenbosch), 1 (1) Jan. 1939, 39-42; (2) April 1939, 56-60.

1140. EBERHARDT, Jacqueline (ROUMEGUÈRE, P.) "Messianismes en Afrique du Sud," Archives de sociologie des religions, 2 (4) July-Dec. 1957, 31-56.
        A survey of independent churches, all called "messianismes," with special attention to the Zion Christian Church and the Nazaretha Church. (AA 10, 105.)

1141. _____. "Christianity and African separatist churches in South Africa," Occasional Papers (London: International Missionary Council), 1 (4) 1960, 9p. (mimeo.)

1142. EISELEN, W. M. "Christianity and the religious life of the Bantu," in I. SCHAPERA (ed.), Western civilization and the natives of South Africa. London: Routledge, 1934. xiv + 312p.
        Pp. 73-76, reasons for separatist movements.

1143. _____ & SCHAPERA, I. "Religious Beliefs and Practices," in I. SCHAPERA (ed.), The Bantu speaking tribes of South Africa. London: Routledge, 1937.
        Pp. 253f., brief reference to traditional prophets; p. 425, brief reference to separatist churches.

1144. ETHIOPIAN CATHOLIC CHURCH IN ZION. Constitutions and Canons of the Ethiopian Catholic Church in Zion. Bloemfontein: the Church, 1918. (B.S.)
        Founded by S. J. Brander in 1904, by secession from the African Methodist Episcopal Church.

1145. ETHIOPIAN CATHOLIC CHURCH OF SOUTH AFRICA. Constitution of the Ethiopian Church of South Africa. (?): the Church, n.d. (1914?).
        With a brief historical preface.

1146. FRITSCH, Gustav. Die Eingeborenen Süd-Afrikas (The South African Natives). Breslau: F. Hirt, 1873. (K.S.)
        Pp. 473f., Ntsikana; p. 477, Nxele; pp. 498-503, Mlandscheni; pp. 503f., Mchlakaza and Nonquas.

1147. GERDENER, G. B. A. Studies in the evangelization of South Africa. London: Longmans, Green & Co., 1911. 212p.
        Pp. 46-53, Ethiopian movement.

1148. _____. Recent developments in the South African mission field. Cape Town: N. G. Kerk-Uitgewers, 1958. 286p.
        Pp. 188-206, "the trends of separatism and independence."

1149. GLUCKMAN, Max. "Analysis of a social situation in Modern Zululand," _Bantu Studies_, 14 (1) Mar. 1940, 1-30; 14 (2) June 1940, 147-174. Also _Rhodes-Livingstone Papers_, 28, 1958, 82p.
   Pp. 61-62, the multiform causes of Zulu separatism. (AA 3, 704)

1150. GRAHAMSTOWN, BISHOP OF. "The Order of Ethiopia," _The Mission Field_ (London: S.P.G.), 46 (543) Mar. 1901, 92-95.
   The reception of Dwane's "Ethiopians" into the Anglican Church, 1900.

1151. GREEN, E. M. "Native unrest in South Africa," _The Nineteenth Century_ (London), 46 (273) Nov. 1899, 708-716.
   Pp. 708-710, a prophet in Tembuland, 1899; pp. 710-713, Ethiopianism and Dwane.

1152. GRIMM, Hans. _Das deutsche Südwester-Buch_ (The book of the German South-west). Munich: A. Langen, 1929. 429p. (K.S.)
   Pp. 17-19, 25f., 107-109, 244, 255f., on Witbooi; p. 26 on Stürmann.

1153. GRUBB, Kenneth S. (ed.). _The Christian handbook of South Africa_. Love-dale, S.A.: Lovedale Press on behalf of the Christian Council of South Africa, 1938. viii + 290p.
   Pp. 145-158, list of "Native Separatist Churches" supplied by the Native Affairs dept.

1154. HELLMAN, Ellen. "Culture contacts and social change," _Race Relations_ (Johannesburg), 15 (1-2) 1948, 30-42.
   Includes separatist churches as self assertion and escape from white authority. (AA 1, 284)

1155. _____. _Sellgoods: A sociological survey of an African commercial labour force_. Johannesburg: South African Institute of Race Relations, n.d. (c. 1951).
   A study of a large retail company near Johannesburg. P. 51, 17% of African workers belong to "unrecognized African Churches."

1156. HEWSON, L. A. (ed.). _Cottesloe consultation_. Johannesburg: South African Member Churches of the World Council of Churches, n.d. (1961). 100p.
   The Report of a Consultation in 1960 at Cottesloe, Johannesburg: pp. 27-30, on causes of, and ways of meeting, the "separatist sects."

1157. HILL, F. "Native separatist movements and their relation to the problem of evangelization," in _Report, Sixth General Missionary Conference of South Africa, 1925_. Cape Town: Nasionale Pers, 1925. 110-118.
   On the causes of these movements.

1158. HINCHCLIFF, Peter. _The Anglican Church in South Africa: An account of the history and development of the Church of the Province of South Africa_. London: Barton, Longman & Todd, 1963. 266p.
   Pp. 200-205, the order of Ethiopia.

1159. HORRELL, Muriel (compiler). _A survey of race relations in South Africa_. Johannesburg: S. African Institute of Race Relations, annually.
   E.g.: 1952-1953, pp. 56-57, separatist church sites; 1955-56, pp. 215-216, recognition of separatist churches; 1957-58, pp. 39-40, prosecution; 1958-59, pp. 33-34, church sites; 1959-60, pp. 27, 128-129, union of separatist churches, and relations with Government; 1961, pp. 133-134, church sites.

106

1160.   HUNTER, Monica. <u>Reaction to conquest</u>. London: O.U.P. for IAI, (1936)
         1961. xxiv + 582p.
              Pp. 349, 543, 562-565, "independent native churches," expecially
              Enoch Mgijima.

1161.   JABAVU, D(avidson) D(on) T(engo). "Lessons from the Israelite episode,"
         <u>South African Outlook</u> (Lovedale), July 1921, 105-106.
              On Enoch Mgijima: the origins of his "Ama-Sirayeli" church, and
              reasons for his success; the Bulhoek tragedy.

1162.   _____. <u>An African indigenous church</u>. <u>A plea for its establishment in
         South Africa</u>. Lovedale, S. Africa: Lovedale Press, 1942. 15p.

1163.   JACOTTET, E. <u>The Ethiopian Church and the Missionary Conference of
         Johannesburg</u>. <u>An open letter to the . . . special conference of the
         African Methodist Episcopal Church held at Pretoria in Aug. 1904</u>.
         Morija (Basutoland): Morija Printing Office, 1904. 30p. Also as
         Appendix to the 1904 Report, see next item.
              The missionary attitude to independent churches.

1164.   _____. Native churches and their organization," in <u>Report of proceedings,
         First General Missionary Conference for South Africa, 1904</u>. Johannesburg:
         Argus, 1904, pp. 108-133.
              A missionary of the Paris Mission suggests a progressive withdrawal
              of European control, in the interests of an indigenous church
              incorporating the truth in Ethiopianism.

1165.   JORDAN, A. C. "Towards an African literature IX: The tale of Nong-
         qawuse: 'The cause of the cattle killing of the Nongqause period,'"
         <u>Africa South</u> (Capetown), 3 (4) July-Sept. 1959, 111-115.
              An eye-witness account of the 1856-7 event among the Xhosa in South
              Africa.

1165A.   JUNOD, Henri A. <u>The life of a South African tribe</u>. New Hyde Park, N.Y.:
         University Books, 1962. 2 vols. (reprint of 2nd. rev. edn.)
              Vol. II, pp. 597-602, the Murimi movement, a chiliastic neo-pagan
              movement which abolished charms, about 1914.

1166.   KARSTEDT, (Franz) Oskar. <u>Englands afrikanisches Imperium</u> (England's
         African empire). Berlin: O. Stollberg, 1937. (K.S.)
              P. 485, Mchlakaza and Nonquas, father and daughter, prophets in the
              1850's, among the Nchlambe.

1167.   KELLERMANN, Abraham Gerhardus. <u>Profetisme in Suid Afrika in akkulturasie
         perspektief</u>. (Prophetism in S. Africa in the perspective of accultura-
         tion). Vrieburg: Zanoni -- Offset, 1964.

1168.   KIDD, Dudley. <u>The essential Kafir</u>. London: A. & C. Black, (1904)
         1925. xiv + 436p. (B.S.)
              P. 407, the absorption of Dwane's movement in the Anglican Church.

1169.   KNAK, D. "Südafrika. (Missionsprobleme . . .)," in <u>Die Religion in
         Geschichte und Gegenwart</u>. Tubingen: Mohr, 2 edn., 1931, vol. V, cols.,
         870-873.

1170. KRATZENSTEIN, Ed. Kurze Geschichte der Berliner Mission in Süd-Afrika
       (Short History of the Berlin Mission in S. Africa). Berlin: Wohlgemuth,
       vol. II, 1878. (K.S.)
           Pp. 77ff., Mlandscheni, mid-19th. century prophet.

1171. KROPF, A. Das Volk der Xosa-Kaffern im östlichen Südafrika nach seiner
       Geschichte, Eigenart, Verfassung und Religion. (The Xhosa-Kafir people
       in Eastern S. Africa, according to their history, peculiarities, con-
       dition, and religion). Berlin: Berliner Evangelische Missionsgesellschaft,
       1889. viii + 209p. (K.S.)
           Pp. 49f, Nxele; pp. 29f. 66-71, 96, Mlandscheni; pp. 30f, 60, 71f,
           95, Mchlakaza and Nonquas.

1172. _____. "Die Lügenpropheten des Kaffernlandes," (The false prophets of
       Kafir land), Neue Missionsschriften (Berlin), 2 (11) 1891. (K.S.)
           Pp. 1-5, Nxele, a syncretist prophet; pp. 5-7, Mlandscheni; pp. 7-
           16, Mchlakaza and Nonquas; traditional prophets.

1173. _____. "Ntsikana, der Erstling aus den Kaffern und ein Prophet unter
       seinem Volk" (Ntsikana, the first of the Kaffirs to be baptized, and a
       prophet among his people), Neue Missionsschriften (Berlin) 2, 1891. (K.S.)
           Early 19th century prophet among the Ngquika (?).

1174. KUPER, Leo, WATTS, Hestan & DAVIES, Ronald. Durban--A study in racial
       ecology. London: Jonathan Cape, 1958.
           P. 83, "minor sects" strong among African population (44.67%);
           pp. 133-135, ecology of African religion.

1175. KUPER, Leo. An African bourgeoisie. New Haven: Yale U.P., 1965. 452p.
           Pp. 204-206, separatist churches; pp. 311-312, Ethiopianism; pp. 136-
           137, 311-312, 314-316, Zionism.

1176. LATOURETTE, K(enneth) S(cott). History of the expansion of Christianity.
       London: Eyre & Spottiswoode, 1939-1945.
           Vol. VII, pp. 227-228, on the causes and features of independency,
           especially in South Africa.

1177. LEA, Allen. "Native separatist churches," in J. D. Taylor (ed.),
       Christianity and the natives of South Africa: A year-book of South
       African missions. South Africa: Lovedale Press, 1927, 73-85.

1178. _____. The native separatist church movement in South Africa. Cape
       Town, Johannesburg: Juta & Co., n.d. (1927). 84p.
           Origin, causes, and features of the movement; the attitude of older
           churches and Government.

1179. LEE, A. W. Charles Johnson of Zululand. London: Society for Propagation
       of the Gospel, 1930.
           Pp. 108-109, why Nqutu District was not much affected by separatist
           churches.

1180. LEENHARDT, Maurice. Le mouvement éthiopien au Sud d'Afrique de 1896 à
       1899. Cahors: Couesland, 1902. 128p.

1181. LEHMANN, Friedrich R. "Eine Form der Religionsmischung in Südafrika. Die
       AmaNazaretha-Kirche in Natal" (An example of syncretism in South Africa.
       The Ama Nazaretha Church in Natal), in Von fremden Völkern und Kulturen.
       Beiträge zur Volkerkunde, Dusseldorf: Droste, 1955, 184-193.

1182. "LELOKO." "Mokete o mogolo Zion City Moria," (Ein grosses Fest in der
       Zion City Moria) (A major festival at Zion City, Moria), Bantu World
       (Johannesburg), 25 (4) 1953. (K.S.)
           On Edward Lekganyane.

1183. LENNOX, J. "The relation of European and native churches," in Report of
       proceedings, Third General Missionary Conference for South Africa, 1909.
       Cape Town: Townshend, Taylor & Snashall, 1909, 82-90.
           Also pp. 90-92, the ensuing discussion.

1184. LEWIS, C., & EDWARDS, G. E. Historical records of the Church of the
       Province of South Africa. London: S.P.C.K., 1934. xix + 821p. (B.S.)
           Pp. 224-5, Dwane's Order of Ethiopia and the Anglican Church.

1185. LININGTON, P. A. A summary of the reports of certain pre-union commis-
       sions on native affairs: church separatist movement. Pretoria: 1924.

1186. LORAM, C. T. "The separatist Church movement," International Review of
       Missions, 15 (59) July 1926, 476-482.
           A review of the Report of the South African Government Commission on
           the 1921 disturbances.

1187. MABOEE, A. T. "Letter in Reply to Beyerhaus, 1961," Ministry (Morija,
       Basutoland), 2 (2) Jan. 1962, 38-40.
           An African's criticism of separatism.

1188. MACMILLAN, W. M. Bantu, Boer and Briton: The making of the South African
       problem. Oxford: Clarendon Press, (1929) 1963. xviii + 382p.
           Pp. 51, 80, 341, Makana, a Xhosa prophet in 1812-1819, and others,
           1853, 1856-1857.

1189. MARKS, Shula. 'Ethiopianism' and the 1906 Natal Disturbances, Paper
       presented to the Society for African Church History, London, 1964.
       9p. (mimeo.)
           Questions the correctness of government and white assertions that
           independent churches had fomented the Zulu rebellion; these assertions
           derive from the "Ethiopian peril" scare, and the government hostility
           to the American mission involved.

1190. _____. "Harriette Colenso and the Zulus, 1874-1913," Journal of African
       History, 4 (3) 1963, 403-411.
           P. 409, the attitude of Bishop Colenso's daughter to the separatist
           movement, and her relationship to P. J. Mzimba.

1191. _____. "Christian participation in the 1906 Zulu Rebellion," Bulletin,
       Society for African Church History (Aberdeen), 2 (1) Dec. 1965.
       (Expected 1966)
           Similar to earlier item.

1192. MARQUAND, Leo. The peoples and policies of South Africa. London:
       O.U.P., 1952.
           Pp. 204-5, brief mention of "separatist churches."

1193. MAYER, Philip. Townsmen or tribesmen. Capetown: O.U.P., 1961. xvi +
       306p.
           Ch. 12, "Red Converts to Christianity," the impact of Bhengu's Xhosa
           Church on rural pagan migrants to East London; sympathetic, detailed.

1194. ____. "Some forms of religious organization among Africans in a South African city," in Urbanization . . . , item 223, 113-126.
   The Bhengu Church as a "face-to-face" society.

1195. MBATHA, Simon. "Sektrörelser i Sydafrika" (Sect movements in S. Africa), Svensk Missionstidskrift, 44, 1956, 39-44.

1196. MELCHIZEDEK ETHIOPIAN CATHOLIC CHURCH. Fundamental principles of the faith of the Melchizedek Ethiopian Catholic Church. N.p.: the Church, n.d. (mimeo.)
   And see item 1144, which is here largely reproduced, with addition of an historical preface.

1197. MERENSKY, Alexander. "Missionsrundschau. Süd-Afrika I" (The outlook for missions, S. Africa), Allegemeine Missions-Zeitschrift (Berlin), 24, 1897, 347-351. (K.S.)
   Includes Ethiopianism.

1198. ____. "Die Äthiopische Bewegung unter den eingeborenen Christen Süd-Afrikas" (The Ethiopian movement among South African native Christians), Allegemeine Missions-zeitschrift (Berlin), June 1903, 261-274, 334-345.
   Based on Leenhardt, item 1180.

1199. MILFORD, Bertram. The white hand and black. London: 1907.
   Fiction: the 1906 Zulu rebellion; pp. 50ff., on Ethiopianism.

1200. MILLIN, Sarah Gertrude. The coming of the lord. London: Constable, 1928.
   Fiction: the South African independents.

1201. MOKITIMI, S(eth) M. "African religion," in Ellen HELLMAN, (ed.), Handbook on race relations in South Africa, London: O.U.P., 1949, 556-572.
   Pp. 564-572, on "separatism"; a good survey with statistics, by an African church leader.

1202. MONTEIL, V. L'Islam noir. Paris: Éditions du Seuil, 1964. 368p. bibl.
   Pp. 183-200, include reference to syncretisms between Christianity and animism. (FA 1, 323-11)

1203. MOON, D. S. R. "Festival of Shembe," BaNtu (Pretoria), 10 (10) 1963, 534-537. Illus.
   Zulu Nazarites' festival at Inanda, Natal.

1204. MORAN, Fernando. Le prophète. Paris: Éditions du Seuil, 1964. 191p. (Translated from Spanish original)
   Fiction: a Zulu prophet founds a church to liberate his brethren, and his movement is studied by a crippled European.

1205. MPUMLWANA, P. M. "Indigenisation of Christianity," Ichthus (Stellenbosch, Students' Christian Association of S. Africa), 14, 1962. Also in Ministry (Morija), 4 (1) Oct. 1963, 14-17.
   (1963) P. 15, historical review of the attitudes to Ethiopianism in the Paris, Scottish and Anglican missions, by a minister in the Order of Ethiopia.

1206.   MQOTSI, L., & MKELE, N.   "A separatist church: Ibandla lika-Krestu,"
        African Studies, (Johannesburg) 5 (2) June 1946, 106-125.
            The Church of Christ, Capetown, 1910, and its later development under
            Bishop Limba; a systematic account. (AA 3, 702.)

1207.   MZIMBA, L. M.   "The African Church" in J. D. Taylor (ed.), Christianity
        and the natives of South Africa, A year-book of South African missions.
        Lovedale: Lovedale Press, 1927, 86-95.
            The causes and aims of the separatist movement.

1208.   NEAME, L. Elwin.   "Ethiopianism: the danger of a black church," Empire
        Review, 10 (57) Oct. 1905, 256-265.
            An assembly of opinions critical of Ethiopianism, with comments on
            the Report of the Native Affairs Commission, item 1253.

1209.   NEWMAN, Bernard.   South African journey. London: Jenkins, 1965. 222p.
        illus.
            P. 26, "Bantu sects" -- impressionistic.

1210.   NICHOLLS, G(eorge) Heaton.   Bayete! 'hail to the king!'. London: Allen
        & Unwin, 1923. 374p.
            Fiction: written in 1913 by a S. African senator; an extreme
            expression of the "Ethiopian scare."

1211.   NORTON, G. R.   "The emergence of new religious organizations in South
        Africa: A discussion of causes, Part II," Journal of the Royal African
        Society (London), 40 (58) 1941, 48-67.
            Based on secondary sources; cites a variety of causes besides race.

1212.   O'HARA, Andy.   "Donne zioniste nel Süd Africa," (Zionist women in South
        Africa), Nigrizia (Verona), 81 (10) Oct. 1963, 18-23. Illus.
            General description of Zionism and 'Protestant Clubs' for women which
            have a strong anti-European feeling. (AA 16, 508)

1213.   (OLIFAN, J. W.) Expose of the Faith and practice of the Church of Christ.
        N.p. (Port Elizabeth?): the Church, n.d.
            Olifan (or Oliphant) founded the Church of Christ in 1910, and signed
            the major portion of this document as "Moderator," i.e., before Limba
            took over the leadership.

1214.   OOSTHUIZEN, Gerhardus C.   "Sondebegrip by die Separatistiese Bewegings
        in Afrika" (The concept of sin in independent movements in Africa),
        Nederduitsch Gereformeerde Teologiese Tydskrif (S. Africa), 5 (4) 1964,
        219-225.

1215.   _____.   "Independent African churches: sects or spontaneous development?
        A Reply to Dr. Alex. van Wyck," Ministry (Morija), 5 (3) Apr. 1965,
        99-107.
            See Van Wyck, item 226. A theological examination leading to
            classification as "post-Christian or anti-Christian cult communities."

1216.   PAUW, B. A.   Religion in a Tswana chiefdom. London: O.U.P. for IAI,
        1960. 258p.
            An important study by an anthropologist, of the churches in a native
            reserve in the northern Cape Province, 1952-1954; typology differing
            from Sundkler's, and cutting across the sociological division into

"European-connected" and "separatist" churches. Appendix II, on St. Paul Apostolic Faith Morning Star Church.

1217. _____. "African Christians and their Ancestors," in V. E. W. Hayward (ed.), item 110, 33-46.
The relationship of independents to ancestor worship, with special reference to South Africa.

1218. _____. The second generation: A study of the family among urbanized Bantu in East London. Cape Town: O.U.P., 1963. xviii + 219p.
Pp. 38-41, independent Bantu churches; 10.4% of his sample belonged to them.

1219. _____. "Patterns of christianization among the Tswana and the Xhosa-speaking peoples," in M. Fortes & G. Dieterlin (eds.) item 87, 240-257.
A minor reference to independents, but relevant for background.

1220. _____. Bantu Christians and their churches. Cape Town: O.U.P., forth-coming.

1221. PAYNE, Adam. "A prophet among the Zulus: Shembe. A power for peace and a restraining influence," The Illustrated London News, 176, 8 Feb. 1930, p. 203.

1222. PELEMAN, M. De Ethiopische Beweging in Zuid-Afrika (The Ethiopian move-ment in S. Africa). Dendermonde (N. Transvaal): St. Pieter en Paulus Abdij, 1937.

1223. PEREIRA DE QUEIROZ, Maria Isaura. "Maurice Léenhardt et les 'Églises éthiopiennes'," Monde non-chrétien, n.s., 74, Apr.-June 1965, 84-101.
(FA 1, 1690)

1224. PERROT, Claude-Hélène. "Un culte messianique chez les Sotho au milieu du XIXe siècle," Archives de sociologie des religions, 9 (18) July-Dec. 1964, 147-152.
An anti-white revolt led by Molageni, 1850-1852. (AA 16, 703)
(FA 1, 549-01/2.)

1225. _____. "Un messianisme sans lendemain: le culte de Molageni chez les Sotho," in Bouaké, item 206.
An Anti-white revolt led by Molageni, 1850-1852. A fuller version is found in the previous item.

1226. PHEKO, S. E. M. "What does Bengo preach?" Our Africa (Johannesburg), 5 (9), May 1963, 6-7.
Illustrations and testimonies concerning Rev. Nicholas Bhengu and his Church in East London.

1227. PHILLIPS, Ray Edmund. The Bantu are coming: phases of South Africa's race problem. London: S.C.M., 1930. 238p.
Pp. 54-56, 'sects' on the Witwatersrand.

1228. _____. The Bantu in the city. Lovedale: Lovedale Press, n.d. (1938).
Pp. 254-259, 264, 274, 278, 286: the "separatist churches."

1229. PRINGLE, Thomas. Narrative of a residence in South Africa. London:
       Edward Moxon, 1840. 116p.
           Pp. 96-100, Prophet Makana among the Amaxosa.

1230. PULLER, F. W. "The Ethiopian Order," The East and the West (London),
       1 (1) Jan. 1903, 75-91.
           The Order of Ethiopia and its relation to the Anglican church, by an
       English missionary.

1231. RATZEL, Friedrich. Völkerkunde. (Anthropology). Leipzig: Bibliograph
       Institut, 1885. (K.S.)
           Pp. 276-277, early traditional prophets in South Africa: Nxele,
       Mlandscheni and Ntiskana.

1232. RICHTER, Julius. Geschichte der Berliner Missionsgesellschaft 1824-1924
       (History of the Berlin Missionary Society . . .). Berlin: Berliner
       evangelische Missionsgesellschaft, 1924. vi + 740p. (K.S.)
           Pp. 109f., Ntsikana; pp. 111f., Mlandscheni, Mchlakaza, and Nonquas;
       pp. 644-647, Mwamafungubo.

1233. ROBERTS, (Archdeacon). The mission field (London: S.P.G.), 44 (528)
       Dec. 1899, 467.
           Note on the danger of the "Ethiopian movement" to "Native
       Christianity," by an Anglican missionary.

1234. ROBERTS, E. L. Shembe, the man and his work. Unpublished M.A. thesis,
       University of South Africa, 1936. (K.S.)

1235. ROUX, Edward. "The Ethiopian Movement," Trek (Johannesburg), 27 July,
       1945.

1236. _____. Time longer than rope: A history of the black man's struggle for
       freedom in South Africa. London: Gollancz, 1948, 398p.; Madison:
       University of Wisconsin Press, 2 edn. enlarged, 1964. xviii + 469p.
           (1964) Ch. 2, "Makana the Prophet"; Ch. 8, also pp. 135, 402, 421,
       "The Ethiopian movement"; pp. 135, 141, Israelite movement of 1909-
       1921.

1237. ROUX, H. A. De Ethiopische Kerk. (The Ethiopian church). Bloemfontein:
       de Vriend, 1905. 39p.

1238. ROYI, Mabel. "Bhenguzu Bhengu! Phakati Kwethu! Back to God (E. London),
       1 (2) July 1955. (K.S.)
           On N.B.H. Bhengu and his church; and see item 1102.

1239. SAUBERZWEIG - SCHMIDT, P. Der Äthiopismus. Die kirchliche Selbständig-
       keitsbewegungen unter den Eingeborenen Südafrikas. (Ethiopianism--the
       independent church movement among the natives of South Africa). Berlin:
       Evangelische Missionsgesellschaft, 1904. 32p.

1240. _____. "Die kirchliche Selbständigkeitsbewegung unter den Eingeborenen
       Südafrikas" (The independent church movement among S. African natives),
       Die Reformation, 3 (43) 1904; 679-682; (44) 1904, 698-700; (45) 1904,
       713-717.

1241. SCHAPERA, Isaac. "Christianity and the Tswana," Journal of the Royal
       Anthropological Institute, 88 (1) Jan.-June 1958, 1-9. Reprinted in
       S. & P. Ottenberg. Cultures and Societies of Africa. New York:
       Random House, 1960, 489-503.
            (1960) P. 498, brief reference to short-lived secessions in 1901
            and 1937. (AA 10, 434.)

1242. SCHNEIDER, Théo. "Les églises indépendentes africaines en Afrique du
       Sud," Verbum Caro (Basel), 6 (23) 1952, 116-26.
            A summary of Sundkler, item 1262, with suggestions for positive
            attitudes by older churches.

1243. ____. "Zion, ruhme Deinen Gott! Ein 'Zionisten' Fest in Norden Trans-
       vaals" (Zion, glorify thy God! A Zionist festival in N. Transvaal),
       Schweizer Mission in Sudafrika (Zurich), 29 (162) 1953, 8-13. (K.S.)
            On Edward Lekganyane's Zion Christian Church.

1244. ____. "Sauvegarder la vérité de l'Évangile: Inventaire de quelques
       obstacles à l'évangelisation en Afrique du Sud," Monde non-chrétien, 41,
       Jan.-Mar. 1957, 18-37.
            The "obstacles" include the "Bantu separatists" where the African
            element increasingly submerges the Christian. (AA 10, 107.)

1245. SCHLOSSER, Katesa. "Passahfest und Leben der 'Israeliten' in Queenstown
       (13, 14, und 15 Apr. 1953)" (Passover and life of the 'Israelites' in
       Queenstown), Wissenschaftliche Zeitschrift der Freidrich-Schiller-
       Universität, Jena, 1953-1954, Math.-Nat. Series, 1, 1953, 147-151. (K.S.)

1246. ____. "Les sectes d'Afrique du Sud en tant que manifestation de la
       tension raciale," in Bouaké, item 206.

1247. SCHULTHEISS. Die bewohner den Ostküste Süd-Afrikas (The inhabitants of
       the East coast of S. Africa). Berlin: W. Schultze, 1854. 21p. (K.S.)

1248. SETILOANE, Gabriel M. W. The separatist movement in South Africa: its
       origins, danger to the church, and comparison with American Negro cults.
       Unpublished S.T.M. thesis, Union Theological Seminary, New York, 1955.
            By a South African theologian.

1249. SHEMBE, J. Galilee. Izihlabelelo zaMaNazaretha (Hymns of the Nazarites).
       Durban: W. H. Shepherd for J. G. Shembe, 1940. (K.S.)
            222 hymns of Isaiah Shembe, edited by the son of the founder.

1250. SHILLITO, E. Fr. Coillard, a wayfaring man. London: Student Christian
       Movement, 1923. 235p.
            P. 107, an early Bantu secession from the Paris Mission, Basutoland,
            1872; p. 228, on the return of Coillard's evangelists from Ethiopian-
            ism.

1251. SHOOTER, Joseph. The Kafirs of Natal and the Zulu country. London:
       E. Stanford, 1857. 403p.
            Pp. 167-195 on prophets or 'seers'; pp. 195-212 on Makana and early
            Bantu prophets.

1252. SOUTH AFRICA. Report and proceedings, with Appendices, of the Government Commission on Native Law and Customs. Capetown: Richards & Son, 1883. Pp. 269-270, Mhlakaza and the cattle-slaughter by the Amaxosa in the 1850's.

1253. SOUTH AFRICAN NATIVE AFFAIRS COMMISSION. Report, 1903-5. Cape Town: Government Printers, 1904-5. 5 vols. (S. & P.)
         Shepperson and Price cite this as an important source on Ethiopianism, which is fully indexed under "Politics" and "Religion" in the subject index, vol. V.

1254. SOUTH AFRICAN NATIVE RACES COMMITTEE (ed.). The South African natives: their progress and present condition. London: Murray, 1908.
         Ch. 7: "The Ethiopian Movement: Native Churches."

1255. SOUTH AFRICA, UNION OF. Report of Native Churches Commission. Cape Town: Cape Times, 1925. 38p.
         A survey of religious organization of the Bantu, and the origins and extent of the separatist movement.

1256. SOUTH AFRICA: NATIVE REPRESENTATIVE COUNCIL. Minutes, Native Representative Council. Pretoria: 1944, 338-349. (B.S.)
         An extended debate between Zulu leaders on the fissiparous nature of separatism.

1257. STEAD, W. Y. "The Order of Ethiopia and its relation to the Church," The African Monthly (Grahamstown), 3 (15) Feb. 1908, 311-331.
         A missionary criticism of the admission of the Order to the Anglican Church in S. Africa.

1258. STEWART, James. Dawn in the dark continent. Edinburgh: Oliphant Anderson & Ferrier, 1903. 400p.
         Pp. 131-132, 185, 371, Ethiopianism.

1259. STUART, J(ames). A History of the Zulu rebellion 1906 and of Dinuzulu's arrest, trial and expatriation. London: Macmillan, 1913. xvi + 581p. illus.
         Pp. 97, 128, 420-421, 521, et passim on Ethiopianism.

1260. SUNDKLER, Bengt G(ustaf) M. "Separatisme en die Sending," (Separatism and Mission), Op die Horison (Stellenbosch), 2 (2) 1940, 63-70.

1261. _____. "Black man's church," Libertas Magazine (Johannesburg), 5 (10) Sept. 1945, 18-37.

1262. _____. Bantu Prophets in South Africa. London: Lutterworth, 1948. 344p.; O.U.P. for IAI. (revised & enlarged) 1961. 381p. illus.
         The best-known general survey; historical, sociological, and theological, of independent Zulu churches. The second edition adds a chapter on independency from 1948-1960.

1263. _____. "Response and resistance to the gospel in a Zulu congregation," in J. Hermelink and H. J. Margull (eds.), Basileia, Stuttgart: Evangelischer Missionsverlag, 1959, 128-145.

1264. _____. "Bantu messiah and white Christ," Frontier (London), 3 (1) 1960, 15-32; Also in Practical Anthropology (Tarrytown, N. Y.), 7 (4) July-Aug. 1960, 170-176.

1265. _____. "The concept of Christianity in the African independent churches," African Studies (Johannesburg), 20 (4) 1961, 203-213.
   A survey of new material on Zulu messianic movements from his further work; Zionist movements in Swaziland. (AA 13, 586.)

1266. _____. "Chief and prophet in Zululand and Swaziland," in M. Fortes & G. Dieterlin (eds.), item 87, 276-290.

1267. _____. "Les prophètes bantou," in Bouaké, item 206.

1268. SUTER, F. "The Ethiopian movement," in Report of Second General Missionary Conference for South Africa, Johannesburg, 1906. Morija, Basutoland: Morija Printing Office, 1907, 107-113. (I.S.)
   Based on answers to a questionnaire on the history of independent churches.

1269. TAYLOR, James Dexter. The American Board Mission in South Africa, A sketch of seventy-five years. Durban: J. Singleton & Sons, 1911. 99p. (B.S.)
   Includes the formation of the Zulu Congregationalist Church in 1896.

1270. _____. "The Rand as a mission field," International Review of Missions, 15 (60) Oct. 1926, 647-661.
   Pp. 651-653, brief references to "separatist bodies or sects."

1271. THEAL, George McCall. Compendium of South African history and geography. Lovedale: Institution Press, 3 edn., 1877.
   Ch. 17, Makana (= Nxele), early 19th. c. prophet.

1272. TRACEY, Hugh. "Zulus find the middle road," Natural History (New York), 64 (8) Oct. 1955, 400-406. Illus.
   Shembe's Church of Nazareth -- popular account with many illustrations. (AA 8, 419.)

1273. UNION OF SOUTH AFRICA. Interim and Final Reports of the Native Affairs Commission and Telegram from Commissioner, South African Police relative to 'Israelites' at Bulhoek and Occurrences in May, 1921. Cape Town: Government Printers, 1921. (U.G. 15-1922)

1274. _____. Report of the Native Churches Commission. Cape Town: Government Printers, 1921. (U.G. 15-1922)

1275. _____. Summary of the Report of the Commission for the Socio-Economic Development of the Bantu Areas within the Union of South Africa. Pretoria: Government Printer, 1955. 211p. (U.G. 61-1955)
   Pp. 20-22, the Tomlinson Report; review of Christianity in South Africa with reference to separatist churches.

1276. VAN ANTWERP, C(ornelius) M(arkinus). Die Separatistiese Kerklike Beweging onder die Bantu van Suid-Afrika (The separatist church movement among the S. African Bantu). Unpublished Ph.D. dissertation, University of Cape Town, 1938.

1277. VAN DEN BERGHE, Pierre L. Caneville: The social structure of a South
       African town. Middletown, Conn.: Wesleyan U.P., 1964. x + 276p.
           A study of a company town near Durban. P. 185, the relation of
           religious affiliation to social status: small "separatist churches"
           have low status, but some townspeople distinguish respectable sects
           from fringe groups.

1278. VERRYN, Trevor David. History of the Order of Ethiopia. Unpublished
       thesis, Faculty of Divinity, Church of the Province of S. Africa
       (Anglican), 1962.

1279. VILAKAZI, Absalom. Isonto Lamanazaretha: The Zulu Church of the Nazarites
       in South Africa. Unpublished M.A. dissertation, Kennedy School of
       Missions, Hartford, Conn. (U.S.A.), 1954.

1280. _____. Zulu transformations: a study of the dynamics of social change.
       Pietermaritzburg: University of Natal Press; London: Bailey Bros.
       & Swinfen, 1962. x + 168p. maps.
           P. 101, separatist churches as a search for a more genuine
           Christianity; Ethiopian leaders' opposition to apartheid.

1281. WAGNER (Père). "Les sectes en Afrique du Sud," in Museum Lessianum,
       item 161, 144-163.
           Ethiopianism, Zionism, especially Shembe's Church.

1282. WALKER, Eric A. A history of South Africa. London: Longmans Green,
       (1928) 1947.
           Pp. 587-588, the Bulhoek incident of 1921.

1283. WARNECK, Gustav. Missionsgegschichte (Missions history). Berlin:
       M. Warneck, 1910. (K.S.)
           P. 287, Ethiopianism.

1284. WELLS, James. Stewart of Lovedale: The life of James Stewart. London:
       Hodder & Stoughton, 1909. 419p.
           Pp. 287-299, Ethiopianism.

1285. WEMAN, Henry. African music and the church in Africa. Uppsala: Svenska
       Institutet for Missionsforskening, 1960.
           Pp. 101-110, "The sects and folk music;" pp. 111-114, the Nazarite
           Hymn Book. Also first-hand description of Shembe's January festival
           on the mountain, Nhlangakazi.

1286. WESTERMANN, Diedrich. Africa and Christianity. London: O.U.P., 1937.
           Pp. 53-56, a brief sketch and evaluation of independent movements;
           South African context.

1287. WILLOUGHBY, William Charles. Race problems in the new Africa: A study
       of the relation of Bantu and Britons in those parts of Bantu Africa
       which are under British control. Oxford: Clarendon Press, 1923. 296p.
           Pp. 70-72, possession and prophets, Ethiopianism; pp. 231-243,
           Mhlakaza and other prophets.

1288. WILSON, Monica and MAFEJE, Archie. Langa: A study of social groups in an African township. Capetown: O.U.P., 1963.
Pp. 91-103, church groups, including various independent churches, in an African suburb of Cape Town.

1289. WOOD, A. V. The Bantu reaction to Christianity. London: Prism, n.d. (c. 1961). 16p.
A popular account, dependent on Sundkler; concentrates on Zionism in S. Africa.

SOUTH WEST AFRICA

1290. BERDROW, Wilhelm. Afrikas Herrscher und Volkshelden (Africa's rulers and folk-heroes). Essen: Berdrow, 1908. vii + 243p. (K.S.)
Pp. 124-158, Witbooi and Sturmann.

1291. DOVE, Karl. Land und Leute in Deutsch-Südwestafrika (Land and people in German S. W. Africa). Jena: G. Fischer, 1900. viii + 124p. (K.S.)
Pp. 110-111, Witbooi.

1292. GÜRICH, Georg. Deutsch-Südwest-Afrika. Hamburg: Friederichsen, 1891. (K.S.)
Pp. 128-137, Witbooi.

1293. KOMAMBO, Katiti. "The development of African nationalism in South-West Africa," Présence africaine, 49 (1) 1964; Eng. edn., 21, p. 98.
African Methodist Episcopal Church influence on national consciousness.

1294. KÜLZ, Wilhelm. Deutsch-Südafrika im 25 Jahre deutscher Schutzherrschaft (German S. Africa in the 25 years of German colonial rule). Berlin: W. Süsserott, 1909. (K.S.)
P. 17, Witbooi.

1295. LOTH, H. "Zur Bedeutung sektenkirchlicher Frühformen im sogenannten Witbooi-Aufstand im Südwestafrika" (The significance of the early sect-church forms in the so-called Witbooi Rebellion in S. W. Africa), Kongressmaterialen der Delegation der D.D.R. des XXV Internationalen Orientalistenkongresses . . . Section XX: Afrikanistik. Berlin: Nationalen Vorbereitungskomitee in der D.D.R., 1960.

1296. MENZEL, Gustav. "Eine neue Sekte in Südwest?" (A new sect in South-west Africa?), Berichte der Rheinischen Mission (Wuppertal-Barmen), 105, Feb. 1955, 33-35.
A report on the proposed secession of the Herero African Church of Evangelists from the Rhenish Mission.

1297. _____. "Die Entscheidung der Herero" (The decision of the Herero), Berichte der Rheinischen Mission (Wuppertal-Bremen), 105, Nov. 1955, 2-7. (K.S.)
The Herero independent church.

1298. MIRBT, Carl (U.C.). Mission und Kolonialpolitik in den Deutschen Schutzgebeiten (Mission and colonial politics in the German colonies). Tübingen: Mohr, 1910. xii + 287p. (K.S.)
P. 194, on early Ethiopianism.

118

1299. OLPP, Johannes. <u>Angra Pequena und Gross-Nama-Land</u>. (Angra Pequena and
       Great Namaland). Elberfeld: Friedrichs, 1884. 41p. (I.S.)
            P. 40, Witbooi.

1300. PASSARGE, Siegfried. <u>Südafrika, Eine Landes-, Volks- und Wirtschafts-
       kunde</u> (S. Africa. A textbook of geography, ethnology, and economics).
       Leipzig: Quelle & Meyer, 1908. xii + 355p. (K.S.)
            P. 186, Witbooi.

1301. REEH, Gunther. "The Half-Opened Door," <u>International Review of Missions</u>,
       50 (199) July 1961, 293-296.
            The neo-pagan Herero Church in South West Africa, from 1956.
            (AA 14, 141.)

1302. SCHINZ, Hans. <u>Deutsch-Südwest-Africa</u>. Olderburg, Leipzig: Schulzesche
       Hofbuch, 1891. xvi + 568p. (K.S.)
            Pp. 196-202, Witbooi.

1303. SCHOLZ, Hans Georg. "Die Selbstständigkeitbewegung unter den Herero-
       Christen. Eine Reise durch das Watersberg-Reservat" (The independence
       movement among Herero Christians. A journey through the Watersberg
       Reserve), <u>Berichte der Rheinischen Mission</u> (Wuppertal-Bremen), 106,
       Nov. 1956, 4-8. (K.S.)

1304. _____. "Magische Umschliessung oder Gemeinschaft der Heiligen?" (Magic
       circle or communion of the saints?), <u>Berichte der Rheinischen Mission</u>
       (Wuppertal-Bremen), 107, Apr. 1957, 5-8. (K.S.)

1305. _____. "Junge Kirche und separatistische Bewegungen in Südwestafrika"
       (Young churches and separatist movements in S. W. Africa), <u>Kirche in der
       Zeit</u> (Dusseldorf), 16, 1961, 197-201.

1306. VEDDER, Heinrich. <u>Das alte Südwestafrika</u> (Old S. W. Africa). Berlin:
       Warneck, 1934. xvi + 666p. (K.S.)
            Includes a ch., "Der Hendrik-Witbooi-Krieg" (The Witbooi War), on
            Witbooi, late 19th. c.

1307. VON BULOW, F. I. <u>Deutsch-Südwestafrika. Drei Jahre im Lande Hendrik
       Witboois</u> (Three years in the Land of Hendrik Witbooi). Berlin: Mittler
       & Sohn, 1897. ix + 365p. (K.S.)

1308. WIENECKE, W. A. <u>Die Gemeinschaft der Ahnen und die Gemeinde Jesu Christi
       bei den Herero</u> (Fellowship with the Ancestors and the Church of Jesus
       Christ among the Herero). Unpublished thesis, University of Hamburg,
       1962.

SWAZILAND

1309. KUPER, Hilda. "The Swazi reaction to missions," <u>African Studies</u> (Jo-
       hannesburg), 5 (3) Sept. 1946, 177-189.
            The growth of "native dissident churches." (AA 3, 726.)

1310.   _____.   The uniform of colour. A study of white-black relationships in
         Swaziland. Johannesburg: Witwatersrand U.P., 1947. xii + 160p.
             Pp. 114, 124, separatist churches among the Swazi; in 1936, 21 sects
             in Swaziland, 13 of the Zionist type.

1311.   _____.   The Swazi. London: IAI, 1952.
             P. 45, brief account of separatist churches.

1312.   _____.   The Swazi: A South African kingdom. New York: Holt, Rinehart
         and Winston, 1963.
             Pp. 67-68, separatist churches in relation to nationalism.

1313.   _____.   "The Swazi of Swaziland," in J. L. Gibbs (ed.), Peoples of Africa.
         New York: Holt, Rinehart & Winston, 1965, pp. 479-511.
             P. 507, "Native Separatist Churches."

The numbers refer to items.

MERLO, M., 869.
MESSENGER, J. C., 509-513.
MIDDLETON, J., 155, 156, 870-872, 927-931.
MILFORD, B., 1199.
MILLIN, S. G., 1200.
MINA, G. P., 873.
MINEAR, P. S., 815.
MINJAUW, L., 732.
MIRBT, C. J. C., 1058, 1298.
MITCHELL, R. C., 157, 158, 514, 515.
MKELE, N., 1206.
MOFFETT, J. P., 914.
MOKITIMI, S. M., 1201.
MOMBASA, L., 874.
MONTEIL, V., 1202.
MOON, D. S. R., 1203.
MOORE, N. O., 956.
MORAN, F., 1204.
MORGANTHAU, R. S., 379.
MORIONDO, B., 875.
MORRILL, W. T., 516.
MORTON-WILLIAMS, P., 517, 518.
MPANGI, 733.
MPUMLWANA, L. M., 1205.
MOOTSI, L., 1206.
MÜHLMANN, W. E., 160, 876.
MURIU, N., 877.
MURPHEE, M. W., 998.
MURRAY, J. P., 1033.
MUSEUM LESSIANUM, 161.
MUSSON, M., 249.
MVENG, E., 277.
MZIMBA, L. M., 1207.

NATIONAL CHURCH OF NIGERIA, 519, 520.
NDANEMA, I. M., 593.
NEAME, L. E., 1208.
NEILL, S., 162.
NEILS, M., 734.
NEUFELD, E., 735.
NEVEUX, M., 380.
NEWMAN, B., 1209.
NICHOLLS, G. H., 1210.
NIDA, E. A., 163.
NIGER DELTA CHURCH BOARD, 521.
NIGER (ANGLICAN) DIOCESE ON THE, 522.
NIGERIA, CHRISTIAN COUNCIL OF, 523.
NIPPGEN, J., 610.
NJAGA, W., 877.
NIKLAUS, R. L., 736.
NORBECK, E., 878.
NORDFELT, M., 915.
NORMAN, L. S., 980.
NORTHERN RHODESIA GOVERNMENT, 1033A.

NORTHERN RHODESIA (ANGLICAN) BISHOP OF, 1034.
NORTON, G.E., 1211.
NOTTINGHAM, J. C., 879, 893.
NWANGORO, B., 524.
NWANGWU, J., 525.
NYANGWESO, 880.
NYREN, J., 737.
NZEKWU, O., 526.

OBATERO, O. I., 527.
O'BRIEN, C. C., 738.
O'CONNELL, J., 528.
OETTLI, W., 381.
OGER, L., 1035, 1036.
OGOT, B. A., 881, 882.
O'HARA, A., 1212.
OJI, B. A., 529.
OKARA, G., 530.
OKE, G. A., 531, 532.
OKPALAOKA, C. I., 533.
OKUNGA, D. N., 866.
OLAGUNJI, B., 534.
OLAYEMI, S., 535.
OLIFAN, J. W., 1213.
OLPP, J., 1299.
OLUSHOLA, J. A., 536.
OMONIYI, B., 164.
OMOYAJOWO, J. A., 537, 538.
ONYIOHA, K. O. K., 539.
OOSTHUIZEN, G. C., 165-167, 1214, 1215.
OSCHWALD, P., 799.
OSHITELU, J. O., 540, 541.

PADMORE, G., 168-170.
PARNIS, R. O., 542.
PARRINDER, E. G., 171, 250, 251, 281, 543-545.
PASSARGE, S., 1300.
PAUL, C., 1128.
PAULME, D., 338, 382-384.
PAULUS, J. P., 739.
PAUW, B. A., 1216-1220.
PAUWELS, M., 806.
PAYNE, A., 1221.
P. E. B., 611.
PEEL, J. D. Y., 546.
PELEMAN, M., 1222.
PEREIRA DE QUEIROZ, M. I., 11, 1223.
PERRAMON, R., 811.
PERROT, C-H., 1224, 1225.
PETERS, J., 740.
PHEKO, S. E. M., 1226.

SMITH, N. L., 899.
SMYTH, H. H., 199.
SMYTH, M. M., 199.
SOBCHENKO, A. I., 760.
SOGA, J. H., 1064.
SOUTH AFRICA (GOVERNMENTAL), 1103, 1252-
   1256, 1273-1275.
SOUTHON, A. E., 327.
SOYINKA, W., 553, 554.
SPECKER, J., 200.
"SPECTATOR," 328.
STEAD, W. Y., 1257.
STENNING, D. J., 933, 934.
STEWART, J., 1258.
STOEVESANDT, G., 329.
STONE, W. V., 1044.
STONELAKE, A. R., 761.
STUART, J., 1259.
SULZMANN, E., 613.
SUNDKLER, B. G. M., 201-203, 1260-1267.
SURET-CANALE, J., 204.
SUTER, F., 1268.
SVENSKA MISSIONSFORBUNDETS, 762.

TALANOVA, E. V., 763.
TALBOT, P. A., 555.
TALMON, Y., 13, 208.
TAMBARAM CONFERENCE, 207.
TAS, F., 764.
TASTEVIN, C., 614.
TAUXIER, L. M. J., 392.
TAYLOR, J. D., 1269, 1270.
TAYLOR, J. V., 209, 258, 935, 1045.
TAYLOR, S., 1046.
TERRY-THOMPSON, A. C., 210.
THEAL, G. M., 1271.
THIEL, V., 615, 765.
THOMAS, H. B., 936.
THOMAS, L. V., 211.
THOMPSON, E. W., 330, 393, 394.
THOMPSON, V., 616.
THRUPP, S. L., 14.
THURNWALD, R., 39.
THWAITE, D., 212.
TORREND, J., 1047.
TOUSSAINT, R. F., 766.
TRACEY, H., 1272.
TSHIMBAYEKE, 213, 767.
TUBOKU-METZGER, C. E., 596.
TURNBULL, C. M., 768.
TURNBULL, T. N., 556.
TURNER, H. W., 214-222, 259-265, 557-559.
TURNER, V. W., 156, 222.

UBA, S., 560.
UBRUN, A., 769.
UCHENDU, V. C., 561, 562.
UGANDA COMMISSION OF ENQUIRY, 937.
UMEH, N., 488.
UNION OF SOUTH AFRICA, 1273-1275.
USHER-WILSON, L. C., 817.

VAN ANTWERP, C. M., 1276.
VAN BULCK, G., 395.
VAN DER BERGHE, 1277.
VAN DER MEERSCH, W. J., 775.
VAN DER POST, L., 224.
VAN LANGEN HOVE, F., 225.
VAN LOCO, J., 776.
VANSINA, J., 777, 778.
VAN TRIGHT, F., 331.
VAN WING, J., 771-774.
VAN WYCK, J. A., 226.
VAZ, J. M., 227.
VEDDER, H., 1306.
VERBEKEN, A., 779.
VERGER, P., 563.
VERHAEGEN, B., 785.
VERRYN, T. D., 1278.
VILAKAZI, A., 228, 1279, 1280.
VON BULOW, F. I., 1307.
VON GOETZEN, 917.
VON HOFFMAN, C., 1059.
VON SICARD, H., 228A.
VON WERDER, P., 122.
VYOTSKAYA, N. I., 780.

WAGNER, (Père), 1281.
WAGRET, J. M., 781.
WALDER, A., 782.
WALKER, E. A., 1282.
WALKER, F. O., 266, 267, 396-398.
WALLACE, A. F. C., 15, 16.
WALLERSTEIN, I., 229, 230.
WALLS, A. F., 597.
WALTER, R., 800, 801.
WARD, B. E., 332.
WARD-PRICE, H. L., 564.
WARNECK, G., 1283.
WARREN, M. A. C., 231, 232, 818.
WATSON, W., 1048.
WATT, W. M., 233.
WAUTHION, R., 783.
WEATHERBY, J. M., 901, 902.
WEAVER, E. I., 565, 566.
WEBSTER, D., 567.
WEBSTER, J. B., 568-574.

WEINBERG, S. K., 33.
WELBOURN, F. B., 234, 819-822, 882, 938, 939, 1049.
WELLS, J., 1284.
WEMAN, H., 1285.
WERNER, A., 235.
WESLEYAN METHODIST MISSIONARY SOCIETY, 334, 399, 575, 576.
WEST CENTRAL AFRICAN CONFERENCE OF PROTESTANT MISSIONS, 784.
WESTERN EQUATORIAL AFRICA (ANGLICAN), DIOCESE OF, 577, 577A.
WESTGARTH, J. W., 578-581.
WESTERMAN, D., 39, 1286.
WHISSON, M. G., 903.
WIEGRABE, P., 335.
WIENECKE, W. A., 1308.
WILCOX, W. D., 956.
WILES, M., 582.
WILKINSON, F. O. G., 966.
WILLAME, J. C., 785.
WILLIAMS, M. W., 406,
WILLIAMS, W. B., 405, 406.
WILLIAMSON, S. G., 336.
WILLOUGHBY, W. C., 236, 1287.
WILLS, A. J., 967.
WILSON, B. R., 17, 237.
WILSON, G. H., 988.
WILSON, H. S., 268.
WILSON, M., 918, 919, 1288.
WINTER, E. H., 155.
WIPPER, A., 904.
WISTE, M., 905.
WISHLADE, R. L., 989, 990.
WITTER, T., 337.
WOBO, M. S., 583.
WOOD, A. V., 1289.
WORSLEY, P. M., 238, 991.

YOULOU, F., 637.
YOUNG, C., 786.

ZAJACZOKWSKI, A., 239.
ZEITZ, L., 240.
ZIEGLE, H., 617.
ZOLA, E., 787.
ZOLBERG, A. R., 400.

MERLO, M., 869.
MESSENGER, J. C., 509-513.
MIDDLETON, J., 155, 156, 870-872, 927-931.
MILFORD, B., 1199.
MILLIN, S. G., 1200.
MINA, G. P., 873.
MINEAR, P. S., 815.
MINJAUW, L., 732.
MIRBT, C. J. C., 1058, 1298.
MITCHELL, R. C., 157, 158, 514, 515.
MKELE, N., 1206.
MOFFETT, J. P., 914.
MOKITIMI, S. M., 1201.
MOMBASA, L., 874.
MONTEIL, V., 1202.
MOON, D. S. R., 1203.
MOORE, N. O., 956.
MORAN, F., 1204.
MORGANTHAU, R. S., 379.
MORIONDO, B., 875.
MORRILL, W. T., 516.
MORTON-WILLIAMS, P., 517, 518.
MPANGI, 733.
MPUMLWANA, L. M., 1205.
MOOTSI, L., 1206.
MÜHLMANN, W. E., 160, 876.
MURIU, N., 877.
MURPHEE, M. W., 998.
MURRAY, J. P., 1033.
MUSEUM LESSIANUM, 161.
MUSSON, M., 249.
MVENG, E., 277.
MZIMBA, L. M., 1207.

NATIONAL CHURCH OF NIGERIA, 519, 520.
NDANEMA, I. M., 593.
NEAME, L. E., 1208.
NEILL, S., 162.
NEILS, M., 734.
NEUFELD, E., 735.
NEVEUX, M., 380.
NEWMAN, B., 1209.
NICHOLLS, G. H., 1210.
NIDA, E. A., 163.
NIGER DELTA CHURCH BOARD, 521.
NIGER (ANGLICAN) DIOCESE ON THE, 522.
NIGERIA, CHRISTIAN COUNCIL OF, 523.
NIPPGEN, J., 610.
NJAGA, W., 877.
NIKLAUS, R. L., 736.
NORBECK, E., 878.
NORDFELT, M., 915.
NORMAN, L. S., 980.
NORTHERN RHODESIA GOVERNMENT, 1033A.

NORTHERN RHODESIA (ANGLICAN) BISHOP OF, 1034.
NORTON, G. E., 1211.
NOTTINGHAM, J. C., 879, 893.
NWANGORO, B., 524.
NWANGWU, J., 525.
NYANGWESO, 880.
NYREN, J., 737.
NZEKWU, O., 526.

OBATERO, O. I., 527.
O'BRIEN, C. C., 738.
O'CONNELL, J., 528.
OETTLI, W., 381.
OGER, L., 1035, 1036.
OGOT, B. A., 881, 882.
O'HARA, A., 1212.
OJI, B. A., 529.
OKARA, G., 530.
OKE, G. A., 531, 532.
OKPALAOKA, C. I., 533.
OKUNGA, D. N., 866.
OLAGUNJI, B., 534.
OLAYEMI, S., 535.
OLIFAN, J. W., 1213.
OLPP, J., 1299.
OLUSHOLA, J. A., 536.
OMONIYI, B., 164.
OMOYAJOWO, J. A., 537, 538.
ONYIOHA, K. O. K., 539.
OOSTHUIZEN, G. C., 165-167, 1214, 1215.
OSCHWALD, P., 799.
OSHITELU, J. O., 540, 541.

PADMORE, G., 168-170.
PARNIS, R. O., 542.
PARRINDER, E. G., 171, 250, 251, 281, 543-545.
PASSARGE, S., 1300.
PAUL, C., 1128.
PAULME, D., 338, 382-384.
PAULUS, J. P., 739.
PAUW, B. A., 1216-1220.
PAUWELS, M., 806.
PAYNE, A., 1221.
P. E. B., 611.
PEEL, J. D. Y., 546.
PELEMAN, M., 1222.
PEREIRA DE QUEIROZ, M. I., 11, 1223.
PERRAMON, R., 811.
PERROT, C-H., 1224, 1225.
PETERS, J., 740.
PHEKO, S. E. M., 1226.

INDEX OF PEOPLES